T0195036

Is the U.S. Office of Personnel Management Responsible for 9/11?

The American Bureaucracy
A Veteran's Eye-Opening Memoirs

Dr. Theodore G. Pavlopoulos
Navy Physicist for Thirty-Seven Years

authorHOUSE

AuthorHouse™
1663 Liberty Drive
Bloomington, IN 47403
www.authorhouse.com
Phone: 833-262-8899

Published by AuthorHouse 01/20/2021

ISBN: 978-1-6655-0807-0 (sc)
ISBN: 978-1-6655-0806-3 (hc)
ISBN: 978-1-6655-0805-6 (e)

Library of Congress Control Number: 2020923132

Print information available on the last page.

Dedication

This book is dedicated to two women, my mother,
Hilda, and my wife, Helen, who accompanied
me on my life's journey. With love.

Contents

Introduction

On September 10, 2001, then Secretary of Defense Donald Rumsfeld used the phrase "a matter of life and death" in a speech to Pentagon personnel, titled "War on Bureaucracy." He stated that the Pentagon's bureaucracy was dysfunctional. The next day, one airplane crashed into the Pentagon, and two airplanes crashed into the World Trade Center. It was the most devastating terrorist attack in United States history. It has been said that old generals just fade away, but that great nations commit suicide. With a dysfunctional federal bureaucracy that has left us ill-equipped to deal with natural disasters, energy shortages, and war, I believe America is committing suicide.

September 11 was a wake-up call for Americans in many far-reaching areas, including security, diplomacy, and immigration. The terrorist attacks should also have been a wake-up call for our poorly functioning federal civil service. Unfortunately, this did not happen. Performance problems at the FBI, the CIA, and other federal departments and agencies have been reported. Unfortunately, no one seems to have a workable solution to these problems. The president, Congress, and the American people seem to have no idea that those sections of the federal civil service system are steadily descending into a very serious human resources crisis. Americans have found many good solutions for their political, social, technical, scientific, and medical dilemmas, but their federal civil service system is still a mess.

In an article released in April 2002, with the title "A Fresh Start for Federal Pay: The Case for Modernization," former director of the U.S. Office of Personnel Management (OPM), Kay Coles James, states that the federal government is looking to bring new talent, new skills, and new energy into its workforce for a modernized federal pay system for the twenty-first century. She continues:

> To attract the best and the brightest in this next generation into public service, we need a pay system that reflects the realities of the modern workforce, where performance and results are emphasized and rewarded. What will such a system look like? The fundamental nature of the federal compensation system was established at the end of the 1940s, a time when over 70 percent of the federal white-collar jobs consisted of clerical work. Government work today is highly skilled and specialized "knowledge work." Yet in the age of the computer, the federal government still uses—with a few modifications—pay and job evaluation systems that were designed for the age of the file clerk. The divergence between the federal pay system and the broader world of work where the war for talent must be fought, has led observers to call for reform of the federal system. To support achievement of the government's strategic goals, a new, more flexible system may be called for, one that better supports the strategic management of human capital and allows agencies to tailor their pay practices to recruit, manage, and retain talent to accomplish their mission.[1]

Unfortunately, former director James's proposal contains a fatal flaw. Besides the high-quality, twenty-first century federal workforce she envisions, high-quality management must also be in place. However, the old "file-clerk type" management structure is still in place in many federal agencies and departments.

Managers who were originally supervisors of file clerks were typical bureaucrats, mainly performing administrative functions. These are poor or unqualified supervisors and managers who have little leadership ability and who lack the qualifications or the experience necessary to supervise or manage their high-quality employees.

For the last thirty five years, with assistance from the OPM, these managers have skillfully resisted the creation of an efficient and high-quality federal bureaucracy. In this type of twenty-first century federal bureaucracy, there is no place for useless "clerk type" managers. In 1980, my workplace, together with the Naval Weapons Center at China Lake, California, entered a so-called demonstration project known as the China Lake Project. About seven thousand navy employees were forced to participate in this five-year project Such demos are human-resource research projects designed to test new civil service personnel concepts, including pay-forperformance. They are conducted under the oversight of the OPM.

The navy's demo was supposed to increase compensation for high-performing employees, improve retention, offer incentives to improve performance, and strengthen recruiting through more competitive salaries. However, before taxpayers' dollars can be used to reward performing federal employees, proper performance evaluation systems must be in place. No such systems were ever developed, although the navy's demo is still in place.

During 2003, Congress discussed introducing new civil service systems that provided pay-for-performance and which would be more efficient for the federal bureaucracy. During these hearings, representatives from the Department of Defense (DOD) and the Department of Homeland Security (DHS) stated that they had selected the China Lake Project as the new civil service system. It was claimed that only the navy's demo had undergone substantial review and that, for the most part, it had been judged a success.

The rationale for the request for a new civil service system was to be able to fight terrorism more effectively. However, Congress and President Clinton were intentionally misinformed by the OPM. The navy's demo system is a total failure, and although required, it was never "substantially" reviewed by the OPM. Implementing the demo, or parts of it, as the new civil service system for federal agencies will seriously jeopardize, not only the American bureaucracy's ability to fight terrorism, but also the very future of America.

After September 11, 2001, it became clear that an inefficient human resources system had prevented sections of the American bureaucracy from communicating with one another. People began to ask whether this attack had been preventable. Did the concerned agencies have any foreknowledge of this terrorist plot? According to *The 9/11 Commission Report*, bits and pieces of information were available to several federal agencies, but the managers responsible were unable to put them together. Why should anyone assume that the old "clerk type" management still in place will be able to put critical information together the next time we have a brewing national crisis?

We have a deeply entrenched clique of "clerk" management that has no incentive whatsoever to reform. These managerial cliques lack the leadership skills and technical qualifications to lead a twenty-first century workforce. The present federal civil service system will break down whenever unqualified management faces difficult and complex situations. This type of bureaucracy is becoming more like the communist bureaucracy that I experienced in East Germany, and less like the merit-based system upon which America was founded. The OPM is fully responsible for the existence of this entrenched bureaucracy.

I am the only employee at the Naval Electronics Laboratory Center (hereafter referred to as "the Center") who fought this oppressive personnel system, and I kept detailed records and notes through each step of my long career with the navy. Therefore, I am able to report how this flawed personnel system works in practice. This is the main reason for my decision to write this book.

I will also discuss the shortcomings of some federal agencies, especially the ones that have adopted the China Lake demo as their personnel system. I have provided a considerable number of references, documentation, and excerpts from professional magazines, journals, and reports—as well as the opinions of fellow federal employees—that support my thesis. I want the reader to form an independent opinion on the working of the federal bureaucracy under the demo. Does the demo really reward performing employees? Will this new civil service system provide America with improved efficiency and effective national security?

I have also proposed some ideas on how to improve the federal civil service system. Because the OPM is directly responsible for the shortcomings of the American bureaucracy, this agency should be abolished. Furthermore, it is of the utmost importance that we improve the qualification requirements of federal supervisors and managers; otherwise, high-quality employees will either quit or not join the federal civil service. As a result, there will never be a twenty-first century federal civil service in place.

This book covers my professional and scientific journey, from my time as a high school and university student in Germany. Some of this coincided with the Nazi regime and the occupation of Eastern Germany by the Russians. After I left Communist East Germany in 1946, I finished my doctorate in 1953 at the University of Göttingen.

I immigrated to Canada, where I began my professional career, followed by immigration to the United States in 1956. From 1965 to 2003, I worked for the navy as a physicist in San Diego, California.

As a navy physicist, I worked on different projects, starting with an extension of the special theory of relativity, microelectronics, and fiber optics, but mostly, I worked on dye lasers and laser dyes. I have provided a brief description of my work. I wish to apologize for the relatively small space allocated for some of this work. However, to understand the work, one would probably have to be an expert in this field, and I did not want to write a physics textbook. Some of this material—where I try to explain the work in some detail—is presented as an appendix at the end of this book.

Working for the federal government, I clashed with my management over performance-and-promotion (merit-principle) issues. It was a difficult decision to write about this subject, but I decided to present parts of my experience because of the timeliness of the federal civil service issue. I have authored and coauthored more than sixty scientific papers in the open literature and was the top international authority in the field of laser dyes. Despite these accomplishments, I was never promoted. During this time, I saw many well-qualified colleagues leave my workplace, the Center.

Chapter 1
The Years in Germany

The Nazis and World War II

My parents, Georgios Pavlopoulos and Hildegard Zelinka, met in Dresden, Germany, where my father was studying economics at the Technische Hochschule (Technical University) of Dresden. When his father suddenly died in Greece, in 1923, my mother and father married in the Russian Orthodox Church in Dresden and left for Greece. I was born on August 20, 1925, in Thouria, near Kalamata.

My parents' marriage was not a happy one, so my mother traveled with me back to Germany. We returned to Greece when I was about five. My father had been working for his uncle, who operated a casino in Loutraki. This small city is opposite Corinth, separated by the Corinth Canal.

This was the time I started noticing my surroundings. I vividly remember the blue sky over Greece. When I was six, I attended the local school. However, my parents could not resolve their differences, so they divorced, and my mother and I returned to Germany. This was in 1933, the year the Nazis came to power in Germany.

For the first few years, we stayed with my grandmother. My mother remarried, to a kind man named Paul Dreher who worked for the Dresdener Bank. Every year, I had tonsillitis with fever. I thoroughly disliked the wet and cold winters in Germany and longed for the blue skies of Greece. I attended grammar school in Dresden. In Germany, at that time, we had classes on Saturday; but the number of students started dwindling when I was about ten because most of my classmates joined the Hitler-Jugend—the Nazi youth movement. They were excused from attending Saturday morning school.

The Hitler-Jugend would also meet on Wednesday evenings. Soon I was almost alone in class on Saturday mornings with the teacher. I, too, joined the Hitler-Jugend. Early one Saturday morning—it must have been 1938—I participated with the HitlerJugend at the opening of the newly-built Autobahn. My unit was positioned on the new Autobahn Bridge spanning the river Elbe. It was a miserable day—rainy and windy. We all got very wet, and it was cold.

We had to wait for hours until Hitler arrived with his entourage. His caravan consisted of about six cars. Slowly his car passed about ten feet from where we were standing. I still remember his white face. I cheered with all my comrades. Little did we know what was in store for Germany—and the world.

When I was fourteen, I attended the private high school of Dr. Wiener. The Germans and Nazis were wrestling with two gigantic problems. The first was their fight against communism. The second was their struggle to understand why Germany had lost World War I.

Americans and the United States were, and still are, of great interest to—and greatly admired by—many Germans. The United States is the home of cowboys and Indians, the Rocky Mountains, and American inventiveness and technology. Also, in the nineteenth century, a large number of Germans had immigrated to the United States. The hostility that many Americans exhibited toward Germany during World War I came as a shock to many Germans. I was exposed to both German history and Nazi propaganda during these years at school—and especially at meetings with HitlerJugend. Here is a brief overview of this propagandized history. It contains what I remember; these views are not my own.

When World War I started, the Allies blockaded Germany's ocean access to shipping in order to prevent goods, ammunition, and food from reaching Germany. The Germans countered with submarine attacks against freight bound for England. America supported the Allies, not Germany. When, in 1915, a German submarine sank a British passenger ship with American children onboard—the Lusitania — anti-German sentiment in the United States escalated.

America declared war on Germany in 1917, stating that it had to fight for the freedom of the seas. President Woodrow Wilson also declared that the Americans were fighting this war in order to end all wars. He then offered his famous "Fourteen Points" to the Germans as a fair foundation for an armistice and as a foundation for future peace. The Germans obliged, disarmed, and agreed to peace negotiations. However, when it came time for negotiations, the Western Allies tried to impose harsh conditions on Germany, and President Wilson's promises vanished.

Germany refused to sign the demands listed by the Allies in the Treaty of Versailles. In response, the Nazis claimed, the Allies continued their blockade of Germany for another six months. During these months, six million Germans, including scores of children, died from the influenza epidemic that ravaged the world. Because of the Allied blockade, this catastrophe hit the Germans especially hard.

Germany's population had been weakened, and had been living on small rations of food during World War I. During these six months, the Nazis complained, there was no mention from the Americans about the "freedom of the seas." The Nazis and many Germans blamed the Jews in America for the catastrophic loss of World War I. The late entry of the Americans into the war had tilted the outcome in favor of the Allies. According to the Nazis, all of this had a logical explanation. The Jews were controlling the press in America, turning public opinion against the Germans. President Wilson's "Fourteen Points," they claimed, were a typical Jewish swindle to trick the Germans into putting down their weapons. America had never had any intention of giving the Germans a fair shake. The Jews of the world were conspiring to enslave all Aryans.

Similarly, the Nazis claimed that communism was a phony ideology. After World War I, the Nazis and the communists were engaged in a bitter fight for control of Germany. After the Nazis came to power, Russia was viewed as a major threat.

Their country's defeat in World War I left many Germans filled with self-doubt. To raise the spirits of all Germans, the Nazis fabricated their race theories. They stated that most of the world's modern cultures, technology, medical advances, and science that had been invented or developed over the last two hundred years had taken place within the geographical triangle spanning Paris, Berlin, and London, as well as in America. This space was the home of the Aryans, the descendants of Germanic tribes. Without the contribution of these Aryans, the Nazis claimed, the world would still beliving in the Stone Age.

On one side were the Western powers allied with America, which was not too sympathetic to the Nazis. On Germany's eastern side was the vast expanse of Communist Russia, an area also unsympathetic to the Nazis. Together, West and East possessed huge human and material resources. Germany had only limited resources.

Hitler and the Nazis were uncontrollably angry over the way Germany lost World War I and over the terrible aftermath of that war. Hitler started World War II in September of 1939 with the invasion of Poland, later invading Russia in June of 1941 and declaring war on the United States in late 1941. The outcome of World War II was easy to predict: Nazi Germany was crushed.

Some still question whether six million Jews really died in German concentration camps. The fact that six million Jews died is entirely conceivable to me. Whenever Hitler learned of another

German loss on the battlefield, another bombing of a German city, or another supply convoy reaching the Russian harbor of Murmansk, he ordered his henchmen to round up more and more Jews in the Nazi-occupied territories for shipment to German concentration camps. However, most of the German population did not know about the mass killings of Jews in concentrations camps during World War II. Anyone who would try to speak about these atrocities would also have landed very quickly in a concentration camp.

Germany Occupies Greece

The sideshow of World War II that most affected me was the Italian occupation of Albania in 1939. On October 28, 1940, Benito Mussolini ordered Italian troops to invade Greece through Albania. The Greeks resisted fiercely, eventually driving the Italians back into Albania. Hitler learned of Mussolini's intention to invade Greece only after the fact Hitler grew furious. Witnesses said this was his first of many fits of madness.

On April 6, 1941, fearing the British would assist Greece, the superior German forces attacked Yugoslavia and Greece. On April 27, 1941, German tanks rolled into Athens. This development caused me to stop attending the meetings of the Hitler-Jugend. My group leader came to our apartment, asking what made me miss the meetings. I explained to him that I was a Greek citizen, and after the hostilities between Greece and Germany, I could no longer be a member of the Hitler-Jugend. He left without saying a word.

The Greeks agreed to sign an armistice with Germany. One of Greece's conditions was the release of all Greek prisoners of war. Because of the bravery that the Greek soldiers had shown in their fight against the Italian invaders, Hitler agreed to this provision and signed the armistice. Greece was the only nation at war with Germany where Hitler granted this concession. German law did not require non-Germans to serve in its army. However, both

Germans and non-Germans could volunteer for the Waffen-SS. This meant that although I was in Germany as a so-called enemy alien, I was not shipped to a concentration camp and was allowed to move freely within Germany.

Both the SA (Storm Battalions) and SS (Protection Units) were Nazi creations. The SA was used in the early days in street fights, clashing with the communists, while the SS served as bodyguards. Shortly after the Nazis came to power, discredit fell on the SA, and its leader, Ernst Röhm, was shot. The Nazis claimed he was a homosexual. Others claim that Röhm was unhappy for not being rewarded a high position after he helped Hitler and the Nazis rise to power. However, the leader of the SS, Heinrich Himmler, had an excellent standing with Hitler. Having a slavish nature, he became one of Hitler's most trusted henchmen, and his SS was expanded.

Studying Chemistry in Chemnitz

One of my high school teachers had kindled in me a keen interest in chemistry. I was mesmerized by how easily chemical reactions changed matter, to become a different substance, possessing totally different properties. After graduation, I decided to study chemistry. As graduation approached, I had to plan my future. At that time, as an enemy alien living in Germany, I was not allowed to study at any of the universities or technical universities. However, I was able to study chemistry at one of the two state technical academies.

Uncharacteristically, the Germans had left two state schools off of their list of schools that disallowed attendance by "enemy aliens." One state school was in western Germany. The second one was near Dresden. The academy in Chemnitz appealed to me because of the possibility of studying chemistry.

In Germany, universities do not have engineering faculty. They grant diplomas and doctoral degrees. At that time, the

Technische Hochschulen (now technical universities) would also grant diplomas and doctor's degrees in engineering. The diplomas are equivalent to master's degrees. Besides engineering, these schools have a science faculty, offering studies in physics, mathematics, chemistry, and other fields. There are many schools offering higher learning, including schools covering the many fields in engineering.

In general, these schools required five semesters of study to graduate. There were also the state technical academies, which were between the technical universities and technical schools. The academies required seven semesters of study to earn an engineering degree. Finally, in the spring of 1943, I completed high school and could not wait for the day that I would start studying chemistry. In Chemnitz, I had found a room within walking distance from the school.

Chemnitz is an industrial city with nearly 450,000 inhabitants and is about two hours southwest of Dresden by train. Not much to my liking, a considerable part of the curriculum consisted of engineering and related courses. It was a tough school, requiring students to show up for forty hours of courses and laboratory work per week.

All over Germany, the shadow of war loomed, and the academy was not immune. When I attended my first class, the number of students was small. The male students were mainly wounded and disabled soldiers. My chemistry class had an unusually high number of females. With bad news arriving from all German fronts, the already subdued mood gradually grew ever grimmer as the war progressed.

There were few foreigners attending the academy; those who did were mostly from Turkey. Most had an accent, but I did not. Soon, I felt resentment from Germans. I knew what most Germans were thinking: Why did I not fight on the Russian front to halt the onslaught of communism?

I enjoyed the chemistry classes because of the good teachers. Mathematics, unfortunately, was only tolerable, and I suffered through the engineering courses. However, I was spellbound by physics. One of my teachers, Professor Brauer, presented an outstanding lecture, and soon physics became my favorite course.

During 1944, the number of German soldiers killed grew and grew. In class, female classmates cried during lectures, having lost a father, a brother, a husband, or a boyfriend. I went to Dresden every third week. There, trying to inquire about classmates or friends, I would hear the same sorrowful news of loss.

During this time, I received a letter from the Waffen-SS recruiting depot, requesting to see me. I had a good idea what they wanted. They asked me why I did not join the Waffen-SS to fight communism. I replied that, unprovoked, the Italians had attacked Greece, followed by an attack by the Germans. Therefore, it was difficult for me to join the Waffen-SS. I received a long lecture on the evils of communism. I said that I wanted to think more about their proposition. Much troubled, I left the recruiting office.

The SS was split into two separate entities during the war. The old SS, among other assignments, was responsible for the concentration camps. The Waffen-SS, "Waffen" meaning "weapons" in German, was similar to the infantry, forming a crack troop of fighters. Due to Himmler's influence, the Waffen-SS had the best weapons. They fought mostly in Russia, although they showed up later on the Western Front. Most units of the Waffen-SS fought bravely—but brutally. Some committed war crimes. For these reasons, the Russians generally would not take any Waffen-SS soldiers as prisoners.

There were severe shortages of everything, and there were air raid alarms day and night. The number of male students in my class had dropped considerably. Every night, a group of faculty, staff, and students were required to stay overnight at the academy to fight the fires started by incendiary bombs, which were dropped in large numbers during the air raids. An air of doom was settling over Germany.

There were more bombings, defeats on all fronts, and unending reports of killed and missing German soldiers. In the east, the fastadvancing Russians were plundering and raping. In Germany, practically all houses and apartment buildings have cellars. These cellars are not basements where people live, but are usually used for storage. Because of the rather long winters in Germany, these cellars mainly store coal for heating. Often, potatoes and other food supplies are also stored there. During the war, these cellars served as bomb shelters. More and more hours had to be spent in these cellars because of the increased bombings. Some shelters had openings in their walls to provide access to neighboring cellars. This allowed people to escape in case their exit became blocked by rubble. In these shelters were benches and chairs, some even had bunk beds. During the winter, people brought blankets with them, but perhaps the most important item was the radio, which provided information on the movements of Allied bomber formations.

Collapse of Germany

Dresden is about 125 miles south of Berlin, in the valley of the River Elbe. Before World War II, its population was about 650,000, making it then the seventh-largest city in Germany. It is an old city and dates back to 1206. Dresden became world-renowned for its fine china and was also known for its Baroque architecture, and was often called "The Florence of Germany."

On February 13, 1945, the sirens drove me downstairs to our cellar. Over the radio came news that very large bomber formations were approaching Chemnitz. Later, the bombers changed direction and continued on to Dresden. After considerable time, a large, second wave of bombers headed for Dresden. As soon as the sirens indicated that the planes had left the area, I hurried upstairs to the apartment. From my landlady's living room, I could see in the direction of Dresden. A deep-red glow lit up the sky. The following morning, we learned that two large formations of Allied bombers had bombed Dresden. The attack had focused on the city's center, causing huge losses of life and destroying vast sections of the city.

Anxiously I waited for a telephone call from my mother, but it did not come. Neither did word come the next day. There was no train connection to Dresden anymore, and it was unclear when the damaged railroad system would be repaired. I borrowed a bicycle from a friend and left for Dresden very early the following morning. It was afternoon when I arrived at the outskirts of the city. Continuing in the direction of the city's center, the destruction caused by the bombing became more and more visible. I had to lift the bicycle over several corpses with heads and other body parts missing. More and more rubble covered the streets. Corpses were everywhere. Many had been burned into grotesque charcoal figures.

The smell of rotting flesh filled the air, immediately inducing the urge to vomit. I turned into a zombie, carrying the bicycle over mountains of rubble and bodies. Our house was located close to the Dresden railroad station, which was on one side of the elevated railroad tracks that lead south to Prague. When I reached the elevated railroad tracks, I could see that the tracks and the train station had been heavily bombed. All around, every house was in ruins.

Finally, I was standing in front of our burned-out house. I couldn't find any message from my mother, so I forced myself to leave. Then I decided to take a closer look. Near the house's entry, under a brick, I found a piece of paper that contained a message from my mother. I have rarely been happier than at that moment. She had written that she and my stepfather were at her uncle's house, in the outskirts of Dresden.

Stepping again over mountains of rubble, followed by a rather long bicycle ride, I arrived late in the evening, more dead than a live. Besides my mother and stepfather, I also found my grandmother and my aunt Gertrud, both of whom had escaped the bombing. After a long sleep, I returned the next morning to Chemnitz.

My mother said that during the attack, burning phosphorus had splashed through one of the cellar windows, igniting the stored pile of coal. They'd had to leave the cellar, and they found some protection under one of the railroad underpasses. When morning broke, they and tens of thousands of other survivors streamed out of the city and into the suburbs.

Back in Chemnitz, it was difficult to pay attention in class. About one month later, on March 5, 1945, I awoke to the noise of airplanes. I was so tired that I hadn't heard the alarm. Now awake, I dressed hastily and ran downstairs to seek shelter in the cellar. When I passed the door leading out to our yard, I could not resist looking outside. When I opened the door, I could hear the loud noise from the many airplanes. I stepped outside and looked up. It appeared as if a huge Christmas tree were hanging high in the sky just ahead of me. After I stepped downstairs to the shelter and had just turned the corner came a huge explosion, deafening me.

During night bombings, the bomber acting as pathfinder would mark the area to be bombed with flares of different colors. Attached to these flares were parachutes. The burning flares generated hot air that counteracted gravitation, letting the flares drift slowly down to earth. This is what made it seem as if a huge Christmas tree were hanging in the sky.

When the attack ended—sometime after midnight—I became concerned about the fate of the academy. I left my apartment quickly to investigate. To reach the academy, I had to pass under the tracks that came from the Chemnitz train station. The tunnel was about a hundred yards long and served as a bomb shelter. Walls had been erected on both sides of the tunnel. Because there was no electricity, the inside of the tunnel was pitch-black.

I had no choice but to use my hands to feel my way along the walls to reach the other end.

When I arrived at the academy, several fires were burning from incendiary bombs that had hit the roofs. The small night watch was discussing what to do, and eventually, we decided to fight the fires. Although there was no water, there were many fire extinguishers throughout the building complex. We split into two groups: One group went to fight the fires, and the other one gathered the fire extinguishers and carried them to where they were needed. After many hours of hard work, we brought the fire under control.

Overall, the academy hadn't suffered too much damage. I learned the next day that a large bomb called a "blockbuster" had hit the middle of the yard on the next block, causing extensive damage to all of the apartments facing the yard. Our apartment building suffered relatively minor damage, with mostly windows blown out. Chemnitz had been hard hit. Many buildings had burned, and in some parts of the city, these fires combined to form firestorms, destroying about 80 percent of the city's center.

A few days later, the head custodian of the academy paid me a visit. He informed me that I had been nominated to receive a bronze medal for bravery on the home front. For a long time, I did not hear anything about it. The next time I saw the head custodian, he looked embarrassed. Apparently, the powers that be had decided that Nazi medals were not appropriate for enemy aliens.

The situation in Germany deteriorated day by day. At the beginning of April, I decided to visit my classmate, Gerhard Hentschel, who was a Swede. As I took a shortcut through the ruins, there was a huge explosion. More explosions followed left and right of me. I was confused, not knowing where to take cover. When the barrage was over, I figured out what had happened. The Americans had arrived and were shelling the city with artillery.

The next day, the citizens of Chemnitz turned out to witness the Americans entering the town. There were more artillery bombardments, but no Americans. During the following days, the bombardments stopped, and people started looting stores. People ran down our street with boxes of soap on their backs and yelled, "There is soap. There is soap!"

Some days later, people again ran down the streets yelling, "The Americans are coming. The Americans are coming!" This circus went on for about two weeks. I went downtown to check on a classmate. When I approached the city's center, I received one of the greatest shocks of my life. Instead of the Americans, the Russians had arrived. For me, it was doomsday. The war was over, and I was now living under Russian occupation.

The Years after the War

My mother and stepfather had moved from the outskirts of Dresden closer to the city and were staying with some friends. These were the days right after the collapse of Germany. At night, Russian soldiers would go from house to house raping women, and the women's screams came from everywhere. I had no idea what I would do if these soldiers entered our house. However, within a few days, Russian authorities worked to establish some normalcy.

My stepfather was concerned about finding work because he had been a member of the Nazi party. Like many other Germans, the bombings and the collapse of Germany had affected him deeply. In addition, all institutions of higher learning in East Germany were either destroyed or closed. Everywhere, the communists wanted to separate Nazis from non-Nazis. The worker who ran the centralheating system had been promoted to director of the academy. I am sure he was a decent man, but what qualifications he possessed to get the academy going again, I did not know.

I was concerned about my future. Communism has been

defined as the dictatorship of an administrative clique—the Politburo. The Politburo was the central policy-making and governing body of the Communist Party in the Soviet Union. This clique claimed that their dictatorship was required to deal effectively with the corrupt capitalist system that exploited workers and started wars to fill its pockets by selling war materials. To prevent war mongering and the exploitation of workers, the Politburo felt that the property of capitalists must be confiscated. The communists claimed that the workers owned the confiscated property.

According to communist ideology, working for such a civil service system guarantees fair treatment of workers, who are now free from capitalist exploitation. In fact, according to communist ideology, they were now working in a worker's paradise.

The Politburo led the communist revolution all over the world and provided oversight of its vast bureaucracy. Graduates from the communist-party school—and other loyal communists—provided most of the management for the vast communist bureaucracy, including technical and scientific leadership. This management was mostly trained in communist ideology, but they were generally not taught how to supervise and manage the entire Russian workforce.

The communist management formed a homogeneous clique whose main interest was to protect its power, its comfortable jobs, and its members' good benefits. Only those with similar political views and openly expressed loyalty to the communist clique were eligible for membership. This clique was very anti-intellectual and obsessed with exercising total control over the workforce.

During frequent rallies that all workers were required to attend, workers' behaviors were studied with suspicion—who was contributing to political discussions, who was jumping up first to applaud, and who was applauding the longest for the communist speaker? Workers who learned how to participate in this exercise did well. All the spoils of this system went to the Politburo and their stooges, the civil service administrators. In short, under communism, there was a workforce laboring under unqualified management in competition with the efficient capitalistic system. Not surprisingly, the communist bureaucracy performed poorly.

To explain this poor performance, the bureaucratic hierarchy evoked one of the main communist doctrines, which claims that the communist bureaucracy could compete efficiently with the ca pitalistic system if only their managers had more power to whip the "lazy workforce" into shape. Because communists were also under constant fear of sabotage, there was an unending hunt for saboteurs. The Politburo was unwavering in its support for the incompetent management clique. Although the Politburo repeatedly gave managers increased power in personnel matters, no improvements in efficiency were ever made.

The workforce was left under total control of its management, without any rights of fair treatment or due process. Dissidents, including many intelligent workers who complained about their unfair treatment and mismanagement, were branded as saboteurs and enemies of the people. They were regularly mistreated by the communist judicial system. Communism provided a hellish workplace for many workers. Meeting some of these communist supervisors and managers, one was always stunned by their suffocating professional incompetence. Unable to produce consumer products of sufficient number and quality, and unable to compete in most scientific and technical fields, communism collapsed in 1991.

My aunt Gertrud's fashion salon was destroyed when downtown Dresden was bombed. With great foresight, she had taken several suitcases with dresses and materials to her uncle. This provided her with a foundation to reopen her old dressmaking business. The city's communist officials assigned her a house for her new business. Communism allowed only small, private firms to exist. Besides working space, the house also had some living spaces and a kitchen, so my grandmother joined her.

To my disappointment, the relationship between my mother and my stepfather deteriorated. He found a low-level job with a local bank; however, he did not follow our urging to try to find a better job in West Berlin or in the western part of Germany. My mother and I decided that we could not live under the communists. She and my stepfather separated, and my mother and I moved to my aunt's house.

There, Gertrud hired several dressmakers. Wives of Russian officers were her most frequent customers. They often brought some food with them that helped to supplement the small rations distributed by the occupying force. My mother decided to become a dressmaker also. If we could leave East Germany, she could support my studies. For me, finding a place to study became a major concern. I had written to several universities in West Germany, asking them to mail me their application forms. During the following months, however, I received very few.

It must have been the spring or early summer of 1946 when I left the house and noticed a man on our street waving and yelling at me. He was one of the few Greeks left in Dresden. Apparently, he was on his way to visit me. He told me that a Greek Military Mission had arrived in West Berlin. They had instructed him to notify all the Greeks he could find to come to Berlin-Charlottenburg to register with the Greek Military Mission. Berlin-Charlottenburg was in the British sector.

When I went to Berlin-Charlottenburg to register, I met Lieutenant Colonel Ypsilantis. He spoke fluent German. The first question he asked me was whether I had served in the Waffen-SS. Fortunately, I had my student pass from the academy with me, showing that I had attended the academy for the last two years of the war.

I also used this occasion to go to the Technical University of Berlin, also in Berlin-Charlottenburg. When I asked for application forms, I was instructed that the deadline for submitting the completed forms was the next day. Because of the bombings, miserable Berlin was the last place I wanted to study. The technical university, like most of Berlin, had been very badly bombed, and there were huge piles of rubble everywhere. Returning to Dresden by train, I was first inclined to discard the application forms. However, when I arrived, I had a change of heart. I spent all night completing the forms. Early the next morning, I went to the Dresden station for the train to Berlin. I boarded the train and went from compartment to compartment and from car to car, asking for someone who lived in Berlin-Charlottenburg. Finally, I found a man who lived close to the technical university. He promised to deliver the completed forms on time for me.

As time passed, I became more and more frustrated. Fall approached, but none of the universities in West Germany had notified me. I realized that I might not be able to start my studies in the autumn of 1946. The only university left was the one in Charlottenburg. I had to go to Berlin and find out for myself. At the Technical University, I was informed that all students who had been admitted had already been notified. On my way out, I remembered to ask whether this included foreign students. No, I was informed, those application forms still had not been considered. From the Technical University, I set out to the Greek Military Mission to vent my frustrations to Lieutenant Colonel Ypsilantis. Many of the universities in West Germany had admitted students who were former Nazis. I also mentioned to him that at the Technical University in Berlin, the admission of foreign students had not yet been decided. He promised to try to help me.

Back in Dresden, I waited anxiously for the mail every day. One day someone knocked at the door. A young man handed me a telegram from the Greek Military Mission in Berlin, informing me that I had been accepted at the Technical University, and that I had to report at once.

Studying in Berlin

Berlin was originally the capital of Prussia. It was the capital of Germany between 1871 and 1945. The Berlin Wall kept the city divided between August 13, 1961, and November 9, 1989. The following is a short summary from Ambrose's *American Heritage: New History of WWII.*

By the fall of 1942, thousands of planes were coming off U.S. assembly lines. On September 8, 1942, both the Washington and London high commands agreed to go ahead with "around-the-clock bombing" in Germany, after a complicated timetable was devised to accommodate the narrow airspace above the British Isles. The Berlin Blitz lasted almost three years. It was described as "Hell on Earth." Bombing raids by the RAF at night and the U.S. ravaged the city day by day. Some raids targeted manufacturing plants and supply lines, while others terrified German civilians. February 14 to 25, 1944, was known as Hell Week as the RAF put 2,300 bombers over Germany at night and the U.S. Air Force another 3,800 during the daytime. The devastation in the cities was immense, and they lay in ruins.[2]

After I had registered with the Technical University, I stayed overnight at the apartment of Mrs. Coban, who was a close friend of my Aunt Gertrud. She had prepared the sofa in the living room for me. That evening, there was no electricity. Bombing had disconnected buried electrical cables in many parts of the city, so Berlin was repairing its electrical lines. In my room, a little light came from a candle. This was a good time to reflect on the past and on my future.

Besides Germany, large parts of Europe—and other parts of the world—were in rubble. During the war, between fifty million and sixty million people had perished—most of them violently. I tried to make some sense of this terrible disaster, but all my reasoning left me in despair. I had survived the war unscathed. Why me? Because I had not been drafted, I had escaped being sent to a concentration camp. I knew from radio and newspapers that many millions had vanished in these concentration camps. The bravery that my Greek compatriots showed against the Italians compelled Hitler to send all Greek prisoners home. This was why I did not end up in a German concentration camp.

I concluded that it was my turn to make a statement; for me, it was payback time. I had an obligation. I owed the Greek soldiers for their stand in the Epirus Mountains. Now I could hear my calling to honor these Greek soldiers: I would strive to excel in research. When I started my studies at the technical university, only two thousand students attended the school because of the massive destruction from the bombings. When the war started, in addition to Berlin, eastern Germany had technical universities in Dresden, Breslau, and Danzig in the east. After the war, based on an agreement between Churchill, Roosevelt, and Stalin, the far eastern part of Germany was annexed by Poland, so Germany lost the technical universities in Danzig and Breslau. Further, the technical university in Dresden was almost completely destroyed, requiring several years to rebuild.

The Technical University of Berlin was located in the British sector. When the East German communist officials needed to rebalance this dire situation in their higher technical educational system, they elevated the rather well-preserved Technical Academy, in Chemnitz, to a technical university.

After the war, life was difficult in Berlin. Food rations were small. For my meals as a student, I had to use the campus cafeteria or restaurants. Often, the amount of food served in public places was too little for the number of ration coupons one had to surrender to buy it. I frequently went to bed hungry. In Berlin, ruin and rubble were everywhere. I had found a room in Berlin-Spandau. This part of Berlin was one of the few places that had been only partially bombed. To commute to school, I had to use the S-Bahn, the widely used elevated electric train.

It took sometime to reach the university. Many cars of the train had lost the glass in their windows, and these openings were often poorly covered. The cardboard or plywood used for their repair often fell out. Traveling during cold weather, especially during winter, became almost unbearable.

After I arrived in Berlin, the relations between the Allies and the USSR started to crumble, without anyone knowing where all this would lead. At school, I finally had the chance to listen to a good mathematics teacher, Dr. Szabo. He had excellent classes in calculus and differential equations. In addition, Professor Ramsauer's lectures in experimental physics were well presented. I badly wanted to leave miserable Berlin. I had not given up my plans to study in West Germany.

My choice was the University of Göttingen. At that time, this city had just under a hundred thousand inhabitants. Luckily, Göttingen and its university had escaped significant damage from the bombing. As a result, the city was overrun with refugees and students. The University of Göttingen, founded by Baron Münchhausen in 1737, was rated among the highest in Germany and soon became a center for mathematical studies. Over the last hundred years, its natural sciences faculty, especially the departments of physics, mathematics, and chemistry, had been among the best in the world. The faculties of the physics and chemistry department have been awarded the most Nobel Prizes of all the German universities. From the mid-1920s to the early '30s, the physics department was the international center for the studies of quantum mechanics.

In 1946, my attempts to gain admission at a West German university had been a total failure. In 1948, I approached Lieutenant Colonel Ypsilantis and asked him to write a letter of recommendation to the University of Göttingen. The admissions office of the University of Göttingen contacted me, detailing the conditions of my acceptance. I had informed them that I was preparing myself for the Vor-Diplom (pre-diploma), the examination that has to be passed by all students after four to five semesters of study. At German universities and technical universities, this examination is the prerequisite for passing the

Diplom Exam (diploma examination). This examination takes place after studying eight to ten semesters. Passing the Diplom Exam is equivalent to earning a master's degree and requires a thesis. The University of Göttingen requested that I pass the VorDiplom with at least a B average in the main subjects: physics, mathematics, chemistry, and one field in theoretical physics.

At the Technical University of Berlin, I received a B in physics, a B in mathematics, and an A in chemistry, but I did not attempt to pass the examination in theoretical mechanics because it was poorly presented.

Politically, the rift between the Allies and Russians had widened—this was just before the blockade of Berlin started. It was time to make plans to travel to West Germany. I went to the Greek Military Mission to inquire about passing through the Russian Zone that separated Berlin from West Germany. Lieutenant Colonel Ypsilantis had only bad news for me. Because of the crisis between the Allies and the Russians, it was no longer possible to put nonGerman civilians on Allied trains. The only way to leave Berlin at that time was to obtain a Russian visa from the Russian Consulate in East Berlin. Ypsilantis added that he did not know anyone who had been successful in obtaining such a visa, but he gave me the address of the Russian Consulate.

I got up very early in the morning to set out for the consulate. It must have been around 6 a.m. when I arrived—but this was not early enough. The consulate was located in a very large villa. The huge waiting room on the first floor was completely filled with visa applicants and was standing room only. About a hundred people filled the room. When the consulate opened for business at 9 a.m., the hopelessness of obtaining a visa became apparent. Every fifteen minutes, only one applicant left the room. Closing time was about 4 p.m. I could easily see that my chances of obtaining a visa were nonexistent.

I decided to try my luck; I had nothing to lose. It was a matter of my freedom. I went upstairs, where I found about seven or eight doors with no signs on them. I knocked at the first door, showed my Greek passport to anyone occupying the room, and said in German that I needed a visa. The occupants of the rooms, who were mostly Russian officers, were perplexed, and I did not know if any of them spoke any German. Each time I tried to speak to one of them, they ran me out of the room. I reached the last door. When I opened it, I found a rather large room with about a dozen civilians sitting or standing around. I asked one of the men why he was waiting. He said that this was the consular office for non-Germans who wanted to obtain Russian exit visas. I had found the right place!

After waiting for about two hours, I was asked to enter one of the small adjacent offices. I found myself sitting in front of a highly decorated Russian officer, who asked me what I wanted. I had come up with a story for just such a question. I explained to him that the living conditions in Berlin were terrible. I said I wanted to return to my homeland, Greece. I said that I could not go south through Yugoslavia because there were no train connections to Greece. I wanted to go west, through France. There I would go south to Marseille, trying from there to reach Greece by ship.

The officer gave my explanation a lot of thought. Finally, he opened his desk drawer and took out a huge stamp. With it, he stamped my passport and signed the visa. When I returned to the Greek Military Mission, Lieutenant Colonel Ypsilantis was very interested to learn how I had obtained my visa. I thanked him for his help, and he reminded me not to forget my homeland, Greece. I assured him that I would not.

The political situation in Berlin worsened. I left for Hanover immediately, where after several hours of travel, my train arrived. I left that train and changed to one going south. In about two hours, we pulled into a small train station. A magic word—magic to me, at least—appeared on the sign of the train station: "Göttingen." I had arrived at the place of my dreams; this was the place where significant contributions to quantum mechanics had been made. When I stepped off the train, I knew I had finally found freedom.

From 1925 to 1930, the University of Göttingen was the international center for quantum mechanics, with Heisenberg one of the most important founders of this field. The wartime climate had made Heisenberg a controversial figure. The Nazis had assigned him to lead their atomic bomb project. However, not much came of it due to the shortage of resources. The controversy resulted when Heisenberg's followers claimed that he had tried to sabotage the project. His detractors claimed, however, that he had eagerly followed Nazi orders. Despite the controversy, in 1946 he became the director of the Max Planck Institute of Physics in Göttingen.

Studying in Göttingen

It was evening when I arrived in GÖttingen, and I had no shelter for the night I went to the city's center hoping to find a place to eat and sleep. I stopped at a Gaststatte (Restaurant/ Hotel) with the name Junkernschenke. A friendly woman managed the restaurant I introduced myself and explained that I had just arrived from East Germany, from Berlin. I asked her if she knew of a place for me to stay for the night. She suggested a small room just under the restaurant's roof. If I liked it, she said, I could have it.

The next day, I asked her if she knew anyone who had a room for rent. The following day, she introduced me to a Mrs. Küchemann. She had a small room available under the roof of the apartment building where she and her husband lived. The room was quite acceptable, and the apartment was within walking distance of the physics and mathematics department of the university. In no time, I had resolved my housing and transportation situations.

Among the courses I attended the first semester was a lecture on theoretical physics, namely, electrodynamics. I needed to take a course in theoretical physics—and pass it—to complete my prediploma. Professor Richard Becker presented the lecture in electrodynamics, which also included an introduction to the special theory of relativity (STR). He had written a textbook on the subject that was widely used by German students. (The STR is briefly discussed in Appendix 1.)

After I had attended Professor Becker's course, I asked him to serve as my examiner. I did not do very well, receiving only a C. When he saw my long face, he consoled me. With my A in chemistry, he said, I had a grade average of B, and I fulfilled the requirement for admission to the university. Still, I was somewhat troubled to discover that I was a slow thinker, and my notes were nothing to brag about. Other students were much faster than I at grasping ideas in physics. My mind struggled with these ideas. The same applied to mathematics. Overall, with the exception of chemistry, I was a mediocre student, and I had to work hard just to be mediocre.

My mother followed me to Göttingen about one year after I started my studies. Until 1949, the old money, the Reichsmark of the Nazi era, was still in use. It became worthless with the introduction of the Deutsche Mark—DM for short. I had no source of income, so it became imperative for my mother to join me in Göttingen. Mr. Küchemann, my landlord, had a friend who worked for the German railroad. He was stationed at the border between East and West Germany and reassembled railroad cars that were to be returned either to East or West Germany. He knew where the Russian border guards were positioned and showed my mother how she could move among the railroad cars to avoid the border guards.

In Dresden, my mother had earned certification as a master dressmaker after passing the necessary examinations. In Göttingen, she went into business tailoring dresses, and her earnings allowed me to continue with my studies. Studying physics in Göttingen, I attended Professor Heisenberg's courses. He presented two different courses, one in quantum mechanics, and the other in his favorite subject, his new theory on elementary particles.

Naively, I attended his favorite course first. During the first hour, Heisenberg spoke about the importance of the universal length in physics. He was very passionate about this subject. A future theory on elementary particles, he stated, must contain a universal length for dimensional reason. Although I did not know it at that time, the first hour of his lecture would influence the rest of my life: I would work to understand the role that the universal length plays in physics.

During the second lecture, Heisenberg presented his new theory on elementary particles that contained a universal length. I was too inexperienced to follow the derivation of his equation. The nonlinear partial differential equation he had developed was difficult to solve. All the mathematics he used was beyond my reach. The following semester, I attended his course on quantum (matrix) mechanics. Heisenberg had developed his own mathematics and his own physics, which made it difficult for me to follow. However, I learned that many of my friends were having the same experience. We discussed our difficulties grasping Heisenberg's physics with one of his assistants. He told us that we were wasting our time attending Heisenberg's courses. He explained we needed to thoroughly master quantum mechanics and possess a strong background in mathematics before we could attempt to understand Heisenberg physics. (A short overview of quantum mechanics is presented in Appendix 2.)

I was consumed by theoretical physics, but I was a slow learner. Some of my friends were specia lizing in theoretical physics, working on their theses. However, when I visited them, I always saw them solving differential equations. Sitting day after day and year after year at a table solving differential equations was not for me. I wanted to conduct experiments and use my hands, so I decided to specialize in experimental physics.

Dr. Theodore G. Pavlopoulos

At the Max Planck Institute

The closeness of the border between West Germany and the Russians in East Germany was constantly on my mind. I wanted nothing more than to complete my studies, graduate, and immigrate to America. For many years to come, America was the only place where physics would advance. In addition, the Russians had obtained the atomic bomb, and consequently, I wanted to put as much distance between them and me as possible.

It was the summer of 1949, and the time had arrived for me to think about my thesis work. First, I had to complete my diploma thesis, followed by the necessary examination. The same applied for obtaining a doctorate. I started to look for a professor who would supervise my thesis work. However, there were too few physics professors, a shortage of equipment, and a very large number of other students who were also planning to start their theses. Several professors told me to come again in six months or a year. This was unacceptable.

My other option was to try the Max Planck Institute for Physics, where Heisenberg was the director. The result was the same. Every physics student in Göttingen wanted to do thesis work at this institute. The Max Planck Institute of Physics was one of many institutes belonging to the Max Planck Gesellschaft (Society), which was the successor of the Kaiser-Wilhelm Gesellschaft, founded in 1911 by Kaiser Wilhelm II. He was a strong supporter of this organization, so it was named after him. After the war, in 1948, the Kaiser-Wilhelm Gesellschaft was renamed the Max Planck Gesellschaft.

These institutes perform basic research independent from universities and industries. At that time, there were over sixty such institutes in Germany. Each institute covered a major field of academic research. These institutes provide research opportunities for prominent university professors, without the burden of teaching. They are mainly supported by the government and are usually much better funded, and therefore better equipped, than universities. One of my friends was Manfred Eigen, who was completing his doctorate at the Institute for Physical Chemistry at the university. Later, Manfred Eigen would receive the Nobel Prize in chemistry, together with G. Porter and R. Norrich, in 1967.

I asked him if he had any ideas about where else I could try to start my thesis work. He asked me if I had heard of Professor Karl Friedrich Bonhöffer. I had not. He said that Professor Bonhöffer had just arrived from the University of Leipzig, located in East Germany, via Berlin. He had brought with him only a small staff. He was setting up a Max Planck Institute for Physical Chemistry in Göttingen.

The German Luftwaffe had operated several large wind tunnels in a building complex just across the Bunsenstrasse from the departments of physics and mathematics. The next day, I visited the institute. Considerable work was going on to convert the building that had housed the wind tunnels into laboratory spaces. Professor Bonhöffer informed me that at this moment, he was too busy with the construction of the laboratory to worry about thesis work; however, he said, a Professor Theodor Förster had come with him to Göttingen, and he might be interested. Professor Förster was unavailable when I visited, but I was advised to leave my address with his secretary.

A few days later, I received a postcard asking me to see Professor Förster for an interview. When I met Professor Förster, he offered me a place to do my diploma-thesis. Because he was working on the fluorescence of organic compounds, he was interested in a physics student who had a background in chemistry. (A short overview of fluorescence is provided in Appendix 3.)

Obviously, I had the proper background, so I started working on my diploma-thesis within a few days. I was the first student from the University of Göttingen to work at the new Max Planck

Institute of Physical Chemistry. However, with the passage of time, more staff and many more students arrived at the institute to work on their diplomas and doctorates. Right next to our institute was another large building, from which the wind tunnel had been removed. It served as an eating place, but it was not a cafeteria. Only lunch was offered, and it consisted of a bowl of German soup and a bun. It was very cheap and very convenient. We ate on primitive garden tables and sat on benches.

At this eating place, Professor Otto Hahn, the president of the Max Planck Society, would often show up for lunch. Professor Hahn, together with Dr. Fritz Strassmann, discovered the fission of uranium 235, and their findings were published in 1938. Their discoveries led to the development of the atomic bomb. Hahn had received the Nobel Prize in Chemistry for this fundamental discovery in 1944. He always sat at the end of the table, and he always looked sad. I never saw him smiling. This puzzled me. With his fame, why would he not smile? Later I learned that he and his wife had lost their only son on the Eastern Front, which had left them devastated.

After completing my diploma-thesis, I passed the examination necessary to obtain my diploma in physics in 1951. Unfortunately, Professor Förster had accepted a professorship at the Technical University of Stuttgart and left Göttingen. I had to look for another mentor to work on my doctorate. The Max Planck Institute for Physics was still overrun with applicants. Fortunately, Professor Hans Strehlow, a staff member at the institute at that time, offered me a place to work in electrochemistry, a subfield of physical chemistry.

Professor Strehlow had a great affinity for Italians. During World War II, he had served in Russia. During one of the German army's hasty retreats from Russia, he found himself abandoned when no German truck would stop to pick him up, although he frantically waved his arms to signal each one that passed. Finally, an Italian truck stopped for him, and he escaped capture by the Russians. Later, he was shipped to North Africa, where the

Americans took him prisoner. They sent him to the United States, where he ended up picking cotton in the South.

Although I would have preferred to do my doctorate in physics, I wanted to complete my studies as quickly as possible and leave Germany. Therefore, I accepted Professor Strehlow's offer to measure the electromotive series in formamide, an organic solvent. The field of electrochemistry covers batteries, electrolysis, electroplating, and corrosion. Because electrochemistry has many technical applications, it is widely studied. This work resulted in two papers published in the *Zeitschrift for Physicalische Chemie (Journal of Physical Chemistry)*, naming Dr. Strehlow and me as authors.

Chapter 2
Leaving Germany for Canada

University of Toronto

During my last years in Göttingen, I had discussed with my mother the idea of going to America. Obtaining information on how to accomplish this proved difficult. Finally, I learned that I could not immigrate to the United States, because, having been born in Greece, I counted toward the immigration quota assigned for Greece. At that time, about 3,500 Greeks were permitted to enter the United States each year. I would have to wait eight to ten years to enter.

This forced me to examine other possibilities. After I considered Brazil, Australia, and some other countries, Canada looked best. The Canadians imposed only two conditions on prospective immigrants. First, the applicant for an immigration visa must occupy a profession that was in short supply in Canada. Second, one had to present a ticket of passage to the Canadian Immigration Office in Hanover.

Going to Canada had another advantage: It bordered America, which was still my ultimate goal. In addition, I had a place to stay there. My mother had a customer who had just obtained her doctorate and was planning to immigrate to Toronto with her husband. She agreed to provide shelter for me during my first days in Canada. My application for an immigration visa was quickly approved, but there was one stipulation: I had to arrive in Canada before a certain date.

Visiting a travel agency in Göttingen, I learned that there was only one passenger ship available for this time period. Unfortunately, this ship would arrive in Canada a few days too late. Again I had to travel to Hanover. Conveniently, the Canadian Immigration Office informed me that the Canadian government had its own ship that would make the date requirement. I had no choice but to book a ticket on this ship. The ticket price was $156, about the same price as the passenger ships. This whole arrangement was a cheap ploy by the Canadian government to make money off poor immigrants. However, during my three years in Canada, I never again experienced the Canadians being cheap, and I greatly enjoyed my stay in there.

The ship left Bremerhaven on December 7, 1953. It was a converted freighter that had been used to transport troops and refugees. Under its lower first deck, all nine hundred passengers were accommodated in huge rooms, packed floor to ceiling with bunk beds. My bed was located at the bow, together with about one hundred other male passengers. I was elated when we set sail late in the afternoon.

I awoke in the middle of the first night. Most likely, it was when we hit the English Channel. The sea was rough, and most of the men in the cabin became seasick at the same time. The stench of vomit filled our dormitory. Although I did not get seasick, I did not get much sleep that night. Because the dining room on board was small, passengers had to eat in four shifts. We used cheap paper cups for milk, juice, or coffee, and I remember that all the liquids served took on the taste of the cup's glue. In the morning when I tried to reach the restroom, I felt like Tarzan, hanging from a limb. The huge waves lifted the ship's bow high out of the water, cementing my feet to the floor. When the bow of the ship reached the crest of the wave, it pitched forward, and the floor suddenly disappeared from under me. I had to hold onto the bedpost in order to stay upright, and every time the ship crested, I felt like I was hanging in midair.

I started exploring the ship, searching for a room to spend the day. I did not want to go back to my bed. Only a small room was available, where the ship's crew spent their spare time. There was room for only thirty to forty people. On the deck, there was a huge pile of small folding chairs without backrests. One had to find a place outside on the ship's deck that was somewhat protected from rain and the very strong winds. Everybody was wrapped in multiple blankets.

The days were long, especially when sitting on those little, uncomfortable chairs. We also had a few parties-dance parties, because there was a gramophone available for music. The room was poorly lit, and the dance floor was one of the huge openings through which cargo had been brought onto the ship, now covered with large planks. The only problem was the waves. When the music started, we had to wait until the ship was horizontal to run and find a partner. Time was short because soon the dance floor would not be horizontal anymore, and everybody would slide and fall to the lowest point. The pile of people would try to get up and reach the dance floor when the ship became horizontal again. Very soon, however, the ship would rear back, and everyone would slide and fall in the opposite direction. After a while, not much dancing was going on, and people gave up and left.

After seven days of stormy weather, we arrived at St. John, New Brunswick. This city had only a small harbor, surrounded by barren countryside. In the afternoon, we boarded a train to take us through Montreal to Toronto. As soon as the train started, officials came through to instruct us not to leave the train. I had trouble understanding why someone who had been booked to go to Montreal or Toronto would want to get off the train. I soon learned that the train passed through the United States to reach our destination. Apparently, German girls would sign up with the Canadian Immigration Authorities to work as domestics in Canada. They would board this train. As soon as the train stopped on United States soil, they would get off the train to find and hopefully marry their American boyfriends.

At the time I arrived in Canada, its population was about fifteen million. In 2013, there were over thirty-four million Canadians. Toronto had a population of about one million when I first arrived. Now the population has swollen to 4.6 million.

After the world wars, Toronto continued to grow with the influx of tens of thousands of immigrants. When I arrived in Toronto, my mother's friends made a room available to me. From a friend in Göttingen, I had acquired the address of a Dr.Schmidt, a German medical doctor who was performing research at the Banting and Best Institute in Toronto. I contacted him, and he agreed to see me. Together, we went to the University of Toronto to inquire about possible employment for me. First, we visited the chemistry department, but I had no luck. However, in the physics department, Professor H. Welsh was interested in offering me a postdoctoral position. During the 1930s, he had studied physics and quantum mechanics in Göttingen and consequently spoke German. During the first weeks of my stay in Toronto, he was very helpful to me. In addition, Lucian Krause, a Polish graduate student, also spoke German. This was helpful in making quick contacts with the other graduate students. The group I was associated with was working on high-pressure physics and on Raman spectroscopy. I was ecstatic that I had found a position where I could perform research. Although the wages I received were not very high ($3,000 Canadian for the year), they were enough to get by.

It was winter in Toronto, but I liked it much better than the winters I had experienced in Germany. It was mostly a dry cold with only a little snow for a few months and not much rain. Now I did not have to worry about finishing my doctorate and examinations.

However, the idea of universal length started to torment me. I had no idea where to start or how to incorporate this constant into physics. Which theory needed to be expanded? Was it quantum mechanics or the special theory of relativity (STR)? I realized that I had to invest considerable time to read more literature on the STR and expand my knowledge of mathematics.

My mother followed me to Canada the spring after I'd arrived. We rented a small apartment, and she found work in one of Toronto's garment factories, not too far from our apartment. I studied the pressure broadening of mercury lines. (Some details of this work are provided in Appendix 4.). I was lucky to discover two new mercury lines. I was getting ready to send my experimental data to a publication when Professor Welsh advised me to halt my efforts. My work had been for nothing; a French group had also discovered the two mercury lines and published their results ahead of me.

I really enjoyed my stay at the university, the work, and the camaraderie with my coworkers. I was able to improve my English, and I enjoyed this new and fun experience. By this time, my oneyear post doctoral research fellowship had ended. Professor Welsh asked me whether I wanted to work in electrochemistry. There was a postdoctoral fellowship available at the British Columbia Research Council in Vancouver. Because of my background in electrochemistry, I gladly accepted this offer. My colleagues congratulated me for having the opportunity to work on the Canadian west coast. They told me that Vancouver was considered the banana belt of Canada.

Vancouver

Professor G. M. Shrum, the director of the Research Council, mailed me a train ticket. My journey to Vancouver took three days. The first section of the trip seemed to take forever, traveling through the province of Ontario, with its thousands of lakes. After we crossed the Prairie Provinces, we finally entered the Rocky Mountains.

The British Columbia Research Council was located on the campus of the University of British Columbia. However, the university was located at a tip of a large peninsula, facing Georgia Street. The university was separated from Vancouver by a large wooded area. At that time, only one main street connected the university with the city of Vancouver.

About two hundred years ago, Captain George Vancouver had landed at this site. Later, the city was named after him. When I arrived in Canada, British Columbia had a very bright economic future. Its huge industrial expansion had left some of its industries in need of technical expertise as well as short-and long-term research. Because of the rapid growth of the province, many of the newer industries lacked facilities for research and development. The Research Council played an active role in assisting the industries in the province in fulfilling their research and development needs.

Among the many projects handled by the Research Council was electrochemical research, directed by Dr. J. D. H. Strickland. Of specific interest were the formation of oxide films on metals and the development of new techniques for measuring the rates of metal ion discharge during electro deposition. There was a need to understand the complex behavior of metal ions during electroplating.

I had found a small room in a student housing area, dating from World War II. The small house was close to the cafeteria. When I arrived, some of the faculty members of the Research Council invited me to their homes. Overall, however, I led a lonely life. As a postdoctoral fellow, I did not belong to the student body anymore, so my association with the students was broken. In addition, I did not belong to the faculty, because I was viewed as a passing visitor.

My mother arrived from Toronto a few weeks later. We moved into a small house on campus, also built during World War II that housed two families. She was able to find work in the nearby kitchen of the university cafeteria.

Dr. Strickland, my new mentor, and I worked well together. To study the kinetics of metal deposition, I used microelectrodes. I collected sufficient experimental data that allowed me to produce a lengthy paper, with Dr. Strickland a coauthor. The paper was published in 1955 in the *Journal of the Electrochemical Society*.

With no entertainment on campus, the only heated building available in the evenings was the library. Getting there from the cafeteria involved walking on an unpaved road through the woods. Because cars also used them, these roads had deep ruts. With the region's abundant rain, most of the time the ruts were filled with water. The early onset of darkness and lack of lights made visiting the library a problem. My feet would sink ankle-deep into the water and mud, and I would have to sit for two to three hours with wet feet in the library. I used the library mainly to read more on the STR.

On weekend evenings, I would venture to downtown Vancouver. There was no bus service at night, so I had to hitch a ride across the woods to reach the nearest bus connection. During the winter months, it rained constantly, sometimes heavily. When I reached downtown, I would have dinner and see a movie. In the theater, I would drape my wet coat over my knees, hoping the coat would dry. Because of the late hour, I had to wait a long time in the rain for the bus. Also, fewer cars traveled through the wooded area in the late evening to reach campus, so I was often left standing in the rain for a long time.

I continued with my work on the kinetics of metal deposition. However, after one year, my postdoctoral fellowship had expired. Dr. Shrum obtained a lectureship at the university for me. I helped students solve physics problems that had been assigned during their regular physics classes. It was the first time I had taught students. I found the Canadian students to be intelligent, but rather poorly prepared for academic study. Most of the students learned the presented material rather quickly, but turned to the teacher too quickly for assistance. It seemed to me that some independent thinking and effort would have provided, not only the answer, but also the intellectual benefits of original thinking.

I started to realize that teaching at a university might not be for me. It took away from my hands-on work in the laboratory. However, this lectureship allowed me to continue with my work at the BC Research Council. I studied the electrochemical discharge characteristics of lead, thallium, silver, bismuth, copper, tin, and antimony ions. I collected sufficient data for a lengthy paper, again with Dr.Strickland as coauthor. This paper was also published in the *Journal of the Electrochemical Society* in 1955.

When the end of the semester came, it was again time to move on. My dream of moving to the United States was very much alive. However, the question of how to get there remained unresolved. I had answered an advertisement in the journal *Nature* to work as a postdoctoral fellow in New Orleans at Tulane University, which resulted in an invitation to come to Tulane University for an interview. That trip was my first time on an airplane. After I had received my new employer's assurance of a job, I also received assurance that they would help me enter the United States.

However, when I consulted with the American Consulate in Vancouver, the news was not good. The only way for me to enter the United States was on a one-year worker's permit. There was a possibility that this permit could be extended for a second year, but I was worried. After having left Canada for two years, would I be allowed to reenter? Finally, I decided to accept Tulane's offer. I reasoned that being in the United States might make it easier to stay.

Tulane University in New Orleans

During June of 1956, I left Canada on a one-year worker's permit and went to New Orleans.

The Biophysics Program was part of Tulane's physics department. Together with a local company, the Biophysics Program had obtained contracts from the Department of the Navy and the Bureau of Aeronautics to work on nonconventional photography. The objective was to develop a practical method for copying documents. At that time, Xerox had not yet invented its copying machines, which would later dominate the industry worldwide.

My mother followed me to America a few weeks after I arrived. She was able to find work in a fashion salon in downtown New Orleans. Unfortunately, there was practically no equipment at the Biophysics Program available for me to perform advanced research on nonconventional photography. The method advanced by the biophysics program was the development of a new copying method, based on the formation of many tiny bubbles to copy images on documents. (A short discussion of this project is presented in Appendix 5.)

I found a method to increase the optical densities of these Mylar films. Large optical densities could be obtained by adding a tiny amount of a light-absorbing compound (a dye) to the plastic-like film. Light would now undergo considerable absorption when it was scattered by the many tiny bubbles.

I also formulated a theory of scattering center formation, taking into account the surface tension of the film and the pressure of the nitrogen. My interest in the role that the universal length played in physics grew and grew. To improve my competence in mathematics, I took private instruction from Dr. Rengli, a Swiss mathematician who was a lecturer in Tulane's department of mathematics. I diligently solved most of the exercises contained in a textbook of advanced calculus that we used.

At the end of my first half-year of working for the biophysics program, I approached Dr. R. Nieset, the director of the Biophysics Program. I asked if he could assist me in finding a way to stay in the United States permanently. He approached Professor J. C. Morris, who was head of the physics department and vice president of the university. He contacted Congressman Hale Boggs. Boggs, in turn, petitioned the Immigration and Naturalization Service, in the U.S. Department of Justice, to grant me first-preference status on the Greek immigration quota. The petition was granted.

I was supposed to leave the United States for Cuba to obtain a permanent immigration visa from the American Embassy in Cuba. However, by executive order, President Eisenhower revoked this requirement from U.S. immigration provisions. Foreign scientists were not required to leave the United States and come back in order to change temporary status to permanent residence.

After a year at the Biophysics Program, I realized that there was no opportunity for me to perform high-quality research. To obtain my own funding, I wrote a proposal to study the optical properties of thin metallic films. At the time, the optical and electrical properties of thin films were poorly understood, and they were different from the bulk materials. If a substance is not present as a thin film or as powder, it is referred to as bulk. After submitting my proposal and waiting for a long time, I started to look for another position.

Convair in San Diego, California, drew my attention. This company was in the process of setting up a new and ambitious research program in solid-state physics. At the time, Convair was heavily involved in building airplanes. The company anticipated that they would be granted tax breaks for performing research, so they planned to hire a rather large group of scientists for a large research program.

After an inquiry, I was quickly hired. To go west, I found a student to help me drive. Toget her with my mother, we started on the long trip. Eastern Texas looked like Louisiana: green and very humid. The scenery changed as we continued our seemingly endless trip through Texas. It was June 1958, so it was dry and hot. The countryside was flat, with some hilly areas in the distance. After driving and driving, we finally reached west Texas, which looked more interesting. We enjoyed driving through New Mexico and Arizona. The student left us in Phoenix.

Entering eastern California, we were disappointed again. The countryside reminded us of western Louisiana and east Texas. The landscape was flat and agricultural, and it was very humid. We were driving through the Imperial Valley. However, the scenery changed rather suddenly as we reached the mountains.

Convair in San Diego

When we arrived in San Diego, the ocean and the deep blue sky reminded me of Greece. Soon, "America's Finest City," as it is called, became the finest city for me. At Convair, however, several setbacks were waiting. When I tried to enter the plant to work, I was informed that I needed a security clearance. Nobody had any idea how long it would take to obtain one. My department manager suggested that I spend sometime in the library at the Naval Electronics Laboratory, located in the Point Loma neighborhood.

The library was near the apartment my mother and I had rented, and was well stocked with books and journals. The librarian proudly informed me that this was one of the best libraries on the West Coast. The library was often used by the naval laboratory's staff and by a few employees from Convair. My supervisor suggested that I review the literature in thermoel ectricity, hinting that some funding for a project in this area might become available. I put in considerable effort to familiarize myself with the subject, having such great resources available to me in the library. However, no funding became available.

Sometime later, my research department management said that funding might be obtained in the emerging field of microelectronics, so I again put considerable effort into studying the literature and traveling to some companies that were beginning to be active in this new field. I also attended some meetings in microelectronics. Like my research in to thermoelectricity, however, nothing came of all my efforts.

When I arrived in San Diego, I had inquired about the possibility of enhancing my background in mathematics. I was lucky: The University of California Extension at San Diego offered many evening courses. Among them were a number of courses in mathematics, including courses at the graduate level. During my next four years in San Diego, I took quite a few mathematics courses. Diligently, I completed my homework, and with the passage of time, I improved my mathematical skills. I also invested considerable time analyzing the role of the universal length in physics.

Today, I would call these attempts amateurish. First, I tried to expand quantum mechanics, but I encountered immense problems. After considerable pondering, I concluded that I could not see any logical way to accomplish this task. My second approach was to expand the STR by somehow incorporating the universal length. It had always bothered me that the universal length was not a universal invariant, like the velocity of light (c) and Max Planck's constant (h). Was there a way to elevate the universal constant to an invariant, meaning it would have the same values in all frames of reference like c and h? (The meaning of c and h are briefly discussed in Appendixes 1 and 2.)

Finally, after two years, I obtained a security clearance, which allowed me to enter the Convair laboratories. Another disappointment came when I discovered that not much equipment was available. I was asked to produce a list of the equipment I needed for my work, but I was informed that I might have to wait for funding. My colleagues explained to me that large companies in America often receive tax privileges for claiming efforts in research. However, the tax savings did not necessarily end up supporting any research efforts. Convair was trying to enter the commercial airplane market, and the company faced stiff competition from other aircraft companies. I suppose that some of their engineering efforts were labeled "research," but these would be called "development" in Europe.

After investing considerable time familiarizing myself with microelectronics, I had to drop this subject. Instead, I was asked to study the new field of lasers. My research group included a German, Hubert Lintz. Previously, he had worked for the United States government. I asked him how he liked working for the American bureaucracy. He said that if you get along with your manager, it is paradise. If not, it is hell.

Unfortunately, it took me many years to fully understand his statement. During my last year at Convair, due to the shortage of funding, our group was shrinking. Without proper equipment, in early 1962, I realized that my career at Convair was ending. About the same time, expanding the STR had become more and more important to me. This interest had slowly turned into an obsession.

I tried to analyze my situation. Professionally, after six years, my decision to come to the United States had not yet worked out. I had very little to show for my time. I had not published a single paper. Possibly, while working for Tulane University, I should have tried to use my postdoctoral position to make my way into Tulane's faculty. On the positive side, I had become a permanent resident of the United States. San Diego had become my home, and it was difficult for me to leave America's Finest City. However, if I wanted to have a successful professional career—which meant conducting research—it was time to move on, even if this meant a sacrifice.

Early in the spring of 1962, I learned that Dr. Lippert from the Technical University of Stuttgart, Germany, would be giving a seminar at the chemistry department of the University of California, San Diego. Because his seminar was related to my research interests, I decided to attend. Dr. Lippert had been an assistant to Professor FÖrster, who had supervised my diploma-thesis at the Max Planck Institute. At German universities, these assistants fill a position between postdoctoral fellow and assistant professors. To obtain a position as professor at a German university, one has to produce a so-called Habilitationsschrift, an extended doctoral thesis. A professor supervises this extended PhD thesis. The assistant has to work dutifully for the professor for many years to complete this requirement. It is a very good arrangement for the professor, having a dedicated coworker performing slave labor. The assistant, who is also called a Privat Dozent in Germany, might also help to reduce his professor's teaching chores.

I explained my peculiar situation to Dr. Lippert. He suggested that I drive with him to Los Angeles. He was going to give a seminar at the California Institute of Technology. After his seminar, I could make contact with some of the faculty members to learn who was looking for a postdoctoral fellow with my background.

After Dr. Lippert's presentation, we spoke first with Professor Anderson, who was a member of the physics department. However, he himself had no funding, nor did he know of any colleagues with funding. Then we talked with Professor Wiles Robinson from the chemistry department, but Professor Robinson didn't have funding for a postdoctoral fellow either. He said that a Professor Mostafa ElSayed of the University of California, Los Angeles, (UCLA) had—or was expecting—funding for his research project. This project might be large enough to support a postdoctoral fellow. We called Professor El-Sayed, who expressed interest in seeing us. There was sufficient time left to go to West Los Angeles and meet him in his office during the late afternoon. Dr. El-Sayed, at that time an assistant professor in the chemistry department, was very interested that I had worked under Professor FÖrster for my diploma thesis. This meant that I had the proper background to work for him. We quickly agreed that I would come to Los Angeles.

The University of California, Los Angeles

While working in San Diego, I had visited Los Angeles several times. This city is located only 135 miles northwest of San Diego. Los Angeles is the second-largest city in America. Because of its fast pace and crowded freeways, it was not my favorite city to visit. When Mexico won independence from Spain in 1821, California became part of Mexico. Since 1848, when the United States assumed control of California, both the city of Los Angeles and the entire state of California have been among the fastest growing in the nation.

The postdoctoral fellowship Professor El-Sayed had available for me paid only $6,000 per year, exactly half the wages I had been earning at Convair. Unfortunately, I had several financial obligations that I would be unable to meet on such drastically reduced income, so my mother volunteered to go back to work. After we moved to Los Angeles, she found employment at a fashion salon on Wilshire Boulevard, not too far from our apartment in Santa Monica.

The move to Los Angeles was one of the best decisions I ever made. The research I conducted was very interesting, and Professor El-Sayed became a lifelong friend. Working under Professor Förster, I had studied the fluorescence of organic compounds in solution. At UCLA, we studied the so-called triplet state of organic compounds. Besides emission of fluorescence radiation, emission of phosphorescence may also be observed from organic compounds. Phosphorescence occurs at a somewhat longer wavelength than fluorescence from the same compound. (Phosphorescence and triplet-triplet absorption are briefly reviewed in Appendix 6.)

When I arrived at the UCLA chemistry department, Professor El-Sayed had a laboratory for me. Fortunately, a monochromator was available, an instrument widely used in spectrographic research. Also available was a detection system, together with other needed equipment. This allowed me to begin experiments at once. My laboratory was located right next to Professor El-Sayed's office. During his office hours, I would hear the students knocking at his door. He spent considerable time trying patiently to help his students. In his place, I would have become very impatient, not being able to be work in the laboratory. I accomplished this work during my first half-year at UCLA; my work resulted in a publication, coauthored with Dr. El-Sayed, in the *Journal of Chemical Physics* in 1963. In 1964, we published two more papers on the polarization of halonaphthalenes in the *Journal of Chemical Physics*, again with Dr. ElSayed as coauthor.

In Los Angeles, the universal length continued to obsess me as I attempted to apply it to the STR. This theory was considered to be perfect. Or was it only almost perfect? As stated, length is not an invariant under Lorentz transformations. This always bothered me. Could it be that an extended theory of relativity existed that contained the universal length as a second invariant, besides the speed of light c? I had concluded that the STR should be used as the starting point. Finally, I remembered that Einstein had not been the first to derive the Lorentz transformations. Poincaré in 1900 had derived the Lorentz transformations by starting from the hyperbolic wave equation that describes the propagation of electromagnetic radiation. Could it be that this wave equation was an approximation? Using my above-described approach, I immediately obtained an extended wave equation.

During the spring of 1964, the UCLA Extension announced a two-week course on quantum mechanics. This was one of many courses that the university offered every year during the summer months to advance the education of professionals. What attracted me most to the course in quantum mechanics was the lecturer: Dr. Edward Teller, also known as the "Father of the H-Bomb."

The summer afternoons were hot and long, and Dr. Teller was limping from a leg injury. Notwithstanding the very formal and dry subject matter, Dr. Teller tirelessly limped back and forth, talking and writing on the blackboard. He presented one of the best lectures on quantum mechanics I had ever attended. It was obvious that he also had a very deep understanding of physics. The lecture took place in the engineering building. During the first days of his lectures, he mentioned that a small office in the basement of the building had been made available to him to hold office hours. Anyone who had questions was welcome to show up during these office hours. Immediately, I decided to take advantage of his invitation. This was an excellent opportunity to present my theory on extending the STR and to solicit his very valued opinion.

In his little office, I outlined my theory on the small blackboard. During my presentation, he listened very attentively. After I had finished, I did not have to wait long for his opinion. He said that he could not find anything wrong with my theory. I was elated when I left his office. It was time to write a short article about my theory for publication in a physics journal. I started to put my thoughts on paper.

In October 1964, I also married Helen, whom I had been dating for four years. In 1960, I had attended a dance at the El Cortez in San Diego with a friend. Next to our table, I spotted Gary Dorer, a colleague from Convair. He was sharing a table with five girls. When he spotted me, he came over to my table and whispered into my ear that the girl sitting with her back to me was Greek. When the music started, I asked her to dance with me. Four years after the first dance with the most wonderful woman I ever met, I was finally able to ask her to spend the rest of our lives together.

The next year, 1965, it was time for me to settle down; my fortieth birthday was not too far off. My years as a postdoctoral fellow were ending. Again, I had to analyze what I wanted to do with my professional career; I had to find a place where I could conduct my life's work. Performing experiments and using my hands, I felt I was touching our creator's work. I was trying to understand his creation. Even if I held the position of a professor at a research university, I would mostly have to teach. Time in the laboratory would be very restricted. Graduate students and postdoctoral fellows perform most of the hands-on research at these universities. Besides teaching, professors mainly supervise the laboratory and perform administrative functions. Nevertheless, I contacted a few universities to inquire about vacancies.

I had no desire to stay in Los Angeles. During my trips to San Diego to see Helen, I would also visit some old friends. I learned that the Naval Electronic Laboratory was hiring engineers and scientists. If I was interested, it was suggested, I should obtain the necessary forms and apply for a position. Because I had left San Diego reluctantly, I wanted to return, so I decided to apply.

During the following months, I did not receive any acceptable offers from the few universities to which I had applied. However, the Naval Electronics Laboratory invited me in for an interview. Most Americans know almost nothing about the importance, huge size, and rather large numbers of the country's military research and development (R&D) laboratories. These laboratories work on large development projects and also on applied and basic research. The basic research parallels academic research; fields that might prove important to future military applications are investigated. Because I was so interested in performing basic research, working for a military laboratory was very appealing to me.

Besides, after my experience with Convair, I was not enthusiastic about working in industry. Every year, the U.S. Government allocates billions of dollars to universities and industries to perform research and development. Scientists at military R&D laboratories are also acting as contract monitors. These scientists evaluate proposals from universities and industries and monitor the progress of these contracts.

Chapter 3
Working for the United States Navy

Battery Ashburn

At the Electronics Laboratory, Dr. Jim Kerrigan, the head of the microelectronics branch, interviewed me. He held a doctorate in chemistry from the University of Chicago. Dr. Kerrigan's branch was pursuing research into microelectronics, also referred to as microcircuits. Because I had some background in this field from my days at Convair, Dr. Kerrigan invited me to join his branch.

The microelectronics laboratories were located in Battery Ashburn. This was one of the former naval batteries on the Point Loma peninsula in San Diego, its gun turrets facing west. This World War II fortification, with concrete walls many feet thick, had its two fifteen-inch guns removed. It was ideal for conversion into a research facility. At Point Loma, the navy's first wireless radio station had been operating since 1906. The laboratory was established on June 1, 1940, as the Navy Radio and Sound Laboratory, the navy's first West Coast laboratory. At that time, its assigned mission was to improve navy communications and to test new radar equipment

I started working as a physicist in August 1965. When I applied for the position, I was informed that I qualified for a GS-14 grade position. However, due to a moratorium on high-grade positions at that time, I began in a GS-13 position. I didn't know this at the time, but I would never be promoted to the pay grade

I qualified for when I was hired. GS stands for General Schedule, the main government pay system.

I had suggested to Dr. Kerrigan that I study the electric and optical properties of thin metallic, semiconductor, and insulating films. This required an update of the proposal I had prepared at Tulane University. Thin films are widely used in microelectronics. By studying the optical properties of these films, one can obtain information on some specific mechanisms that determine their electric conductivities. The conductivity depends on the thickness of the films and is different from the conductivity of the bulk material.

During my first interview with Dr. Kerrigan, I asked him about the laboratory's policies regarding the publication of research results in the open literature. Besides secret reports, and technical reports and notes, military laboratories also publish in the open literature. These are publications in journals that are available to the public; for example, they can be viewed in libraries. The most prestigious journal publications are "refereed." One and sometimes even two "referees" have carefully reviewed scientific manuscripts before publication. The referees employed by these scientific journals are top scientific specialists on the subject of publication. Only if the quality of the manuscript meets the highest scientific standards will they be published.

He assured me that he and the management of the laboratory encouraged their scientists and engineers to publish. I also asked him if I could publish my short paper on the extension of the STR, listing the laboratory as my place of work. He told me that this would not be a problem. Consequently, after I arrived at the laboratory during August 1965, I worked on two projects simultaneously. The first was to get ready to perform experiments on thin films, which required ordering all the instruments I needed to perform the proposed work. The second was to publish my paper on the extension of the STR.

I faced time constraints on both projects. Because I had just started my new job, I wanted to show rapid results for my employers. Therefore, I planned to publish only a short research note on the theoretical paper, which would allow someone else to follow up on the extension of the STR. This would allow me to quickly start concentrating full-time on my work in the laboratory.

I knew that I would encounter difficulties getting my very controversial paper accepted for publication. Although the proposed theory was an extension of the STR, it collided with some of the most important results of the STR, which were held dear in the scientific community. In a short time, I had put together a brief letter. It mainly proposed the extended wave equation (referred as equation (2) in the paper) to replace the wave equation (referred to as equation (1), which the STR is based on).

By the middle of September, I had completed the paper, and it had passed through the necessary channels that would give me permission to publish it in the open literature. I mailed the manuscript, which bore the title "Ultra Special Theory of Relativity, Which Contains a Universal Length as a Second Invariant, Besides the Speed of Light," to the editor of Physical Review Letters. On October 4, 1965, the editor, Dr. S. Goudsmit, replied that based on a referee's report, my paper could not be accepted for publication. The referee's report stated:

> *The manuscript of T. Pavlopoulos is original in content ... The choice of equation (2) seems quite arbitrary, and it does not make any sense to publish an equation by itself without working out some of its consequences. I suspect equation (2) completely determines a privileged coordinate system up to the Euclidean group. On the whole, I would not recommend publication of this in its present form.* [3]

After the negative response from Physical Review Letters, I tried to have my paper published by *Physics Letters*. The editor of the journal, Dr. Parry, replied: "According to the referee report, this paper contains highly speculative proposals, and should not be published until more work, either experimental or theoretical, has been performed."[4] During November, I had tried my luck and submitted my paper to *Il Nuovo Cimento*. *Il Nuovo Cimento* is a highly respected Italian journal on theoretical physics. However, the referee of this journal suggested that I try to find the group of invariance, meaning finding the transformations that leave equation (2) invariant. The referee stated that studying limited cases and other formulas in the text did not make much sense when the transformations and their meanings and consequences were not discussed. However, his request to produce the group of transformations was beyond my mathematical ability.

I had to agree with the referees. I was not a theoretical physicist who was working full-time solving mathematical problems. I had a new job where I was required to perform, so I could not invest all of my time in my paper. In early 1966, I submitted my manuscript to *Naturforschung*, a German journal that often published theoretical papers. By this time, I had expanded the paper to seventeen pages. However, *Naturforschung* also rejected my paper. I submitted the paper to the regional secretary of the American Physical Society to be able to present it at the society's meeting in Austin, Texas, from February 23 to 25, 1967. During the fall of 1966, I also submitted my paper to the Japanese journal *Progress in Theoretical Physics*. However, this did not advance my case. Professor H. Yukawa, a Nobel Prize winner in physics, stated that the paper was unacceptable for publication in his journal. I further expanded the paper.

After a year of rejections, my self-confidence was shattered. I could feel the stress mounting as I ran out of options. I could not see a way to continue. Wrestling with myself to stop my seemingly hopeless struggle, I endured sleepless nights and started to have nightmares. One morning, when the night gave way to the day, the bedroom seemed to be full of shadowy figures of Greek soldiers. They were the soldiers who had fought the Italians during World War II in the Epirus Mountains. I could hear their silent message. They urged me, "Go on, go on, go on ..."

The next morning, shaken, I went to work I decided to calm down and rethink my situation. Maybe there was some way to continue. I wondered if I should reread the correspondence I had received during the last year. Had I overlooked something? I started from the beginning. The rejection letter from Dr. Goudsmit from *Physical Review Letters* was the first one I studied. The report of the referee stated: "The manuscript of T. Pavlopoulos is original in content. On the whole, I would not recommend publication of this in its present form."[3]

Suddenly, I realized that I was working on an "original manuscript"—namely, on the extension of the STR. Actually, this was a huge compliment. By now, I had to agree with the referee that the short, somewhat flimsy paper had not deserved to be accepted for publication. In the meantime, I had considerably expanded the paper and had also worked out some consequences of equation (2). Now the paper might have a better chance to be accepted for publication.

On October 28, 1966, I sent the revised and expanded manuscript to Dr. Goudsmit. I asked him to reconsider the paper for publication and to submit the paper to two different referees. After several weeks, I received two evaluations. The first referee had nothing flattering to say about my theory. The second referee wrote:

> *Contrary to the author's assertion, the suggested waveequation (2) does indeed seem to single out a preferred frame at rest, that frame in which the speed of a quantum of given energy does not depend on the direction of motion of the quantum, therefore violating the principle of special relativity. The possibility exists, and is well known, that departures*

from the principle of special relativity might exist but be significant only at very small wavelengths. It might be permissible to publish a note to this effect giving an example of such a theory. The author should clarify whether his theory obeys the principle of special theory of relativity, and if so the paper could then be considered for The Physical Review (not the Physical Review Letters, in my opinion).[5]

Finally, I could see the possibility of successfully publishing my paper in the most prestigious physics journal. After revision, I resubmitted my manuscript. During February 23 through 25, 1967, at the meeting of the American Physical Society in Austin, Texas, I presented a short version of my paper. At the presentation, attendance was small, only about five or six people. Nobody asked any questions. A postcard, dated May 10, 1967, informed me that my manuscript had been forwarded for publication in *The Physical Review*. My paper, on the "Breakdown of Lorentz Invariance," was published in September of 1967.[6]

I received many postcards asking me to furnish a reprint of my paper. However, no college or university invited me to present a seminar on my theory. At work, I informed only my managers of the acceptance of my very controversial paper for publication— nobody else. At home, until very recently, I had never discussed this work with my family or with any friends. Quite simply, I did not want to be considered a kook who wasted his time trying to disprove Einstein's STR. I submitted the follow-up paper with the title "The Special Theory of Relativity and the Problem of the Universal Constants" to *Nuovo Cimento*. This time, I had no problem getting it published. Again, I received many requests for reprints but no invitations to present a seminar at any academic institution.

Dr. Theodore G. Pavlopoulos

Working in the Laboratory

When I started at the Naval Electronics Laboratory, I had ordered the necessary equipment to perform my experiments on thin films. This included optical equipment, a monochromator, detectors, light sources, and other needed equipment. In addition to this equipment, I also needed a good vacuum system to produce clean, thin films. Heating metals to very high temperatures in a vacuum will cause them to evaporate. The metal vapors will condense and form films when they hit a cold surface. Preferably, one should use the ultra-high vacuum systems to obtain clean films that are not contaminated by traces of air. Fortunately, a new breed of ultra-high vacuum systems had become commercially available. The laboratory had ordered several of these systems, but their delivery took much longer than expected.

Most of the other equipment arrived before them. Some of the equipment I had ordered could easily be used for spectroscopic studies on organic compounds, similar to the experiments I had performed at UCLA. While I waited for the vacuum systems, I put the other equipment together to begin measuring the triplet-triplet absorption spectra of organic compounds. Dr. Kerrigan did not mind.

The delivery of the ultra-high vacuum systems was postponed and postponed, so I continued with the measurements of triplet-triplet absorption measurements of some organic molecules. Unfortunately, the management of the laboratory removed Dr. Kerrigan from his position—and from the laboratory. All of this was a total surprise to me. I had never seen such a thing happen in the civil service. Possibly, management might have believed that Dr. Kerrigan's background in chemistry had alienated him from the electronic engineers in our branch. However, at that time, there were other positions available in the laboratory that could have used a chemist. It was a big loss for me—even more so than I realized at the time.

Dr. Kerrigan was the only mentor I ever had at the laboratory. Dr. Perkins became his successor. He had started at the laboratory just a few days before me. He was an older man, with a friendly and jovial appearance. His job at the laboratory was to set up the crucial semiconductor processing facility needed to obtain microcircuits. However, Dr. Kerrigan had had a low opinion of Dr. Perkins.

Dr. Kerrigan had once asked his three principal investigators, Dr. Perkins, Dr. Christy, and me, to write a technical note. Such technical notes are in-house publications. In this note, each of us outlined in some detail our future technical and scientific plans in support of the ongoing microelectronic efforts. Dr. Kerrigan remarked that Dr. Perkins's contribution was of poor quality and that he had never published a single paper in the open literature.

To me, and apparently to our management, Dr. Perkins appeared to be a very busy person. Several times I had tried to visit him during my afternoon coffee break for a short chat. Most of the time, he asked me to leave his office because he was too busy. Both of us had started as grade GS-13 physicists, but his appearance of being busy must have impressed our upper management and contributed to his quick elevation to branch head. For about two years, the moratorium blocking high-grade promotions to GS-14 at the Center had been lifted. Now Dr. Perkins's promotion to GS-14 came quickly. Only a short time later, he promoted other branch members from GS-12- to GS-13-grade physicists and engineers.

None of these employees held doctorates. They were performing experiments, but no results were collected or were suitable for publication in the open literature, or even for a technical note. At the same time, many other employees at the Center were being promoted to GS-13 and 14. I did not understand why I and some other deserving employees were not promoted. My experiments on phenazine yielded exceptionally good results, and I was able to quickly prepare a paper for publication. I gave it to Dr. Perkins for processing. After several months of waiting.

I asked him what had happened with my paper. He replied that my paper was right there, in his desk. He said that all my papers were only good to be collected in archives.

Looking angrily at me, Dr. Perkins asked, "Don't you know what you did?" I called our division head at that time, Mr. Mitchel, and asked him the shortcomings of my paper. "Nothing serious," he replied. "You might have difficulties finding my weak pencil marks. I corrected a few minor typos and added a comma." Only much later did I learn that Dr. Perkins's reaction to my paper was typical of poor managers reacting to high-performing employees.

The results of my experiments on the triplet-triplet absorption of phenazine and some other organic molecules were published in two papers in the *Journal of Chemical Physics*. Over the years, many scientists have cited these articles in their publications. During this time, the laboratory had been enlarged and was elevated to the Naval Electronic Laboratory Center (NELC). In the following years, the name of NELC changed many times, but it always maintained its designation as a center.

In the rest of this book, I will mostly refer to my place of work as "the Center." In a memo of September 12, 1969, Mr. D.W. Liddell, my new division head at that time, outlined promotion criteria. These improper promotion procedures are still used even today. To be promoted, your management has to rank you according to your "worth to NELC."

> In my evaluations "worth to NELC encompasses three main factors—technical ability, leadership, and motivation. These are of course subjective criteria, which are the opinions of the rater but are applied uniformly within the organization.[7]

It had never been explained to me how an employee demonstrates "worth." At that time, I had no idea of the existence of classification standards, nor that the classification of positions is the backbone of the federal civil service. Nobody instructed me on proper promotion procedures. These standards enforce merit principles, namely, fair treatment of employees.It took me several years to learn the legal background on how employees are supposed to be promoted.

Back in the laboratory, the ultra-high vacuum systems finally arrived. I immediately started to get my system working. These systems presented a considerable improvement over the older systems, producing much better vacuums. They used stainless steel traps containing charcoal. In the older systems, air and water molecules were absorbed on the walls inside of the vacuum system. These molecules were difficult to remove, slowly diffusing into the vacuum, reducing its quality. The new vacuum systems were made entirely out of stainless steel. This made it possible to heat the entire vacuum system, breaking the strong bond between absorbed air and water molecules and the metal walls of the vacuum system. After heating and pumping, these traps are submerged in liquid nitrogen making them very cold. Under these conditions, the charcoal efficiently absorbs air and water molecules, further reducing gas pressure in the vacuum system. This process is repeated several times to obtain very low pressures.

These systems are very labor intensive. I did not want to waste my time in the lab performing low-level technician work, operating the time-consuming vacuum systems. Although we had several technicians in our branch, they were assigned to other employees, who had very limited research experience. I discussed this matter with Dr. Perkins, but it was not resolved. Therefore, I asked him for a transfer, but he would not let me go.

Dr. Perkins had spent many years behind his desk, ordering new equipment to set up our semiconductor processing facility, which was crucial for fabricating microcircuits. When the equipment arrived, it was stored for a long time in the halls of the battery, until it was moved into his large semiconductor fabrication laboratory.

There was no sign that this equipment was ever installed or operational, or that any activity took place. I made an appointment with the Center's technical director, Dr. Bergman. I asked him to help me transfer to another place with in the Center. He was very much against the idea. He said that he had great plans for me. Microelectronics was very important to the navy, and he was planning to provide microcircuits for the entire U.S. Navy. Shortly, he said, the microelectronic branch would be expanded to a division, and there would be a lot of research for me.

I disagreed with Dr. Bergman. Microelectronics was, not only important for the navy, but also for many other applications in industry, the military, as well as households. Soon there would be a worldwide effort to produce microcircuits cheaply. Industry had already started investing huge amounts of capital to advance this exceptional and important new technology. I could not see how our small efforts at the Center, together with our cumbersome governmental procurement system, could compete with the onslaught of research and products by a conglomerate of industrial giants. I would only be wasting my time trying to compete under these circumstances.

Changes in Funding

Generally, the U.S. government funds its departments and agencies by so-called block funding needed for their operation, including employees' salaries. The Center received most of its funding directly from the Pentagon. Around 1970, a fundamental change took place in the way funding was provided to the Navy's Research and Development (R&D) laboratories when their source of funding was switched to the so-called Naval Industrial Funding (NIF). The R&D laboratories receive only a small block of funding from the Office of Naval Research (ONR) for their basic research—also called independent research (IR)—and for some special projects.

This required R&D laboratories to go to the Pentagon and other agencies to obtain most of their funding, in competition with industry and universities. When the change in the sources of funding occurred, the navy exhibited poor leadership by providing its R&D laboratories with clear instructions on how to implement this order. Consequently, within the R&D laboratories, the question arose who should write proposals and go to Washington, DC to solicit funding? Officially, the commander (the captain) is responsible for securing funding for his command. However, most of these captains have no clue where to go, whom to contact, or how to write and present R&D proposals, nor do they know how to direct the research or development work.

At the Center, the task of requesting funding was delegated to the technical director, who transferred the task to the department heads. From there, the responsibility went to the division heads. During the early days, a few divisions and some branch heads would participate in obtaining funding; the rest of the burden went to employees. Today, employees carry most of the load, with only few branch heads—and, very rarely, division heads—participating. Since that time, employees have been increasingly pressured by their management to obtain funding. This requires scientists and engineers to write proposals, make technical or scientific contacts with potential sponsors, pitch their ideas over the telephone, and present their proposals in Washington, DC.

If these proposals receive funding, the employees supervise the work and, on completion, travel again to Washington, DC to report their progress. Employees write final progress reports, in the form of internal technical notes or papers to be published in the open scientific literature. Employees who were successfu lly pressured by management to perform managerial functions— namely, successfully obtaining funding—are preferred for promotion. Today, the same type of poor leadership the navy showed in 1970 is mirrored by much of our federal management today.

Difficult or complex assignments by upper-level managers are simply dumped on underlings and then forgotten. Managers never worry about how the orders are carried out. In the private sector, success or failure is judged on the color of the bottom line. Is it black or red? Did we have higher profits this year compared to last year? Since the introduction of NIF funding at the Center, the question has been: H ow much funding is being brought in?

The overall performance of the organization is now a minor concern. This funding issue cast a shadow on my work at the Center from 1970 until I decided to retire in 2003.

Working on Blue/Green Lasers

In 1969, a Dr. P. Fletcher had obtained a department head position at the Center. Previously, he h eld a position at the NASA Electronics Laboratory in Boston. I learned that Dr. Fletcher was very much interested in electro-optics, especially in establishing a blue/green dye laser capability at the Center. He reasoned that these lasers could play an important role in naval underwater communication and illumination systems. (Lasers are briefly discussed in Appendix 7.)

At that time, lasers were rather new. Today, besides their use in research, lasers have found a wide application in welding, isotope separation, recording, optical communications, and many other fields. I decided to meet with Dr. Fletcher to discuss a possible transfer to his department. When we met, he was very interested in having me join the dye laser effort. To my surprise, he managed to pull me out of the microelectronics branch. I realized immediately that the field of dye lasers and laser dyes was the field I should be actively pursuing. I planned to invest all my energy and time to succeed. I had experience with the fluorescence of organic compounds from working on my diploma-thesis at the Max Planck Institute. Laser dyes are strongly fluorescing organic compounds. I also had an extensive background studying the triplet state of organic compounds from working as a postdoctoral fellow at UCLA. Combining these two fields immediately made me a top expert in the field of laser dyes.

Among the first organic compounds to exhibit laser action were organic compounds used for coloring fabrics. Now, all organic compounds capable of exhibiting laser action are called laser dyes. Fortunately, I had also spent my time well at Battery Ashburn, setting up equipment and measuring the triplet-triplet absorption spectra of organic compounds.

When I joined the electro-optics division of his department, Dr. Hood was the division head. He had just returned from London, where he had obtained a doctorate in physics. The department where he earned his degree was the birthplace of fiber optics. When Dr. Hood returned to the Center, he established a fiber-and integrated-optics branch, headed by Dr. Albares. This may have been the first fiber-optics effort in America.

Mr. W. Richard, the head of the laser branch, had also just arrived from NASA's laboratory in Boston. Right after I was transferred into his branch, he lectured me on the importance of developing a blue/green dye laser capability. He instructed me on the importance of obtaining funding from the Pentagon, because possessing this capability was an important trump card. He also assured me that if I succeeded in establishing a blue/green dye laser capability within one year at the Center, I would be promoted to GS-14.

Meanwhile, about three years had passed since my paper on the STR, "Breakdown of Lorentz Invariance," had been published. However, in the physics literature, there was no follow-up of my work whatsoever. Leaving Battery Ashburn, I took all of my spectroscopic equipment with me to my laboratory located on Top Site of the Center at Point Loma. I moved into a laboratory that was large enough to accommodate my spectroscopic equipment. Soon after I arrived at my new workplace, my equipment to measure absorption of triplet-state of organic compounds, including some laser dyes, was operational. Laser dyes, besides exhibiting strong fluorescence, must also exhibit low triplet absorption over their fluorescence spectral region.

It was important to further refine this equipment to be able to measure the weak triplet-triplet absorption present in laser dyes. From equipment available in the laboratory, a flash-lamp-pumped dye laser was put together. Employing the newly constructed dye laser and using the commercially available laser dye aminoacridine, impressive outputs of blue/green laser light was obtained. The lab's management was very impressed with our progress and invited many navy and civilian dignitaries to admire our new advances in the blue/green laser field.

Some funding for our small program became available. We tested the different laser dyes available from commercial sources. Soon it became clear to me that the laser dyes that were available commercially performed poorly. Their lasing efficiency was low, and all of them suffered from various degrees of photodecomposition. This required changing the dye solution frequently, a serious drawback for practical applications.

In laser dyes, their laser action spectral region closely covers their nuorescence spectral region. I measured the triplet absorption of some commercially available laser dyes, which showed that there was too much triplet absorption present over their fluorescence (laser action) spectral region, explaining their poor laser action efficiency. I concluded that new, more efficient laser dyes were needed.

Dr. Perkins was transferred to Dr. Fletcher's staff when Dr. Bergman expanded the microelectronics branch to a division. Apparently, the new division head didn't have much use for Dr. Perkins and removed him, not only as a branch head, but also from the microelectronics division entirely. Dr. Perkins served for several years as a gofer to Dr. Fletcher. He went to the airport to pick up dignitaries and showed up when Dr. Fletcher had his regular brown-bag meetings with the employees. Dr. Perkins never had any comments, suggestions, or questions at these meetings.

I mention Dr. Perkins's career in some detail because he was a quintessential civil servant. From all the papers I had published during my time at the Center, together with our newly operational blue/green dye laser, it was obvious to my management that I was performing at the GS-14 grade level. Finally, during November 1971, all the necessary signatures and documentation for a promotion package were prepared and submitted for my promotion to GS14. However, I was not promoted because of another moratorium on high grades. Sometime later, Dr. Hood was transferred into a staff position, and Mr. Richard replaced him.

During 1971, continuous-wave (CW) lasers became commercially available. Unlike pulsed lasers, CW lasers operate continuously. With the aid of a lens, one could focus the CW laser beam on a very small sample area of a cell, containing the dye solution. This generated very high light intensities, creating high concentrations of triplet-state laser dye molecules. Employing CW lasers as excitation sources for organic compounds presented a major advance in the field of triplet-triplet absorption spectroscopy. This allowed me to perform experiments to study the relationships between laser dye molecular structure and their triplet-triplet absorption.

These relationships proved helpful for the synthesis of new and more efficient laser dyes. First, I focused my interest on the coumarin laser dyes. They formed an important family of laser dyes, covering the spectral range between blue and green, including the important blue/green spectral region. Evaluating the ongoing experiments, I also discovered an important relationship between dye molecular structures and the spectral location and intensity of triplet-triplet absorption.

This information provided guidelines on how to develop new laser dyes.

I collected my results in a paper entitled "Prediction of Laser Action Properties of Some Organic Dyes from Their Structure and Polarization Characteristics of Their Electronic Transitions." This paper was published in the *1973 IEEE Journal of Quantum Electronics.*

After the promotion moratorium was cancelled, my management did not reintroduce my promotion to GS-14. During this time, other employees at the Center were constantly being promoted; often nobody had any clue as to why. This included scientists who were promoted to GS-14, who were also performing research work, but who were often less qualified than me, performed less difficult research, and had published fewer articles.

One day, while I was trying to retrieve a letter from the outgoing mail, I ran across a newly prepared position description without a name on it. This promotion to GS-14 had been prepared with the assistance of the Center's personnel office. I realized that it had been prepared for the promotion of one of my coworkers. It contained inflated criteria on qualifications and scientific contributions. It finally started to dawn on me how many employees were being promoted at the Center. Once management had decided whom to promote, the personnel office was contacted to add promotion criteria, whether they applied or not, to the candidate's position description from the classification standard.

By now, it was 1973. Since I had joined the laser branch late in 1969, I had submitted and published eleven papers in the open literature. My managers and I finally collided over the promotion issue. As a result, I was informed that my position would be abolished. Position abolishment means you are fired.

They claimed that there was no funding for me to continue with my work. But firing a federal civil servant is not that simple. In lieu of position abolishment, I was allowed to stay in the same electrooptics division, but I was transferred to Dr. Albares's integrated optics branch. Some of my equipment was stored at Convair. Despite the claim that there was no funding for my research, over the following years the blue/green laser program experienced a huge increase of funding.

Integrated Optics

The mission of the integrated optics branch was to be the navy's leading effort in fiber optics and integrated optics technology, specifically to investigate new phenomena and applications in guided wave optics. At the time, the integrated optics branch was expanding, hiring a considerable number of new physicists, some with PhD degrees. Most experiments conducted in the branch focused on optical fibers and integrated optics.

Optical fibers are used to transmit optical signals. The flexible, thin optical fibers consist of light-transmitting materials like glass, quartz, and sometimes plastics. Optical signals are transmitted based on the principle of total reflection and zigzagging. (A short overview of integrated optics is provided in Appendix 8.)

At that time, there were considerable obstacles in the way of using optical fibers to replace electrical wires in communication systems. Many electric circuit elements had to be translated into their fiber optical counterparts. Dr. Taylor, a GS-13 theoretical physicist, and Dr. Martin, a skillful GS-12 experimental physicist, carried out the main efforts of the branch. Dr. Martin had recently obtained his PhD from the University of California, San Diego, under the difficult conditions of working part-time at the Center.

Both Drs. Taylor and Martin performed exceptionally well, publishing a considerable number of papers in the open literature. However, Dr. Taylor was unhappy with his GS-13 pay, and Dr. Martin was even unhappier with his GS-12 grade, the same rating as most technicians at the Center.

There were also the newly-hired PhD physicists, who had their own ambitions of being promoted. One of these, Dr. Caton, a Canadian, had obtained his PhD in electrical engineering from the University of California, Berkeley. He used to joke that the Center was probably the only place where Bachelor of Science graduates from the California state colleges were supervising PhD graduates from the University of California. Finally, Dr. Taylor was promoted to GS-14, but Dr. Martin was not, so he left the Center for the Lawrence Livermore National Laboratory. His small but very active group was dissolved.

In 1975, I was selected as a member of the New York Academy of Sciences. This honor is reserved for scientists who have provided exceptional scientific leadership and who were recognized nationally and internationally. During my 1976 annual performance review, I notified my management that my position description was not properly graded. In the laboratory, I produced optical waveguides in optical filters. The resulting paper, "Fabrication of Channel Optical Wave Guides in Glass by CW Laser Heating," was published in the *Journal of Applied Physics* in 1974. In addition, I filed for, and was later granted, a patent for the process I had developed to produce the optical wave-guides. For practical applications of integrated optics, rigid, single-mode fiber-to-fiber interconnections of high-coupling efficiency are of utmost importance. The method for providing them should be simple and usable for field applications.

I helped to develop such a method, working with two branch members. The best coupling efficiency between the two fibers was 80 percent. This work was published in *Applied Optics* in 1977.

I knew what was wrong with my position description and the reason it was not classified at the GS-14 grade. First, I did not receive sufficient credit for my unusual qualifications and experience. Second, I did not receive sufficient credit for working as an independent senior scientist, without assistance from my supervisors. On December 21, 1976, as required, I submitted an updated position description to the Center's personnel office, notifying them that I was performing at a GS-14 level. Upon submission of such a request for reclassification, the personnel office was supposed to reclassify the request within one hundred and twenty days.

Chapter 4
The American Civil Service System

The General-Schedule Pay System

The General Schedule (GS) is the American government's main pay system, covering about half of the federal workforce. It consists of fifteen grades. Each grade consists of ten steps, through which employees advance based on their length of service. An employee passes through the first step after fifty-two weeks of service. The same amount of time is required to pass through the second and third step to reach the fourth step. The fifth, sixth, and seventh steps each require 104 weeks. To pass to the eighth, ninth, and tenth steps, each requires 156 weeks. Altogether, to pass step-by-step through all of the grade levels requires eighteen years of service.

Beyond the fifteen grades, there are the super grades, namely, the senior-executive service (SES) grades, ES-1 through VI, which are reserved for high-ranking managers and technical directors.

The GS classification system is set forth in Title 5, U.S. Code Chapter 51. In 1883, Congress passed the Civil Service Act (CSA). Before that date, the civil service system in America operated under a spoil system: the party in power deter mined who would work and who would not. With the passage of time, more CSA rules and procedures were introduced, with merit principles becoming the backbone of the system.

To work for the government, civil servants were required

to pass competitive examinations. The number of civil servants increased from year to year, especially during World War II. To enforce merit system principles, the Civil Service Commission (CSC) was established, serving both management and employees, leading to criticism for having a conflict of interest in serving both groups. During his campaign, President Carter promised the American people that if elected, he would clean up the bureaucratic mess in Washington. On March 2, 1978, in his message to Congress, he complained about the deficiencies of the federal civil service. He stated:

> *But this system has serious defects. It has became a bureaucratic maze, which neglected merit, tolerated poor performance, permitted abuse of legitimate employees' rights, and mired every personnel action in red tape, delay, and confusion. Most Civil Service Employees perform with spirit and integrity. Nevertheless, there is still widespread criticism of federal government performance. The public suspects that there are too many government workers, that they are underworked, overpaid, and insulated from the consequences of incompetence.*[8]

The resulting congressional hearings examined the poor performance of the American bureaucracy. Several federal civil service managers complained bitterly about their lack of power to deal with poorly performing employees. Because of those hearings, Congress initiated provisions that gave managers even more power to promote, hire, reward, and fire employees. The Civil Service Reform Act (CSRA) of 1978 dissolved the CSC and assigned many of the personnel administrative functions to several other agencies.

As we will see, the CSRA had a significant impact on the performance of the entire federal civil service system. The duties of the CSC were taken over by the following agencies: The Merit

System Protection Board (MSPB) concerns itself with protecting employees against managerial abuses of merit system principles. In addition, MSPB judges hear appeals resulting from disciplinary actions against employees, such as suspension, firings, grade reductions, and reductions in force (RIFs). The MSPB also conducts studies of the health of the federal civil service system. The Office of the Special Council (OSC) has jurisdiction over so-called prohibited personnel practices and protects whistle-blowers from reprisal actions. The Equal Employment Opportunity Commission (EEOC) handles discrimination cases. The last of the major agencies that have taken over the duties of the former CSC is the Office of Personnel Management (OPM).

The Office of Personnel Management

For most Americans, the OPM is an unknown federal agency. However, it is a very important one. The OPM's job is to ensure that federal personnel management programs and systems enable the government to serve the American people effectively. Specifically, the OPM is responsible for reviewing agency and department adherence to laws, regulations, and merit principles. At the same time, the OPM supports agencies and departments in recruiting, hiring, and retaining the diverse merit-based workforce. This includes advising Congress and the president on how to apply merit principles related to the selection, promotion, and performance pay of civil service workers. The OPM also bears official responsibility for maintaining federal classification standards and considers employee complaints about proper classification of their positions. The OPM has authority to conduct demonstration projects under Title 5, U.S. Code Chapter 47, which defines a demonstration project as:

> ... a project conducted by OPM, or under its supervision, to determine whether a specific change in personnel

management policies or procedures would results in improved Federal personnel management.

Some of these projects provide agencies with greater autonomy to develop personnel systems for their own needs. For example, some demos try to allow managers more freedom to adjust pay for performance rewards, similar to private industry. Different demos experiment with different personnel management concepts, and the OPM is required to provide consultation, oversight, and assistance during the five-year term of these projects.

Because the MSPB deals with managerial abuses of merit principles, including protecting employees from unfair disciplinary actions, the OPM operates as though its mission is to defend management when accused by employees of violating merit principles. Whenever the OPM finds that management has not adhered to laws, regulations, and merit principles, the OPM never holds management accountable. In short, this agency is anti-merit, which is to say, anti-employee and extremely pro-management.

Because the OPM does not know how to improve the workings of the federal bureaucracy, it has a penchant for listening to management's suggestions for improving the federal civil service. Clerk-type management, left over from the age of the file clerks, uses this power to stifle the advancement of high-performing and high-quality employees, while protecting mediocre and poorly performing employees.

The American civil service system is supposed to operate according to certain merit system principles (MSP), as outlined in the Title 5, U.S. Code 2301, as listed below:

Merit System Principles

1. *Recruit qualified individuals from all segments of society, and select and advance individuals on their merit after fair*

and open competition, which assures that all receive equal opportunity.

2. *Treat all employees and applicants fairly, without regard to political affiliation, race, color, religion, national origin, sex, sexual orientation, marital status, age, or handicapping condition and with proper regard for their privacy and constitutional rights.*

3. *Provide equal pay for substantial equal work and recognize excellent performance.*

4. *Maintain high standards of integrity, conduct, and concern for the public interest.*

5. *Manage employees efficiendy and effectively.*

6. *Retain and separate employees on the basis of their performance.*

7. *Educate and train employees when it will result in better organizational performance.*

8. *Protect employees from arbitrary personal favoritism or coercion for partisan political pursuit*

9. *Protect employees against reprisal for the lawful disclosure of information in "whistleblower" situations (i.e., protecting people who report things like illegal and/or wasteful activities).*[9]

The above merit principles, except for a few revisions, have been in force for many years. The introduction to a 1996 MSPB survey with the title: "Adherence to the Merit Principles in the Workplace," stated:

> *The merit system principles, which were articulated into statute in the 1978 CSRA, are a set of values for federal public service that date back to the beginning of the merit based civil service system in 1883. The principles address basic human resources activities. These activities—including selections, promotions, and actions to deal with performance*

problems—define the goal that all federal managers are expected to strive for when managing their workforce.

While some of these principles were added in later years (such as protection for employees against reprisal for the disclosure of waste, fraud, and abuse in the civil service system), most of them have always been key to the operation of a merit-based system, and central to the ability of the U.S.government to serve the public.

Why are these values so important to our system of government? They are meant to ensure that processes and systems the government uses for selecting and maintaining the federal workforce will result in a competent workforce that serves the best interest of the American people. Our strong belief expressed through the principles is that the workforce should be able to operate free of improper external influences in order to provide the best service possible to its client, the American taxpayer. In addition, the merit principles send a clear message that all individuals should have the opportunity to participate in the operation of our government if they so desire and are qualified.[10]

MSPB's above statements on how the American civil service should operate make nice reading. These principles are supposed to provide fair treatment for all employees and allow them to operate in an efficient civil service system that serves the public interest. However, these MSP statements contain a serious flaw: it is only voluntary for management to adhere to these merit principles.

The OPM is supposed to ensure that management follows merit principles, including protecting employees from favoritism and selection of employees on grounds other than their qualifications. But when management violates these merit principles and an employee uses the available routes to complain about these abuses, the employee rarely succeeds. In the rare case where the employee does succeed, there is no punishment for management.

Among the merit principles that management most often and deliberately violates is in selecting candidates for supervisory or managerial positions. They are mostly selected from the in-house pool, without fair and open competition, nor fulfilling proper experience or qualification requirements. For this reason, the American federal civil service system is not really merit-based, making it ineffective and inefficient.

Employee attitude surveys conducted by the Merit System Protection Board (MSPB) support these observations. Unfortunately, it seems, nobody, including the president, our complacent Congress, or the OPM, seems to have taken these surveys seriously.

Classification of Positions and Promotions

To understand how federal management cheats the American taxpayer, consider some details on how federal employees are paid and promoted. Hundreds of thousands of federal workers, supervisors, and managers are overpaid, with better pay and better fringe benefits than the private sector, while producing inferior results, but with a very high degree of job security.

The General Schedule (GS) classification system is set forth in the U.S. Code Title 5, U.S. Code Chapter 51. The OPM has the responsibility of interpreting and enforcing the provisions of the law and managing the application of the GS system in the federal government, but the OPM is ignoring its oversight responsibilities.

The GS classification system is based on three fundamental principles:

(1) *The need to identify positions with appropriate qualification standards.*

(2) *That there be substantially equal pay for substantially equal work, and*

(3) *Variation in pay should be in proportion to substantial differences in the difficulty, responsibility, and qualification requirements of work performed.*[11]

To enforce these principles, every employee in the federal government must have a position description, and these descriptions must accurately describe the difficulty of the position, its responsibilities, and the qualifications required for an employee to perform the assignment. To divide employees into pay levels, classification standards must be used. These standards developed by the OPM determine employees' GS grades and are the legal basis for every employee's pay.

Good descriptions are necessary to provide a sound basis for classifying positions properly and for ensuring that employees receive equal pay for substantially equal work (Title 5, U.S. Code 2301). Only after working with the government for almost ten years did I became aware of the existence of classification standards and position classification.

Over the years, I also learned that the civil service system provides two separate types of promotions. There are competitive, also referred to as merit promotions, and incumbent-developed, also referred to as noncompetitive, or accretion of duties promotions. Merit-based promotions for supervisory and managerial positions are competitive and must be advertised. According to the merit system principles that are supposed to regulate the U.S. civil service, there must be fair competition among candidates for the advertised position, and the best-qualified applicant must be selected. Therefore, this type of promotion is also called a merit promotion.

Unfortunately, this is not necessarily true in practice. An example of an incumbent-developed promotion is the noncompetitive promotion, a common promotion for scientists. Consider a young scientist who has published extensively in the open literature and over the years becomes nationally known for his or her accomplishments. This scientist qualifies for an incumbentdeveloped promotion. Obtaining additional academic degrees also may lead to an incumbent-developed promotion. There is no competition for this type of promotion. When classifying positions, the use of classification guides and standards is mandatory.[12]

The Research Grade-Evaluation Guide (RGEG) determines the grade levels of scientists perfor ming basic to applied research.[13] In the guide, employees' qualifications, contributions, professional standing, and supervision received determine grade levels. Supervision received means how much supervision does an employee receive from his supervisor. Research means the systematic, critical, intensive investigation toward the development of new or fuller scientific knowledge of the field being studied. The work of these scientists spans a wide range of functions, from basic and applied research to development, testing, and evaluation. According to the RGEG, research capability, as demonstrated by graduate education and/or research experience, is a significant factor in determining the selection of candidates and their pay.

The four factors that determine the grades of research positions are:

I. The research situation or assignment
II. Supervision received
III. Guidelines and origina lity
IV. Qualifications and scientific contributions

To evaluate the grade of positions and how much each position gets paid, points are assigned to factors 1-111. Two, four, six, or ten points can be allotted to each factor. Significantly, factor IV is double-weighted, so that points assigned to this factor are four, eight, twelve, or twenty. This emphasizes the importance of qualifications, stature, and contributions (for example, scientific publications) of the incumbent, which have a major impact on the level of difficulty and responsibility of the work performed. The grade of a research position results from adding all of the points of the four factors.

Grade Determination Chart
Classification Grade Total factor points
GS-11: 8-12
GS-12: 16-22
GS-13: 26-32
GS-14: 36-42
GS-15: 46-54

Although the use of classification guides and classification standards are supposed to be mandatory, if management does not follow the above instructions, no harm will come to them. Consequently, at many federal departments and agencies, there are often great pay differences among federal employees performing work of similar difficulties and possessing similar qualifications.

When I started working at the Center, my management had assigned me six, six, six, and twelve points, adding up to thirty points, a rating of GS-13. However, I should have been assigned ten points for Factor II because I did not receive any supervision while performing my research. I should have been assigned more than twelve points for Factor IV, not only for my scientific contributions, but also because I was among the best-trained scientists working for the Center. In addition to my academic degrees, I had spent seven years as a postdoctoral fellow, performing research in four different fields in physics and physical chemistry.

The RGEG recognizes that research positions are affected by changes in performance that occur gradually over time. The guide emphasize the importance of constantly reviewing positions. However, after working at the Center for over thirty-seven years, my positionwas ever reviewed during the required yearly performance evaluation meeting with my supervisors, and I was never promoted.

Position classification is supposed to be the backbone of the federal civil service system, enforcing merit principles by determining the pay federal employees receive. In practice, management does not always carry it out. This applies to more than just the Center—it is a widespread problem.

Quick Fixes

On the rare occasions when Congress meets to discuss civil service matters, someone always suggests that management should fire poorly performing workers after fifteen days, instead of the required thirty. Most Americans would agree with such a regulation. However, after working for many years for the American bureaucracy, I disagree, at least in part. A quick improvement on the federal civil service could be obtained by firing, not only poorly performing workers, but also poorly performing management after fifteen days, instead of thirty.

Poorly performing management is almost never fired. During his runs for president in 1991and 1995, H. Ross Perot often voiced his anger about the poorly performing federal bureaucracy. He was especially disgusted by the poor service he had received from a postal clerk. He suggested that citizens should be allowed to fire bureaucrats on the spot any time they received poor service.

This is the wrong approach, but it would work very well if the firing of the clerk who provided poor service would automatically trigger the firing of his or her supervisor. Employees provide poor service only when they have the impression that their supervisor does not care how they perform.

The GS pay system provides pay for federal employees mostly based on longevity. This system, with some justification, has been criticized. It has successfully been argued that some employees perform better than others and, consequently, should receive more pay. Significantly, the Civil Service Reform Act (CSRA) of 1978 also introduced pay-for-performance structures. This quick-fix scheme is strongly supported by management and has become one of the primary goals of the OPM.

One source of Americans' confusion about the working of their federal civil service system results from their views of its management and employees. Many Americans, knowingly or not, assume that managers in the federal civil service system have been carefully selected and are highly qualified. They believe managers possess an entrepreneurial spirit on par with managers in the private sector and that they are benevolent, idealistic, accountable, and very interested in improving employees' performance.

By contrast, the public sees civil service employees as inept and lazy. Therefore, pay-for-performance concepts are now widely hailed as presenting the royal road to improving the performance of the American civil service. However, this pay-for-performance scheme raises important questions, although they are rarely asked.

There are devils in the details. For example, one crucial question is what happens to management when there is performance but no performance pay is provided to the employee? Abandoning the current "merit-based" federal civil service has repeatedly been proposed to Congress in response to the reality that the enforcement of merit principles matters less and less for the American civil service. However, Congress has sternly rejected these proposals. Consequently, the OPM is constantly bragging that the American civil service is based on merit principles. At the same time, the OPM eagerly listens to every proposal from clerk managers on how to weaken or even a band on merit principles.

Civil Service Management

I use the expressions of "clerk," "poor," "unqualified," and "incompetent" management. In the beginning, "clerk managers" were supervisors of file clerks; they were typical bureaucrats, namely performing mostly administrative functions. Poor or unqualified supervisors and managers possess limited or no technical or scientific qualifications or experience, and little or no leadership ability to manage their high-quality employees.

Sometimes, I use these three designations interchangeably. In the federal civil service, the word "supervisor" refers to a person directly supervising employees. "Manager" refers to a higher-level management position. Often, I just use "management" to mean both supervisors and managers.

Private business in America works exceptionally well compared with the federal civil service system. No wonder many people argue that the poorly functioning civil service system should be run like a business. It might be helpful to give a short overview on just how private business and federal bureaucracies differ.

Private businesses provide products and services. They compete against other providers. For businesses to operate and survive, a healthy bottom line is the clearly defined goal. This means ever-growing earnings per share or return on equity. Staying too long in the red (loss per share or negative return on equity) may lead to business failure. Working for the private sector, managers and employees both expect pay and hope for job security. American culture approves of employees and managers who contribute to maintain or improve profits.

Civil service organizations, on the other hand, have a mission to provide a variety of services with consistency. Taxes have to be collected, mail has to be collected and distributed, and law and order has to be enforced. Providing these services with consistency is critical. In exchange for long-term employment and job security, civil service employees generally receive lower wages than the private sector.

Wages for management range from good to very good. Besides job security, the civil service also provides reasonable pension plans. For management, meeting the bottomline is not important; often there is none. However, the taxpayers who pay for these services expect that these services will be provided efficiently.

For cost-efficient operation of both the private sector and bureaucracies, it is necessary to hire qualified managers and high performing employees. When hiring employees and managers, both in the private sector and in bureaucracies, one ideally hires someone who is also loyal and who has a compatible personality. This creates an enjoyable workplace.

For private business, however, the loyal and compatible person may not help the bottom line. If not corrected, this is one of the main reasons businesses fail. For private businesses to succeed, employees and managers who are sometimes not enjoyable to work with are tolerated.

So far, all of this is common knowledge. However, at this point, we discover the inherent weakness of the federal bureaucracy. In some bureaucracies, including both America's and that of the former USSR, these loyal and compatible managers and employees are almost never removed. In the poorly functioning American civil service, loyal and compatible employees are routinely handpicked from the in-house pool for managerial positions and promotions, regardless of their lack of qualifications. This is a deliberate and flagrant violation of the first merit-system principle—namely, to "Recruit qualified individuals from all segments of society and select and advance individuals on their merit after fair and open competition, which assures that all receive equal opportunity."[9]

To understand this problem, one has to understand the working of bureaucracies. What people routinely overlook is the issue of management's concern—or overconcern—for their own job security. Hiring and rewarding qualified management and high-quality employees may actually threaten the job security, not only of incompetent managers and supervisors, but also of mediocre ones.

Good managers and high-quality employees may band together in protest and have their poor managers removed.

Incompetent members of management fear this because there are few or no wellpaying openings available for them in the private sector if they are removed from their cozy civil service positions. For unqualified and incompetent management to rise through the ranks, increase or maintain job security and comfortable working conditions, they must refrain from hiring and promoting high-quality management and employees.

As long as a poorly performing manager or employee is not obnoxious, why remove him or her? The replacement employee might present future problems. The taxpayers are paying anyway, and ignoring poorly performing employees does not affect the pay of management. What may look like a poor performance is often acceptable to unqualified management.

Purely for the sake of self-preservation, incompetent managers want iron control over performance pay and thoroughly dislike position classifications. Position classification determines pay. However, this pay is closely linked to the qualifications or experience of both workers and managers. But qualifications and experience are precisely what incompetent managers and their cronies' lack

At the Center, whenever a supervisory or managerial position had to be filled, a crony was appointed as the "acting head." However, this crony would not necessarily be the best choice from the inhouse pool. After about three months, he would be promoted to the position permanently. Apparently, the crony now had the necessary subject knowledge or experience to qualify for his new position. At the same time, over the last few years, national advertisements for high-quality federal employee and managerial positions have almost completely disappeared. Cronies from the in-house pool are filling most supervisory or managerial openings, and there has been a steady increase in management lacking the qualifications or experience needed to manage employees.

These practices explain the various failures of the American bureaucracy. This type of civil service system has no checks and balances, and no changes are in sight. There is neither oversight nor accountability. One can only expect more failures of this system in the future.

Private enterprises extensively advertise openings for their top managerial positions. MBA graduates from top universities are selected for top managerial positions in private industry as well. This is also the case in universities, which often advertise, not only nationally, but also internationally for new faculty and top administrative positions.

For officers in the military, well-trained graduates of military academies are given preference for leadership positions. Even where civil service management has the power to get tough with poorly performing employees, these employees rarely have their pay reduced or get fired, leading to a lack of open positions for new talent and expertise from the outside.

The OPM is failing miserably in its mission to inform Congress and the president on these widespread and deliberate merit-principle violations. Because many of these supervisors and managers have professional limitations, lacking qualifications and/or experience, they are constantly looking for "useful" employees to do their jobs. In many federal agencies and departments, employees perform their supervisors' daily work. They work on their supervisors' pet projects, writing proposals and technical reports to obtain project funding, contacting and visiting potential project sponsors, and managing and supervising the projects.

We have close-knit, mostly unqualified managerial cliques, where candidates for management positions are handpicked from the inhouse pool. Only loyalty to the management clique is required. Here, the old cliche applies: "Birds of a feather flock together."

There is job security in numbers. Clique members view an attack on one member as an attack on all members. The clique neither forgets nor forgives. As a clique member, one knows that no matter how poor his performance, the clique will never let him down. The civil service system will break down whenever unqualified management faces difficult or complex situations. The performance of the Federal Emergency Management Agency after Hurricane Katrina in 2005, presently, the IRS scandal, and Benghazi are perfect examples.

Another critical difference between federal employees and the private sector—as well as other, more local, government civil service—is the doctrine of supreme immunity. You cannot sue the government if you do not have permission to do so. The government does not hold itself responsible for most of its employees' actions, even if one can show that the employee acted negligently or in bad faith.

Federal employees cannot sue their bosses personally with civil lawsuits. Managers do not have to pay for damages out of their own pockets, even if it is shown that they are at fault. The Supreme Court has ruled, "If management personnel face added risk of personnel liability for decisions they believe to be correct responses . . . they would be deterred from imposing discipline in future cases."[14]

In the past, when clerk management was supervising filing clerks, this immunity made some sense. Also, in cases where high-quality management is in place, this immunity makes some sense. If these managers occasionally make poor decisions, one should not harass them with strict accountability. However, what happens when you have mostly unqualified management in place, often making poor managerial and personnel decisions, while supervising high-quality employees? You have a disaster in the making. If we want to build a high-quality federal workforce for the twenty-first century, wouldn't it be better to protect high-quality employees from the actions of incompetent management? Presently, only their next higher level of management can hold supervisors and managers accountable for mismanagement and merit-principle violations. But what if the next level of management looks the other way? Mismanagement is rarely punished. In rare cases, bad managers are moved into staff positions—with all of their benefits intact.

Consider Dr. Perkins's case, my former supervisor at Battery Ashburn, as an example of an employee who did not perform but was promoted to a supervisory position. Again, he did not perform, being transferred to a cozy position behind a desk, where he continued to collect his GS-14 pay. The key issue for the functioning of a twenty-first century workforce is the protection of high-quality employees from supervisory abuses such as merit violations.

Overpaid Federal Civil Service Employees

Over time, a high percentage of employees, not only in private industries, but also in the federal government, especially in technical and scientific fields, experience technical obsolescence. In private industry, employees with obsolete skills are terminated, or given a reduction in pay, or are retrained. In the federal civil service, this obsolescence is called "erosion of duties."

Employees who suffered erosion of duties hold over-graded, or overpaid positions. In a strict sense, these employees are poor performers, receiving compensation they don't deserve. To enforce fair treatment of federal employees according to the merit principles upon which our civil service system is based, their positions must be properly classified. There must be consistent intra-agency classification to ensure equal pay for substantially equal work.

In many federal agencies and departments, management tolerates a high percentage of employees who occupy over-graded positions, saying that these employees are overpaid. This has been going on for many years. The Center is a typical example. For many years, the Center's management has certified that many employees' positions were classified as current, when in fact they were overgraded.

Periodic Review

> *In addition to the day-by-day work of describing and classifying new or changed positions to reflect current duties assigned and reported by supervisor or employees, all positions should be reviewed periodically by competent classification specialists to insure that positions are properly classified.*[15]

Downgrading of positions is very rare. In thirty-seven years at the Center, I have never seen it happen. Management is simply too lazy to initiate such an unpleasant action. When reclassification falls behind, overall performance declines because unqualified employees continue to receive inflated pay, and deserving employees are not promoted. This is one of the primary reasons why many valuable and high-quality employees leave the federal civil service.

Under these circumstances, there never will be a modernization of the federal workforce. Clearly, the OPM is responsible for making sure that rules and regulations pertaining to merit principles, such as position classification, are properly executed. However, for many years, the OPM has not notified the president and Congress about the widespread problem of over-grading and management's other merit-principle violations, resulting in a very high cost for taxpayers.

The Center protected its overpaid and over-graded cronies and employees from losing any pay at the expense of underpaid, deserving and performing employees by entering a demonstration project, which is still in place today, and which is on its way to being adopted throughout the federal civil service.

In a section of the November 21, 1975, edition of the Center's internal journal, *NELC Calendar*, Secretary of the Navy J. William Middendorf discussed a crisis that seemed to exist within the Department of the Navy. He addressed classification and pay of the navy's civilian personnel. He stated:

> *Three cardinal principles are governing the classification of positions and the pay of Department of Navy civilian employees were declared last week in a message from the Secretary of the Navy. One that employees have the right to have their positions classified at the level indicated by application of Civil Service Standards to the duties and responsibilities contained in official position descriptions. A classification appeal system, with an option outside the chain of command, safeguards this right. Two, that taxpayers have the right to require that taxes be spent wisely and not used to pay for overgraded positions or over-structured organizations. Three that military and civilian managers have the responsibility to see that all subordinate positions are economically structured and properly classified.*
>
> *"Recent inspections by both our own and Civil Service Commission personnel indicate that a serious amount of over-grading and over-structuring may exist in parts of the department," Sec. Middendorf said. He advised commands to*

review their organizations and, where necessary, to take corrective action to insure that proper classification and position management principles are adhered to at all levels.[16]

There was no reaction from the Center's management. In a memo distributed to all employees and managers at the Center, Mr. R.R. Kraatz, the head of the Center's personnel office at that time, also discussed over-grading at the Department of the Navy and especially the over-grading of high-grade (GS-13/14/15) positions at the Center. Excerpts of this memo of May 26, 1976, are presented below.

NELC managers and supervisors have expressed concern and a lack of awareness regarding the high-grade (GS-13/14/15) problem within the Department of the Navy.

They are especially concerned with the impact of "control" and "reduction" imposed by Secretary of the Navy on the current high-grade complement, as well as on the morale impact on employees who are eligible for promotion into high-level position. Rightly so!

They view the policy as a major dilemma and need a full explanation of how higher management will deal with the problem. This paper attempts to explain the problem by discussing the circumstances leading to the high-grade situation; the attempts to reverse the trend; the need to impose restrictions; essential actions required of managers and a look into the future.

The problem that confronts NELC, which stands alone among the Naval R&D labs as having the highest percentage of GS-13/14/15 engineers and scientists to its total engineer and scientist population, is to effect a realistic reduction in the high-grades without impairing its technical capacity. In that regard, it is imperative that our young professionals at the lower grade levels be able to perceive career opportunities that do not come to a bureaucratic halt at the GS-12 level. In looking at the NELC situation, direct attention must be focused on a general conception of grade GS-13 as the full performance, or "journeyman," level.

In view of the 1960s environment, which helped produce this structure, coupled with the pressure to carry over the same classification procedure, one could easily and logically perceive that GS-11s and GS-12s are headed for the GS-13 journeyman level. This conception and practice requires thorough review for us since NELC has the highest ratio of GS-13 to GS-12 engineers and scientists in the entire Navy R&D Laboratory community. Further, the very nature of the Civil Service Classification Standards precludes the GS-13 level from being the full-performance or journeyman level. In fact, the Commission Standards, as interpreted by the Department of the Navy, characterize GS-11 as the journeyman for engineers and scientists. At that level, the standards describe independent performance with the ability to seek out research, analyze, coordinate, and formalize findings with minimal technical direction.

However, it is recognized that the very nature of the RDT&E laboratory environment provides an opportunity for a higher level in achieving the independent performance. In that regard, the GS-12 has been accepted in such an environment as the journeyman level. Again, the demanding character of the Standards at the GS-13 level permits that level to be described on an individual basis. The laboratory's high-grade structure is largely determined by the decisions which management officials make with respect to their own organization, the allocation of responsibilities, the definition of job content, and the structuring of work processes. Similarly, the review and approval of the establishment of new positions or the upgrading of current and old positions are what positions management and sound-classification principles are all about, and they will become increasingly more significant in the laboratories' attempt to defuse its high-grade situation.

Continuing with position management and classification practices of the past without due consideration of today's environment will invariably solidify an unfavorable image from DOD and Navy Department officials, and could possibly result in further revisions of management authority and right to manage; witness the drawing back by the Secretary of the Navy of the authority to classify GS-15 level positions and the requirement to seek prior approval before staffing such positions. In doing so, the Secretary has centralized such authority and has tasked the Navy's Office of Civilian Man power Management (OCMM) to revise relative management procedure and reporting requirements in order to control and reduce the number of GS-13 through GS-15 level positions within the Navy Department Other more extensive measures have

been advocated at the Secretarial level and may be
implemented if the result on the high-grade control
is less than successful.[17]

On February 22, 1977, the Center (NELC at that time) merged with the nearby Naval Undersea Center (NUC) to become the Naval Ocean Systems Center (NOSC). The next month, our personnel office, without having taken any action, returned the updated position description I had submitted in 1976. The personnel office stated that the merger had resulted in a major reorganization, which would require new position descriptions from all the Center's employees. Mr. William Riley, the new head of the Center's personnel office, in a memo sent on June 27, 1977, requested that all employees at the newly formed Center submit new and updated position descriptions.[18] Along with all the other employees, I submitted a new and updated position description to the Center's personnel office.

Outside Assessment of the Center

In 1978, inspectors from the Western Field Division of the Office of Civilian Personnel (WFDOCP) in San Diego visited the Center from January 3 to January 20 to conduct an on-site evaluation of civilian personnel management at the Center.

A friend of mine gave me the WFDOCP's report. This evaluation described massive merit-principle violations at the Center—namely, a highly over-graded and correspondingly overpaid workforce. To correct these violations, the WFDOCP emphasized reclassification of all high-grade positions (GS-13, 14, and 15) at the Center. At the time, I was unaware that this report would set into motion profound changes, not only at the Center, but also in the entire American civil service system. Here is an excerpt of the most relevant portions of the WFDOCP report.

Overall Assessment

The more serious personnel management problems and their interdependency came into clear focus when viewed within the context of Position Management. Although at the first glance the following areas might seem to be distinct and separate problems, they coalesce and form a very complex overall personnel management problem that is amenable to solution only through a comprehensive, indepth combined position management/ classification review that examines all facets of the problem.

These areas are: the relatively large number of high-grade positions which are misclassified; a highly segmented organization with attendant questions of span of control and restrictions of supervisory authority; organizational pressures resulting from high-grade quotas, including GS-12s and others performing work above their present classification; major shifts in technical emphasis of some positions and incumbents who exhibit technical obsolesce and cannot perform their assigned duties; and overly broad RIF (Reduction in Force) competitive levels which, if continued, would prevent corrective action on many of the other problems without excessive disruption in the placement of personnel, no one of these problem areas can be dealt with effectively by itself, they all must be tackled together as a composite before workable solutions can be devised.

Position Classification

The primary source of data for evaluation of the position classification program was [an] audit of a nonrandom sample of positions. In all, one hundred and twenty-two positions were reviewed. Six of these were documentary reviews only, the balance being audited with the incumbent and/or the supervisor of the position. The sample was selected from among positions with the highest potential for error and with emphasis upon higher-grade levels. Approximately 85 percent of this sample required correction of some type.

The commonest problem was the poor quality or currency of position descriptions and the lack of any significant documentation to support or explain the basis for the classification action. In fact, approximately half of the sample was found to be improperly over-classified for a variety of reasons. There are also some administrative problems with the position classification program, which require attention. Some are the result of poor past practices, pressure, or failure to report significant changes in positions as they occur.

There are several major areas to be reviewed that are central to the effective use of Center manpower and its impact on mission accomplishment—these are: the relatively large number of misclassifted positions at highergrade levels; the highly segmented organization structure with attendant questions of effective span of control and restrictions on supervisory authority; organizational pressures resulting from high-grade controls, including GS-12s working at higher levels; major shifts in technical emphasis for certain positions or technical obsolescence of incumbents of certain positions; an overly broad RIF competitive levels that would affect displacement of newer professionals. The intertwining of these various problems is the factor that determines that magnitude of effort needed in the PM review. Unless these problems can be resolved on a comprehensive, integrated basis, NOSC cannot manage its personnel resources and billets most effectively for mission accomplishment. For example, the failure to resolve a combination of position management/classification problems is blocking effective use of the high-grade quota for employees now performing at levels above their present classification in work, which NOSC considers highly, mission essential. Failure of the Center to correct existing PM and classification problems will ultimately affect significantly on cost and mission accomplishment.

Position Classification: Technical Accuracy

A large number of high-grade positions are inaccurately classified. Discussion: Based on a nonrandom sample of predominately high-level positions, it must be concluded that a significant number of high-level positions (GS-13 and above) are misclassifted one or more levels too high. The problem cases listed in Appendix 8 are estimated as representing (very roughly) from 30 to 50 percent. Some of the positions were initially misclassified through improper application of standards, erroneous job information, or pressures exerted in the past. Many present misclassifications are the result of technical obsolescence, gradual erosion of duties, shift in project emphasis or funding levels, changed demand for specific skills or reluctance on the part of employees to change. With the passage of time, it is virtually impossible for an outside review team in many cases to pinpoint the cause of the error, as it now exists. However, some of them are the results of the merging of the two laboratories. Close review of the classification case listing shows that many also have existed for years. Rather than simply rewriting and having positions reclassified, a review from the position management standpoint should be combined with the review of the cited and similar positions.

Recommendation

Conduct a thorough position-management-and-classification review of high-level positions to identify, document, and correct classification errors.[19]

Captain Gavazzi on May 5, 1978, in a memo addressed to the entire Center's workforce, stated:

The Center will undertake immediately a Position Management Review and Classification Survey of all GS-13, GS-14, and 15 positions. The purpose of the survey is to ensure alignment and proper grading of all GS-13, 14, and 15 positions in accordance with good position management practices and Civil Service Classification Standards.[20]

Captain Gavazzi, on May 19, 1978, also stated in a memo to the Director of the Western Field Division, Office of Civilian Personnel:

The Naval Ocean System Center is undertaking an extensive Position Management Review and Classification Survey of approximate 700 High-Grade positions.[21]

Also, on May 19, 1978, Captain Gavazzi addressed a memo to the Director of Civilian Personnel, via the Director of Navy Laboratories. Authorization was requested to delay downgrading up to December 31, 1979.[22] In a Department of Defense (DOD) directive of July 28, 1979, to the office of the Secretary of Defense, the military departments, the organization of the Joint Chiefs of Staff, and the defense agencies, the follow ing policy was stated:

Policy

It is also the policy of the Department of Defense that civilian positions will be properly classified in accordance with 5 U.S.C. Classification decisions will be made solely on the basis of published standards and authorized classification principles and policies. The classification policy is a cornerstone of sound position management.[22]

Effective Date and Implementation

This Directive is effective immediately. Forward two copies of implementing documents to the Assistant Secretary of Defense (Manpower, Reserve Affairs, and Logistic) within 120 days.[23]

Mr. Leo T. Rickwa, a member of the second survey team from the Chief of Naval Operations, also conducted a position-classification review of the Center. In a memo dated Ma rch 2, 1979, he summarized his classification-survey results.

Of the 219 positions his team reviewed, fifty-six were over graded, and seven were under-graded. In his memo, he also provided guidelines for proper position management, including conducting Center-wide position classification.[24]

Mr. Rikwa also enclosed in his memo a Naval Research Laboratory (NRL) Instruction #12340.4 of March 20, 1978, on the subject of "Performance Appraisal and Promotion of Professional Personnel in the Research Directorates." Apparently, Mr. Rickwa hoped that the Center's management would adopt a similar approach in promoting high-quality employees. This instruction provides guidance on how to develop and maintain a superior technical or scientific workforce for the twenty-first century. However, the Center's management did not follow his recommendations, apparently being totally uninterested in either addressing the issue of over-grading or in advancing under-graded, high-quality employees.

The NRL instruction states:

Background

The most important asset of any scientific organization is its professional staff. Continuous growth and development of scientific skills are essential to the future of the Laboratory. This instruction sets forth promotion criteria based on demonstrated professional growth. Enclosure (1) establishes policy for promotion of individuals based on professional growths. Essential to its application is the continuous and meaningful appraisal of professional personnel. This appraisal must include a careful analysis of each professional employee's performance in his position and a comparison with others in similar positions. The appraisal must inform the professional employee of how his work meets, exceeds, or fails to meet requirements. Current performance, and ways to improve that performance, if needed, will be discussed with employees on a continuing basis.

Enclosure (1)

2. It has been and will be the policy of NRL to promote its professional personnel on merit and demonstrated accomplishments. It is incumbent upon the laboratory in these times of rapidly changing technology, which are complicated by the numerical restrictions on high-level positions, to restate, not only this policy of merit, but also to amplify those factors which are considered to be indicative of professional growth. These factors, in addition to minimal civil service requirements, are creativity, productivity, (specific accomplishments), formal recognition (awards, committee membership, etc.), and maintenance and growth of professional skills.

3. A special assessment will be made in the case of professional supervisory personnel. In addition to the foregoing factors, consideration will be given to evidence of the demonstration of technical leadership. Technical leadership includes the guidance and motivation of subordinates in their assignments, and the innovation and detailed guidance of programs. Primary emphasis will be placed on internal Laboratory administrative skills. In addition, an appraisal will be made of the supervisor's technical outlook; his/her active participationin the development of new programs with system commands and other Navy groups; his/her responsiveness to necessary program changes; and his/her ability and interest in carrying on constructive dialogues with Laboratory Directorate on policy matters.

4. The laboratory maintains that the maintenance and continued updating of professional skills are requirements for promotion. We can be justifiably proud of the leadership NRL has provided the Navy research community during the last 5 decades. To insure that we do not manifest the symbol of scientific decay, "technical obsolesce," we must constantly examine our personal professional knowledge to see that it is current. The Laboratory, through its scientific education program, provides ample opportunity for the individual to be exposed to a wide range of academic environments. Supervisory personnel must pay particular attention to this area and provide the necessary motivation to their subordinates to participate in the "learning" experience.[25]

In summary, judging from the WFDOCP's assessment: "In fact, approximately half of the sample was found to be improperly overclassified for a variety of reasons."[19] According to Mr. Rickwa's estimate, "Of the two hundred nineteen positions his team reviewed, fifty-six were over-graded, and seven were under-graded."[24]

With about three thousand employees working at the Center, this would have required the removal of hundreds of employees from their over-graded, meaning overpaid, positions. It was plain that, for many years, the Center's management had been falsely certifying hund reds of position descriptions as accurate, when, in fact, they were not.

The very high percentage of overgrated positions at the Center strongly suggests that a similar situation exists at other federal agencies and departments. This prevents them from modernizing their workforce to accomplish their missions. Neither the WFDOCP's[19] recommendations nor the DOD's directive[23], nor Mr. Rickwa's[24] assessment were followed by the

Center. Massive downgrading would have allowed the Center to promote many hundreds of deserving high-quality employees and to hire at higher entry grades.

For almost three years, I asked my management, as well as the personnel office, about the status of the new position description I had submitted. Every time, I was instructed that the classification of all the newly submitted position descriptions was progressing slowly due to the large number of position descriptions submitted and the small number of qualified classifiers available.

Chapter 5
The Navy's Demonstration's Project

Demonstration Project Proposed

During 1978, Congress passed the Civil Service Reform Act (CSRA) that included demonstration projects. These research projects are designed to test new approaches to personnel management. They terminate five years from the date on which the project takes effect, except that the project may continue beyond that date to the extent necessary to validate the results of the project.[26]

The Center's management realized immediately that by entering such a research project, the Center might be able to protect all the over-graded, overpaid employees, including the management's cronies. All these employees, many of whom were handpicked by management for promotions, would thus avoid painful downgrading, and their overpayments would be preserved. In addition, management obtained total control over who would be rewarded and promoted, without providing any workable appeal resources for victimized high-quality employees.

Despite the abuses that could and did occur under the terms of the demo, this system is now on its way to being adopted throughout the federal civil service. The primary purposes of the demo were to test a pay-for-performance system—a provision originally proposed by the 1978 Civil Service Reform Act and eagerly supported by the OPM—and simplified position classification. On March 20, 1979, Captain Drayton, the Center's acting commander at that time, simply terminated the classification survey of high-grade positions.[27]During the summer of 1979, in order to meet the required number of participating employees, the Center talked the Naval Weapons Center (NWC) at China Lake, California, into entering the demo project together. Shortly thereafter, technical director Dr. H. Blood informed all the Center's employees on November 13, 1979, that the OPM had accepted the Center and NWC's proposal to conduct a demo. During the spring of 1980, Congress also approved the demo, apparently impressed by the ambitious scientific evaluation of the demo to be carried out by the University of Southern California.

The final version of the demo was published in the Federal Register on April 18, 1980, under the title "An Integrated Approach to Pay, Performance Appraisal, and Position Classification for More Effective Operation of Government Organizations."

Congress approved the demo based on the myth that poor performance of the federal bureaucracy is based solely on the poor performance of its workers. Those who adopt this view speculate that by granting management more flexibility in personnel matters—namely, introducing pay-for-performance schemes and simplifying position classification—high-performing employees will stay at their jobs, and new high-quality employees will be attracted to civil service.

At the same time, so the theory goes, non performing employees will be forced to leave. However, using position classification, the power to deal with underperforming but overpaid and over-graded employees does exist and always has—but it is almost never used. If they wished to properly classify the Center's employees, the Center's management did not need the greater power in personnel matters that the demo granted. Excerpts from the Federal Register about the demo are reproduced here. Only a small section of the demo's complex scientific evaluation plan is presented.

External evaluation team participants were members of the faculty of the University of Southern California (USC) School of Public Administration. The faculty members included a professor of research methodology; two professors of public administration, with specializations in personnel administration; an associate professor with a specialty in research-and-development administration; and two associate professors with degrees in economics.

The outline of the demo provides wonderful reading, but management was not required to follow or implement all the changes the demo proposed. The excerpt below is followed by some comments, with further evaluations to follow. I shortened the outline of the demo, omitted a table that lists provisions of laws and regulations that were waived under the demo, and omitted most of the evaluation procedure proposed by the USC.

Introduction

The purpose of this project is to demonstrate that the effectiveness of federal laboratories can be enhanced by allowing greater management control over personnel functions and, at the same time, expanding the opportunities available to employees through a more responsive and flexible personnel system. In order to accomplish this purpose, changes are proposed that include (1) a more flexible, manageable, and understandable classification system; (2) a performance appraisal system that links performance objectives, compensation, and organizational effectiveness; (3) an expanded application of the merit pay concept. Together, these changes can help managers to operate with more authority, responsibility, and skill to increase workforce and organizational effectiveness and efficiency.

It is anticipated that the project will demonstrate that public managers can be trusted to take these new and changed responsibilities seriously, and that they will act in the best interest of the public service, their organizations, and their personnel. It is also expected that the creation of a management-centered personnel system will, to an extent far exceeding that of the present system, stimulate managers to respond creatively to the problem of goal-oriented manpower management, to develop the required skills, and to economize in their uses of the resources allocated to them. Finally, the project will actualize the principle that public managers, once given the tools and resources, should be held accountable for their decisions and practices with regard to personnel administration, and that such accountability is an essential ingredient of effective and efficient administrative action.

This project addresses problems in key areas within the existing personnel system. The project proposes solutions for these problems, outlined below, by giving managers the authority and accountability to increase both the efficiency and effectiveness of the workforce by stimulating individual and organizational performance. It is expected that this approach to personnel resource management will prove adaptable to a wide spectrum of federal organizations.

Classification

The current classification system is confusing and complex; to a large extent, it diminishes the manager's role in setting pay and gives position-classification classifiers an inordinate degree of responsibility in this process. Neither managers nor employees understand the current method of classifying positions; they see the system as one that impinges on their flexibility. The system delays recruitment actions, which must wait for positions to be classified. It also limits managers' ability to transfer personnel from one functional area to another; delays occur while managers wait for positions to be classified or find that the position to which an employee is to be moved is not classifiable at the appropriate grade level.

Classification of positions consumes the time and energy of the personnel staff and precludes their involvement in assisting managers with other critical personnel resource problems. In addition, the complex classification system causes some professionals to lea ve the federal service for private industry, where managers can more readily reward performance, contributions, and res ponsibility with pay.

Performance Appraisal and Merit Pay

The performance appraisal systems existing prior to the CSRA were unsatisfactory to both supervisors and employees. This project will increase the importance of performance appraisals because it provides that these systems will have close links with pay decisions. Any system becomes meaningless without pay incentives to reward good performance or withhold incentives from low performers. While the supervisor may have high expectations for subordinates' performance, a system that does not translate these expectations into meaningful management actions cannot be effective. The planned change ensures that this translation will take place.

A major problem area in the current system is the Jack of sufficient incentives and rewards for good performance and meaningful sanctions for poor performance. The CSRA changes in the merit pay concept addresses this problem. The participating Centers feel, however, that they do not apply to enough of the workforce. The rigid classification system also works counter to the principle of flexibility for incentives and disincentives. In addition, the present practice of granting "automatic" step increases for virtually all employees limits a tool that managers could better utilize. An effective recruitment tool that is denied to taday's federal organizations is the ability to offer to recent college graduates or other potential employees the incentive that their pay will increase to keep pace with their performance and responsibilities.

Methodology

The project is geared to the CSRA of 1978, existing public and private personnel systems, and anticipated additional Civil Service legislation in the area of classification and pay. The project provides a closely linked classification, performance, and compensation system. Specific proposed changes include the following:

1. *Five levels of classification for the initial increment.*
2. *Broad pay bands within classification levels, with individual pay adjustments annually by placement into one of five basic incentive pay groups.*

3. *Development of general classification/performance standards.*

4. *Individual placement in incentive pay groups during a performance appraisal process based on Performance by Objectives. Classification /Performance / Qualification Standards. The classification levels for professionals will differentiate between broad groups of employees as follows:*

Level I.   *Entrance and training position.*

Level II.   *Advanced training and specific task performance and development to full performance levels.*

Level III. *Journeyman performance-level positions and supervisors.*

Level IV.   *Senior technical specialists, supervisors, and managers. These levels are sufficiently distinct that they can be easily understood by managers; correct placement will therefore be more certain.*

The classification system will be modeled on industry and university practices. Position descriptions can to a large degree be standardized and presented in a side-by-side format that presents the position description along with a limited number of general performance expectations. These performance standards, matched to the level of difficulty, will in most cases be supplemented by individualized documented performance goals and expectations that will serve as a combined basis for incentive pay decisions.

Development of Performance Standards

Performance standards or objectives will be developed for each individual covered by the project.

These standards will specifically address the most important aspects of each employee's position, will be general enough to describe what is expected, and at the same time allow for maximum internal flexibility. Both Centers will also explore industry performance standard systems for inclusion or modification to fit the standards for certain occupational groups.

Management Approach

While the performance appraisal system attempts to set specific standards communicated and understood by management, supervisor, and employee, it will still require judgments by those recommending and determining pay increases. Effective operation of this system will therefore require direct action in instances where supervisory personnel consistently exercise poor or detrimental judgment in the performance appraisal process. These poor supervisory judgments will be reflected in supervisor's pay determinations or in removal from their supervisory functions. The furtherance of this project by complete and equitable judgment of subordinate performance will be a performance element for each supervisor. The use of high supervisory expectations will ensure that supervisors will also be accountable for their increased flexibility in managing their personnel resources. The "pay based upon performance" concept, when fully implemented, will result in a redistribution of current pay resources based upon individual and unit performance measured against predetermined standards. Properly developed individual standards and unit objectives that focus on mission requirements, individual and organizational productivity, and management goals will ensure that employee rewards are tied directly to greater efficiency and improved agency operations rather than to longevity or other artificial measures of worth.

Evaluation Plan

In order to assess project outcomes and to evaluate the feasibility of applications to other federal organizations, a comprehensive and methodically rigorous evaluation model is being developed. The evaluation effort will include (1) preimplementation criteria setting and baseline data collection, (2) multidimensional performance measurements and trend evaluation at specified states of the demonstration project, and (3) a summative-phase comprehensive assessment of the project's overall impact on a set of outcome measures. In addition to the above-mentioned measures and data, there will be an ongoing monitoring of existing records and reports on the laboratories.

Unconstructive measures will be kept on such basic considerations as the profile of the scientific and engineering workforce of the laboratories. When methodologically justifiable, control group data will be obtained from other navy laboratories not involved in the project. The evaluation staff will be drawn from internal and external sources. Qualified laboratory staff members will work with members of the School of Public Administration of the University of Southern California on the design and execution of the evaluation package.[28]

Pay-for-Performance and Performance Standards

Pay-for-performance is one of the centerpieces of the navy's demo, which has now been adopted by several agencies and departments. A performance appraisal system is supposed to link employees' performance and compensation to their organizational effectiveness. Its advocates claim that pay-for-performance constitutes an expanded application of the merit pay concept.

Although pay-for-performance has been hailed as a common sense solution to the problems of the civil service, many details have to be considered for this concept to work in practice.

The OPM had required that the Center develop a performance evaluation system, including performance standards for each employee according to its needs. Here we again encounter one of the major shortcomings of the American civil service management: the OPM takes this complex and difficult assignment, dumps it on somebody else, and then simply forgets about it.

Pay-for-performance is a complex and very difficult subject. It first requires defining what constitutes performance for each job category. One must have an evaluation system in place that measures performance success. Then, for each job category, one must define what constitutes excellent, good, satisfactory, marginal, and unacceptable performance. But at the Center, this had to be accomplished, not only for each job category, but also for each of five demo levels. For some job categories, like supervisors and managers, it is difficult or almost impossible to define performance in every case. After all these performance concepts have been defined, they must be made known and understood by all employees—a Herculean task. Further, it must also be understood that pay-for-performance must be provided whenever there is performance. One cannot expect employees to work diligently all year long, only to be informed by their supervisors during their performance evaluation that financial rewards are not forthcoming—and that there is also no guarantee for the future. This means that a workable independent appeal system must be in place. Without these strict requirements and safeguards, favoritism in the hands of biased management will generate a hostile working climate and prompt high-performing and high-quality employees to quit. A very important question arises: What happens to supervisors if they do not properly reward employees for their effort? According to the outline of the demo:

> *Effective operation of this personnel system will require direct action in instances where supervisory personnel consistendy exercise poor or detrimental judgment in the performance appraisal process. These poor supervisory judgments are supposed to be reflected in the supervisor's pay determination or removal from his supervisory functions.*[28]

However, the Center's personnel office and its management never developed any performance-appraisal system for its employees.

Pay-Banding

The navy's demo project claims that pay-banding is another important personnel tool to reward high-performing employees with pay raises. This allows management to pass performing employees through increasing levels of pay without promoting them. The demo bands several GS pay grades into levels. GS-5, 6, and 7 became level DP-I, which includes entry-level and training positions. GS-9, 10, and 11 were DP-II, the advanced-training and specific-task-performance level. GS-12 and 13 became DP-III, the journey man and supervisor level, and GS-14 and 15 were DP-IV, which includes senior technical specialists, supervisors, and managers. According to Mr. Kraatz's memo, the GS-12 grade has been accepted in the RDT&E environment as the journeyman level:

> *This conception and practice requires thorough review for us since NELC has the highest ratio of GS-13 to GS-12 engineers and scientists in the entire Navy R&D Laboratory community. Further, the very nature of the Civil Service Classification Standards precludes the GS-13 level from being the full performance journeyman level.*[17]

However, pay-banding was the Center's gimmick to protect hundreds of over-graded employees from having their inflated pay reduced. Putting hundreds of GS-13-graded employees, mostly holding BS or BA degrees but performing at the journeyman GS-12 grade, into the demo's journeyman DP-III level (which included both GS-12 a nd 13) automatically protected them from downgrading and a loss of pay. In addition, the demo also protected many nonperforming GS-14 and GS-15 employees from losing their inflated salaries by putting them into the DP-IV level.

Simplified Classification Standards

In the demo, position description and classification standards are the same. Classification standards are necessary to ensure pay equity within the federal civil service system. For the federal government to compete with the private sector for talent, there must be a working position classification system in place to provide proper pay for high-quality employees. Otherwise, the war for talent will be lost.

The GS system's third principle states, (3) The principle that variations in range of basic pay for different employees should be in proportion to substantial differences in the difficulty, responsibility, and qualification requirements of the work performed.[11] When classifying scientific positions in factor VI, qualifications and scientific contributions are double-weighted relative to factors I, II, and III. Similarly, other position descriptions that include supervision and managers also highly value qualifications or experience. However, for years the Center's management, as well as management at other agencies and departments, has been badmouthing the present classification system. The demo states:

> *Neither management nor employees understand the current method of classifying positions: they see this system as one that impinges on their flexibility.*[28]

Although the management of the Center claimed that the demo's simplified and shortened classification standard and the General Schedule standards were compatible with each other, this is not true. In the demo standards, qualifications and/or experience requirements are not properly spelled out—nor are assignments of duties and supervision received. The fact is that incompetent managers do not want to understand the GS position classification system; their willful ignorance protects their employment and that of their cronies. These managers want the "flexibility" in position classification so that they can promote cronies, who either lack or are very short on the necessary qualifications and/or experience to do their jobs. This "flexibility" is of key importance to management in controlling, not only who is properly paid and who is not, but also who moves into managerial positions and who does not, regardless of qualifications and/or experience.

Although the demo has simplified classification standards, in practice, they are not used to classify positions. Under the conditions laid out in the demo, the Center's personnel office played only an advisory role in position classifications matters.

The commanding officer, the captain, was appointed as the chief classifier at the Center. However, the captain was among the last people at the Center qualified to make difficult and complex personnel evaluation decisions on position classifications for management and high-quality employees. This suggests that the Center's management wanted to have an official in place to rubber-stamp high-level promotions (DPIV) of the management's cronies, who might otherwise have lacked the proper qualifications and/or experience to be promoted. It is difficult to understand why the OPM and Congress did not recognize such an obvious swindle.

Adverse Actions

The demo introduced drastic changes with regard to adverse personnel actions. Many of these rule changes reduced or abolished employee protections and rights that were guaranteed in the CSRA of 1978. Under the demo, employees did not have any rights to have unfair performance evaluations appealed to the Merit System Protection Board. When an employee appeals to the MSPB, management must prove that its adverse action against the employee was justified. For example, when appealing a performance rating to the MSPB, for the agency to succeed, it must have a sound performance appraisal system in place. However, no such appraisal system is in place at the Center.

With some exceptions, such as Equal Employment Opportunity Commission violations, the demo makes available to employees only highly pro-management, in-house appeal routes for position classifications and performance ratings. The originators of these appeal routes sought to abolish the application of merit principles for unfairly treated and dissatisfied high-quality employees. The bias inherent in the in-house appeals system gives these employees the clear message that their organization does not want to treat them fairly.

Some of these in-house appeal routes require an employee's upper chain of management to review the complaint. In most cases, this means the manager of the supervisor who initiated the adverse action—the same manager who approved the adverse action in first place. In many cases this is also the same manager who handpicked the accused supervisor for promotion to his present position. How can the manager be neutral?

Another reason for blocking employees' appeals to the MSPB regarding performance evaluations, and to the OPM regarding position classifications, was because someone outside the Center might have become aware of its gross mismanagement, including violations of basic merit principles. As my own example will show, no employee can prevail by using the in-house appeal routes to challenge the appropriateness of their position descriptions. Since marginalized employees had only in-house appeal routes available under the conditions of the demo, most of them either shut up or quit. Is this the system we plan to adopt to govern our entire civil service, in the hope of improving it?

While all of this was going on at the Center, I had continued to follow the literature on the Special Theory of Relativity. Besides two or three papers that claimed that the theory did not hold for the range of the universal length I had proposed, there was no sign of any interest in my work. I came to conclude, after waiting for many years, that I had barked up the wrong tree.

I had invested immense energy, time, and effort, but apparently it was all for nothing. I criticized myself for wasting my time and energy and was angry at myself for having had phony drea ms. I tried to stop thinking about my work on the STR, but my mind would not obey. I realized I badly needed to concentrate on other ongoing work. In desperation, one day in 1980, I dumped all the literature on the STR that I had accumulated over the years into a trashcan.

The Start of the Demonstration Project

The demo, started on July 13, 1980, created a management-centered civil service system that provided the Center's incompetent management with huge power over promotions, performance rewards, and hiring. At the same time, the ma nagement's cronies and many hundreds of over-graded employees continued to receive large financial benefits. In the following sections, I will describe in some detail how the Center's management abused their power in civil service personnel matters.

Together with all other Center employees. I entered the demo with the obsolete premerger position description that had been issued to me in 1973 when I was transferred into the integrated optics branch—the same position description I had brought to my management's attention in the fall of 1976, claiming it was improperly graded. This 1973 position description was automatically converted into a Level DP-III scientist description. This description was the same for all of the other scientists holding classification GS-12 and 13, regardless of the academic degrees they might hold.

At the beginning of the demo, its originators anticipated that the OPM would fund the cost for the independent evaluation during the five-year duration of the project. Directly responsible to the OPM, the School of Public Administration of the University of Southern California (USC) in Los Angeles was supposed to provide an independent scientific evaluation of the project, oversee the collection of research results, and collect data for evaluating the performance of the Center and its partner in the project, the Naval Weapons Center.

Upon conclusion of the five-year experimental period, in 1985, USC planned to make an assessment of the impact of the demo. USC would also assess the degree to which the experiment had proved effective and efficient in meeting the stated goals and objectives of the demo. The demo required the Center to develop a performance evaluati on system, together with performance standards, according to its needs. At the beginning of the demo, the Center's management and personnel office experienced difficulties developing such a complex evaluation system, including performance standards, for all of its employees. This undertaking was quickly and quietly dropped in 1982. This made the scientific evaluation of the demo by USC's faculty superfluous. It then became impossible to prove that financial rewards-namely, pay-for-performance-resulted, not only in improved employee performance, but also in an overall improvement in the performance of the Center. Because performance appraisal systems were never developed for any job categories, there could never be proper rewards for performing employees. The entire performance appraisal process became mean ingl ess. The OPM hired Cooper and Lybrand, a management consulting company, to perform the evaluation of the demo project I did not see Cooper and Lybrand's evaluation report

At this point, the OPM should have sounded an alarm and informed Congress about the failure of the demo. This would have required Congress to cancel the project. Instead, later in 1982, to cover up the serious shortcomings of the navy's demo project, the OPM took over the outside evaluator function of this critical personnel research project from USC. At this time, the OPM knew that the Center had failed to develop any performance appraisal systems and that, consequently, the Center's management would dish out taxpayers' money arbitrarily to their favorite employees. Although the pay-for-performance experiment had failed badly, the OPM's plan was to deceive the president, Congress, and the American people.

The End of the Integrated-Optics Program

Mr. Altman, a member of my branch, had started to construct an experimental setup to fabricate optical fiber couplers. He heated two fibers with a tungsten coil in a vacuum system and then stretched and twisted them. A helium/neon CW laser beam was coupled into one of the fibers. A photocell measured the intensity of the laser light coupled into it at the other end of the fiber. However, before the experiment was complete, Mr. Altman was assigned to another task, and I was asked to continue his work

To filter out the red light from the heating coil, I used a mechanical chopper to chop the red helium/neon light with a lockin amplifier. This allowed me to measure the chopped helium/neon laser light that had been coupled into the second fiber, making it rather easy to follow just the coupling process. As soon as efficient coupling was observed, the heating cycle was disrupted to prevent the two fibers from melting together. Mr. Altman and I published a paper together in *Applied Optics* in 1980 and obtained a patent on our ideas.

The fiber optics branch consisted of a rather large number of high-quality employees. About the same time our paper was published, newly hired PhDs began to leave the branch due to the lack of promotions. With the rapid expansion of the fiber optics industry, many well-paying jobs became available in the private sector. Sometime later, Dr. Taylor also departed for Thompson Ramo Wooldridge in Thousand Oaks, California. He claimed that his support base at the Center had been eroding.

Suddenly, as the only senior physicist left in the fiber optics branch, I had to struggle to keep several programs going. Under these circumstances, I would have preferred to work on laser dyes and dye lasers than fiber optics. Our division underwent reorganization. For reasons that are still not quite clear to me, the integrated optics branch was dissolved. Overall, the branch had performed well. This was the end of one of the most successful programs I had seen at the Center.

To my surprise, the microelectronic division continued to operate at Battery Ashburn. After considerable time, they developed the ability to fabricate microcircuits. There was a considerable demand for obsolete microcircuits for military equipment. Over time, many microcircuits had to be replaced, but the industry was not producing them any longer, their volume being too small.

For some time our branch was without a branch or division head. This was the best time for me to make a career change. I wanted to return to my old field, working in dye lasers and laser dyes. I asked our secretary to prepare the necessary paperwork to have all my equipment returned from Convair. During this unusual situation, the acting branch and division heads would sign almost any paper put in front of them.

I found an almost-empty laboratory and simply moved into it. I assembled all my equipment and confiscated everything useful to me from the vacated laboratories of Drs. Taylor and Martin. In no time, my new dye laser laboratory was operational.

High power lasers are needed for defense against enemy air plains and possibly can also be used against missiles. Among lasers, only organic dye lasers qualify for upscaling, because they are liquid lasers. Pump power supplied to a laser is never converted 100 percent into laser light, but some power is converted into heating the laser. Therefore, if you want to operate a large laser over a longer time period, you must use a liquid laser medium like an organic laser dye solution. Liquids are simply cooled by circulating them in an cooling system.

First, I wanted to verify my experimental theory on laser dye mixtures, the work that had resulted in a paper published in *Optics Communications* about two years previous.

I came up with the compound perylene, which fulfilled the proper requirements as a booster. The laser dye was Rhodamine 110. Its fluorescence spectral region, which mostly coincides with the laser spectral region, also coincided with the low triplet-triplet absorption of the booster dye. I published a short paper on this work in *Optics Communications* in 1981.

It was always my ambition to find a theory that predicted laser action properties from the spectroscopic parameters of laser dyes. The proposed theory that calculated a figure of merit for several laser dyes agreed rather well with the laser action properties of several laser dyes.

These conclusions were published in *Optics Communications* in 1981.

The results again pointed to the importance of synthesizing new laser dyes that would possess a small triplet extinction coefficient. I had called these new classes of compounds "high-efficiency laser dyes." From then on, my entire ambition was directed toward obtaining these high-efficiency laser dyes, especially blue/green laser dyes, because of their importance for naval applications.

Because of the lack of funding for this work, my acting division branch head, Dr. M. Kvigne, asked me to change my field of research and consider moving into signal processing and possibly transfer to the code ("code" refers to an organizational unit) that performs this function. This field of signal processing had attracted considerable attention at that time. I cooperated and installed a mode-locker into my CW laser to produce trains of very short laser pulses. Short pulses are needed for optically controlled data sampling. The laser setup was working. However, this project was cut short because the new code also ran into funding problems.

Chapter 6
Classification Appeals

First Classification Appeal

In 1981, I entered my sixteenth year at the Center at the same level where I had started. I thought the time had finally arrived for me to be promoted, because according to the outline of the demo, our new system was "modeled on industry and university practices." This included the university practice of "publish or perish." Because I had published extensively in the open literature and was internationally known for my scientific contributions, I should have been given preference for promotions under this provision of the demo right after its introduction.

Throughout my time at the Center, I continued to make contributions to the scientific community. However, among the scientists selected for level DP-IV promotions, rarely could one find a person of university-professor quality. According to Mr. Kraatz's memo, most of the Center's technical employees held bachelor's degrees.[17] Now, many of these employees are DP-III (GS13) ratings, the demo's journeyman-level of work. My performance was much higher than the journeyman level. The level DP-IV is reserved for employees performing at the senior technical specialist level.[28]

Anyone considering working for the federal government, especially in the scientific or engineering fields, should study the following pages on appeals very carefully. The clerk management of the federal civil service wants to promote only employees who they feel belong in the organization, even if these employees are not qualified.

As required under the demo's provisions, I filed an in-house classification appeal on February 17, 1981, addressed to Mr. Wilcox, who was then our associate technical director. I asserted that for a long time I had been performing at the senior technical specialist level DP-IV. I pointed out that when I started working for the Center, I was doing GS-14 level work while assigned a GS-13 grade. I had worked in frontier areas of spectroscopy, and I had complete freedom to select my own field of research. My work was concerned with exceptionally difficult and complex scientific problems.

To support my claims, besides my educational qualifications, I described the large number of scientific contributions I had made, consisting of twenty-seven papers published in the open literature. The papers I had published during my employment at the Center represented one of its most advanced research efforts. My publications had a significant impact on the field of my research, which led to the enlargement of other ongoing research projects at other research institutions.

None of my past or present supervisors had appeared as coauthors or contributors to the research effort leading to these publications. This supported my claim that I was working as an independent principal investigator. I was working in areas that were characterized by the absence of guidelines and that required a high degree of originality, judgment, resourcefulness, and independent decision making. To document my scientific standing and qualifications, I also attached thirty-two enclosures. They consisted of invitations to give seminars at universities and scientific meetings and requests to referee colleagues' papers for publication in the open literature.

My qualifications and accomplishments far surpassed any requirements specified for the position and for most other scientists occupying the level DP-IV (GS-14/15) position employed in government R&D laboratories. My professional standing was comparable with that of a highly regarded full professor at one of the major universities. Membership in the New York Academy of Sciences, which I was selected for in 1975, was reserved for scientists who had provided exceptional scientific leadership and who were recognized nationally and internationally.

All these facts and documentations did not impress Mr. Wilcox. I explained that I had tried—without success— many times during the past fifteen years to have my position description updated and reclassified. On May 7, 1981, my request for promotion to DP-IV was denied. Mr. Wilcox stated that my prior efforts in dye lasers and fiber optics had been curtailed, and he speculated that my work in optical signal processing would fall within the level DP-III description.[29]

The DP-IV Scientist classification standard is listed below. As mentioned, classification standards also served as position descriptions for employees.

September 25, 1980
Level IV Scientist

This level differs from the Level III Scientist in the demonstration of outstanding technical leadership in a frontier area, which will influence major projects, proposals, and direction of major work. The scientist is a recognized authority whose ideas form a basis for research/development ideas by others. Consults with very important, high level Navy or DOD committees and provides scientific leadership. Usually, the scientist has made a significant number of scientific contributions in the form of publications, patents, and articles that have had a major impact in the specialty area. Typically, the scientist's work will present the latest state-of the-art in the field. May also serve on panels and committees charged with the planning of broad Navy resources to develop new systems/programs.

The assignment is usually concerned with the most advanced and/or controversial work being conducted by the organization. The scientist has substantial impact in areas of investigations that have, to date, been considered without value or have not been developed. Because of the scientists' outstanding reputation, assignments are often personally assigned by sponsors or high naval officials. Breakthroughs usually include information of fundamental significance.

The importance can be seen through application of this information to follow-on projects using the incumbent's concepts and methodology. The scientist, as a program leader, determines the direction of the technical work subject only to general administrative review. These projects are normally divided into several assignments that are normally divided into several Level II/ and IV scientists and engineers. The Level IV scientists review the work of others, providing coordination and critical insight into the process.

At this level, the scientists are recognized technical authorities in an important field covering all facets of work assigned. Technical supervision is minimal. Administrative direction is provided by sponsors and higher management for such items as funding, resources, and agency's policies. The scientist often conceives and develops major proposals for requirements of the Navy. The scientist is often fully responsible for the planning, directing, and success of a broad program. Technical findings are accepted as the best information available, and agency planning efforts are based, in large measure, upon the scientist's recommendation.

This level represents top technical effort in a major field of unexplored work where there is little or controversial theory to guide experimentation. Incumbent may conceive, plan, and conduct pioneering work of outstanding scope, difficulty, and complexity in unexplored or heretofore unpromising areas of investigation. Incumbents at this level may be technical-program managers of a major research effort of national significance and scope. Based on their level of expertise, they serve as recognized authorities and expert consultants to a large laboratory and/or at the agency/interagency levels.[30]

Transfer to Sea-Site

To run a successful laser-dye/dye-laser research program, I needed funding. Around April of every year, there was a call for in-house proposals to perform independent research (IR) at the Center. In 1982, together with other employees, I presented a proposal during the spring meeting. Dr. E. Cooper was heading this IR program, and Dr. J. Silva acted as his assistant. The IR program at the Center is part of the Office of Naval Research (ONR) In-house Laboratory Independent Research (ILIR) program. This program supports basic research at navy laboratories with the goal of encouraging navy scientists and engineers to pursue innovative, high-risk, high-payoff research projects that will contribute to achieving the Center's mission, which includes research and development. These are the policy guidelines for independent research programs:

> *A successful IR program serves several beneficial purposes. These include developing and maintaining professional expertise; fostering contacts with academia, industry, and other DOD laboratories; and enhancing the SPAWARSYSCEN SAN DIEGO reputation by publishing and patenting important research results.*[31]

During the summer of 1982, I was able to review a list showing the evaluations and rankings of proposals submitted by other employees in my department. Of the twenty-six submitted, my department's management ranked my proposal last. Because I had complained to management about not being promoted, this was to be expected. I visited Dr. Silva to discuss my proposal's low rating. He stated that he and Dr. Cooper had ranked my proposal among the best. However, the very low rating I received from management put my proposal in the middle of the overall ranking, too low to qualify for financial support.

I suggested writing a petition memo for funding, directly addressed to Dr. Blood, the Center's technical director. In this petition, I would outline in more detail the objectives, background, and expected benefits of my proposed research. Dr. Silva said that this was a good idea. Some funding was still available, and both he and Dr. Cooper would hand-deliver the proposal to Dr. Blood. Within a few days, Dr. Blood assured us that my proposal would be funded. This was one of the very few pieces of good news I ever received from the Center.

During my stay at the integrated optics branch, I had published seven papers in the open literature. Even if I continued to perform and published more papers, my management would not support my promotion. Because of the poor support from my management, I decided to transfer.

I visited several different divisions and branches within the Center to look for a new home. This included the chemistry/biochemistry division. When I talked to the division head, he did not show any interest in assisting me with my transfer into his division.

However, an old acquaintance of mine from UCLA, Dr. A. Zirino, was also working in this division. During the fall of 1982, I visited the chemistry/biochemistry division again. Dr. Zirino had become acting head of one of the chemistry/biochemistry branches. The division head had left for a two-year stint to work for the ONR office in Japan. I asked Dr. Zirino to talk to his acting division head.

In no time, a transfer was arranged because I had IR funding for my project. I left Top-Site, my old place of work, without regrets. I had worked there for twelve years and produced eighteen open-literature publications, but I had nothing to show for it.

The laboratories at Sea-Site were located at the end of the Point Loma peninsula, positioned next to the new lighthouse and close to the cliffs. Just stepping outside of the laboratory, one could hear large waves splashing against the cliffs and the constant screaming of seagulls.

I was elated to move to Sea-Site. I hoped this would allow me to flush out all the remnants of my thoughts about the breakdown of the Lorentz invariance. I decided that I should focus all my efforts on success in the laser dye field. There was much work to do, and I was one of the best-trained scientists in this field, outside of the universities. I had brought with me Dr. Taylor's CW-ion argon laser, the same one that had produced the channel optical wave-guides in filter glass.

For many years, since the first observation of laser action from dyes in 1966, Rhodamine 6G had been the king of laser dyes. As a new goal, I was considering concentrating on developing a new laser dye that would be even better than Rhodamine 6G. Using a more efficient and photo-stable laser dye would open more fields for their application. Because of the accumulation of photo-decomposition products over time, spent dye solutions must be replaced. A more efficient and stable dye would reduce the frequency with which the solution would have to be replaced.

As mentioned, excessive triplet-triplet absorption of organic compounds is detrimental to laser-action efficiency. To conduct a successful laser dye development program, it would be essential to have an experimental method available to measure these small triplet absorption coefficients more accurately and conveniently.

After I had developed a more sensitive method, I used it to measure triplet absorption coefficient values over the spectral regions of laser actions of many commercially available laser dyes. These additional measurements further supported my original belief that all their absorption coefficients were too high. I hypothesized, therefore, that a new laser dye with a smaller triplet absorption coefficient over its laser spectral region should possess much higher laser action efficiency.

Now I was in a position to start an ambitious laser-dye research program, studying the relations of laser-dye efficiencies (low triplet-triplet absorption) to their molecular structures. By using the small dye laser I had available, I could also start working on obtaining new laser dyes and quickly test their efficiency and photostability. However, I would need additional funding to find a chemist to synthesize new laser dyes.

During July of 1985, we were informed that Congress had agreed to extend the demo project for another ten years. The OPM claimed it needed this time to evaluate the research results they had obtained on the demo project. However, there were no research results collected on the demo, because no performance measuring system had been developed.

U.S. Senate Hearing

On July 8, 1986, the U.S. Subcommittee on Civil Service conducted a hearing at the Center under Senator Ted Stevens.

At the hearing. Mr. Kirk Davies, an engineer, complained that he had not been promoted to DP-IV (GS-14/15) Level.

Kirk Davies: *My name is Kirk Davies. I have been with civil service at NOSC for fourteen years. I came over from General Atomic. I was hired as a GS-13. By the time the demonstration project was put into effect, I just had reached the top of the thirteenth level. So right now I'm a DP-III, essentially topped out I received this little card through the mail: "The Demonstration Project—What Is It?" One of the statements on there says, "Pay for performance." In my case, that can hardly be true. Every time I get an evaluation, I realize I'm up against the stops. There is a brick wall between a DP-III and DPIV, which seems like it is almost impossible to hurdle unless you get into management I asked my supervisor during the last two annual reviews I've had what, if anything, is wrong with my job, my performance, and he said, nothing. I design instrumentation systems, basically, and this equipment works. Just as I designed it I asked him, "What can I do to get a promotion?" and he told me that there is absolutely nothing I can do. The only chance I have of getting to DP-IV is to watch the NOSC paper and see when a DP-IV opening comes along. Most of these are management positions.*

However, about two or three years ago, a DP-IV engineer's position opened up. I went down to the personnel office and read the job description, and it seemed to me like it fit me to a tee, and I started to take steps to apply for this position. I was told, since I was a DP-III, I could not apply for this DP-IV position.

Senator Stevens: Why?

Mr. Davies: Because that was the rule. Those are the rules. I had to be a DP-IV in order to apply for this engineering position.

Senator Stevens: Wait a minute. I don't like things I don't understand. Are these people still here? Mr. Hillyer?

Mr. Hillyer: Yes.

Senator Stevens: How do you get from III to IV?

Mr. Hillyer: There are two ways: You can apply for a position that's advertised as a IV. Some are reserved for lateral transfer, which I suspect was the case there, but I don't know. Some are not. You can—you can grow in a position either through accretion of duties or creation of expertise. The requirement to be a DP-IV professional technical person is to have national reputation in your field.

Senator Stevens: Is this equivalent to the break between the GS-15 and the SES?

Mr. Hillyer: No, sir. It's roughly between the old 13 and the old 14, GS-13 and GS-or GM-13 and GM-14. That's kind of the same criteria applied there to be technical GM-14, and then—

Senator Stevens: It's going from 13 to 14 of the old system?

Mr. Hillyer: Yes sir, approximately.

Senator Stevens: But this ladder ends at III; right?

Mr. Hillyer: No, sir. If you have national reputation in your field, published in the open-literature journals or are nationally recognized, it's possible to get to be a level IV employee without going into management And we have a significant number of them that do. On the other hand, we self-impose a limit of level IVs we allow on the Center. And I admit that we have more people who are qualified on the Center to be level IV than we have room to promote; and that's simply to limit the cost of doing business on the Center and, frankly, to restrain external criticism for the grade creep. So the captain and I artificially set criteria—not completely artificially—for the number of promotions we'll allow to level IV. We base that on the number of people who have left, past experiences, growth at the Center, the number of professionals at the Center, and some judgmental things on the cost of doing business, and we limit the number of level IVs that we can hire.

Senator Stevens: Okay.

Mr. Hillyer: It wouldn't make sense for this organization to be all level IVs, sir.

Senator Stevens: I understand that, but if I were on the top of a III, I'd want to know how I'm going to get to IV, or I'm going to leave. That's why I'd sort of like to understand that it seems like an arbitrary break that I did not think was there. Does the same thing exist, say, between I and II? When I reach GS-8, how do I get to GS-9? A different job?

Mr. Hillyer: No, sir. We don't have limits on most of those promotions. The journeyman level is Level III. Promotions to Level III generally happen as the *individual grows and gains experience and, in some cases, education. We look at a Level IV as technical, as somebody with special talents.*

Senator Stevens: Okay. Now under the old system, what would happen to you, Mr. Davies?

Mr. Davies: Well, under the old system, the department I worked for at that time—and I had a pretty good rapport, I felt confident that, given a short period of time, I would have been a GS-14.

Senator Stevens: But when you reach the top of thirteen, you would have to have a different position to have a fourteen, wouldn't you, in terms of job description?

Mr. Davies: I don't think so. I think that the step between thirteen and fourteen was much easier than that between DP-III and DP-IV.

Senator Stevens: I see. Okay. We will look into it. That is an interesting question.[32]

Unfortunately, Senator Stevens never looked into this question. Although I considered Mr. Hillyer to be one of the better technical directors we had at the Center, apparently he had a problem understanding merit principles: "The captain and I artificially set criteria—not completely artificially—for the number of promotions we'll allow to level IV." According to merit principles, employees performing at the level IV are entitled to level IV pay. Under the demo, high-quality employees are held financially accountable for mismanagement—namely, for the over-grading at the Center.

Over the last twenty-six years, the Center had limited the number of promotions drastically, especially to the important level DP-IV to fight the so-called grade creep. There are two reasons for the grade-creep. One has been described in detail. Many employees who entered the demo were occupying over-graded and overpaid positions and were blocking the promotion of many qualified employees, mostly from DP-III to DP-IV. The other reason is pay banding.

Employees who were earning performance rewards were able to move from the bottom to the top of their pay-bands, passing through two or three GS grades without being promoted. This automatically raised the average grade level at the Center; it became about one grade higher than its sister laboratories not covered by the demo. No wonder there was external criticism of the grade-creep.

At that time I met a Dr. Winterfeld, a young physicist who had been hired at the Center at the DP-II level (GS-II). He had earned his PhD in physics from Stanford University. He left after spending several years at the Center, never advancing much, and having his career damaged.

Many other DP-III (GS-13) senior scientists with doctorates at the Center also complained bitterly to me that most employees holding BA or BS degrees were also collecting DP-III (GS-13) journeyman pay. For high-quality employees, the move from GS-13 (DP-III) to GS-14 (DP-IV) is the most important promotion. It recognizes a high degree of talent, creativity, and accomplishments. GS-14 is where the action is.

The creators of the demo had claimed that their scheme would provide "Enhanced recruitment of quality candidates."[28]

I cannot see how eliminating or drastically reducing promotions for many years, especially the number of DP-IV promotions, together with hiring new employees at low levels over a very long period, can retain high-quality employees or attract new ones.

In addition, Mr. Hillyer had stated: "The captain and I artificially set criteria." However, promotion, as well as performance criteria, must be made known to all employees. There is no place for fabricating "artificially set criteria." This violates basic merit principles—yet the system that permits this abusive practice was allowed to continue at the Center. Where was and where is the OPM, which was supposed to have oversight over position classification and strict implementing of merit system principles, namely, equal pay for substantially equal work? Is this what Kay Coles James, the OPM's former director, meant when she said, "A fresh start for federal pay: the case for modernization"?

1986 Classification Appeal

On November 17, 1986, I again filed a classification / reconsideration appeal. I stated that the appeal was based on my continuing and long-term sustained productivity, the exceptional difficulty of the work that I performed, and the unique qualifications required in performing my tasks. I stressed that I had never become involved in any intense investigation into the field of signal processing, and my main effort continued to be in the field of dye lasers—as well as marketing proposals. Additionally, in the time since my last appeal, I had also produced still more papers for publication in the open literature. This was the twenty-second year at the Center during which I had been working without the benefit of a properly classified position description. I again enclosed a considerable amount of documentation related to performance criteria, consisting of a list of my open-literature publications, and presentations I had given at conferences, seminars I had led at universities, requests to review the papers of other scientists submitted for publication, and the impact of my work expressed in letters from colleagues.

I stated that Mr. Wilcox's decision in 1981 not to promote me lacked any reference to my qualifications, duties, or responsibilities. The failure to apply these criteria was an abuse of managerial discretion that constituted a harmful procedural error.

I also complained that the 1981 classification did not refer at all to performance standards applicable to DP-IV performance. Mr. Wilcox's rationale that my work in the dye laser field had to be curtailed due to lack of sponsor funding and that my technical efforts had to be redirected ignored the fact that other scientists routinely changed subfields without reclassification or downgrading. His decision was influenced by hypothetical loss of project support and sponsor funding, and it was without any known precedents and contrary to regulations. He had placed undue emphasis on future work and funding, which, at best, relied on speculation.

On July 16, 1987, I received the results of my classification appeal from Deputy Technical Director Talkington, who had succeeded Mr. Wilcox. It was based on the evaluation of Mrs. Alice Smith, a personnel management advisor who had reviewed my submission and talked to my managers. Mrs. Smith concluded that the current classification of my nonsupervisory scientist level DP-III position was appropriate for my position. She fabricated the following three new promotion criteria:

1. *Projects involve the latest state-of-the-art research in a frontier area, which will influence major projects, proposals, and direction of major work.*
2. *The incumbent is concerned with the most advanced and/or controversial work being contacted by NOSC. Research results have a significant Navy-wide impact.*
3. *The incumbent provides "expert" consultation to higher-level Navy/DOD/interagency committees; provides scientific leadership; and has substantial contributions in the form of presentation, papers, and publications.*[33]

The work of scientists spans the entire spectrum of basic and applied research, from development to testing and evaluation. A scientist performing basic research, meaning work directed toward increasing knowledge and understanding of the physical world, will generally not provide "expert" consultation with higher-level Navy/DOD/interagency committees. Basic research may have navy-wide impact ten or twenty years from now. For example, a scientist working on the development of a new type of torpedo may provide "expert'' consultation to high-level committees, but may not have".. [a] substantial contributions in the form of presentations, papers, and publications."

Applicable criteria from the DP-IV Scientist standard are:

> *Usually, the scientist has made a significant number of substantial contributions in the form of publications, patents, and articles that have had a major impact in the specialty area. Typically, the scientist's work will present the latest state-of the-art in the field.*

> *The Level IV scientist reviews the work of others providing coordination and critical insight into the process. The assignment is usually concerned with the most advanced and/or controversial work being conducted by the organization. The scientist has substantial impact in areas of investigation that have, to date, been considered without value or have not been developed. This level represents top technical level effort in a major field of unexplored work where there is little or controversial theory to guide experimentation.*

> *Incumbents may conceive, plan, and conduct pioneering work of outstanding scope, difficulty, and complexity in unexplored or heretofore unpromising areas of investigation. Typically, the scientist's work will present the latest state-of the-art in the field.*[30]

In Mrs. Smith's newly fabricated performance criteria, she expressed the wishes of the Center's management, who wanted

Is the U.S. Office of Personnel Management Responsible for 9/11?

to promote employees who obtain large funding for large development projects that provide funding for many workers. These employees also supervise these workers. With these newly fabricated managerial promotion criteria, employees can now be promoted to DP-IV without competition, through the noncompetitive promotion route, referred to as accretion of duties. Supervisory and managerial promotions require a competitive merit-based selection process. At the Center, employees mostly obtain funding and supervise workers. There is also in place a large managerial clique, mostly performing administrative functions. In such an organization we have "over structuring,"[16] which is very costly to the taxpayer.

Mr. Hillyer's Memos

During 1986, Mr. Hillyer, the Center's technical director, complained in his memo:

> *There has been a significant decline in the number of invention disclosures submitted by NOSC technical personnel (about 50 percent of what it was just five years ago).*[34]

In a memo dated August 13, 1987, Mr. Hillyer lectured all employees and managers on the importance of formal reporting. Formal reporting includes technical notes, conference proceedings, and open-literature publications. Conference proceedings generally consist of a one-page, single-spaced summary of scientific or technical work that an employee has presented at a scientific or technical meeting or conference. This memo is presented below.

> 1. *NOSC is experiencing a serious decline in its 1987 formal reporting. Compared to 1986, report production has decreased by 34 percent for documentation prepared by*

137

NOSC scientists and engineers. I am particularly surprised by these statistics, as our in-house technical base work has expanded by 20 percent, which should be reflected by an increase in reporting and not by a decline.

2. *Formal reporting of technical work is a fundamental precept in the scientific and engineering profession and attests to the professionalism of performance. In addition, formal reporting, i.e., that is available in the Defense Technical Information Center, is a DOD and Navy requirement designed to avoid duplication work; to support the information requirements of scientists, engineers, and managers; and to advance national RDT&E efforts.*

3. *It is very important that we improve our performance in this area. To accomplish this improvement, please remind your technical people of the following policies: Formal reportin is considered a part of the performance rating of scientists and engineers. Formal reporting is considered a part of the evaluation process when considering scientists and engineers for promotion. The performance of NOSC managers (technical department, division, branch heads) includes meeting NOSC requirements on formal reporting.*

4. *To accomplish this improvement will require that time and resources for preparing reports will be made available to our scientists and engineers. It will require that you, as managers, increase their awareness concerning reporting requirements and encourage reporting as a part of their professional stature. By doing this, we will be able to help maintain the accuracy, completeness, and currency of DOD's database of reports, as well as increase the Center's professional stature.*

5. *To help me monitor performance in this area, Code 96 will provide me with quarterly reports on NOSC publications.*

R. M. Hillyer.[35]

Working with Professor Boyer

At the Office of Naval Research (ONR), I contacted Dr. George Neese, whom I knew from the ONR meetings on photochemistry. The ONR is one of the most prestigious government funding agencies for basic research. They provide grants for exceptional university professors who perform basic research. A small portion of their funding is also provided to researchers who perform outstanding basic research at naval laboratories.

I asked Dr. Neese for support for my laser dye synthesis improvement program. Following the usual protocol, he requested a proposal. Sometime later, he told me that there was an Office of Naval Research (ONR)/Navy laboratory supplemental research program. If the Navy laboratory could come up with some funding for my research, the ONR would match the rest. Fortunately, I had independent research funding. This would make it possible for me to fund a chemist to perform the laser dye synthesis. I asked Dr. Neese to suggest a chemist. He referred me to Dr. Guard, the ONR's organic chemist, who, in turn, highly recommended Professor Joe Boyer from the University of New Orleans. I contacted the professor, and he declared unhesitatingly that he was ready to participate in such a laser dye synthesis program. In addition, he had some postdoctoral fellows working for him who were also eager to participate.

I explained to Professor Boyer that the first requisite was an organic compound that exhibited strong fluorescence. I asked him if he remembered any organic compounds that would satisfy this, no matter how unusual their structures. I would study any of them. A few weeks later, he mailed me a rather simple compound, belonging to a family of organic compounds called syn-bimanes. To my surprise, this laser dye lased about as efficiently as some commercially available coumarin dyes. Together with Professor Boyer and his coworkers, we published a letter, in 1986, in the *Journal of Applied Physics*.

Professor Boyer and his group synthesized more synbimane laser dyes. We subsequently published four more papers on the subject of these new laser dyes. Although these compounds showed surprising photo-stability in water and efficient laser action, none of the compounds showed any exceptionally high efficiency.

The discovery that the syn-bimanes exhibited laser action presented a major advancement in the field. These observations suggested that closely related derivatives of the syn-bimanes might also show laser action, and hopefully, some would exhibit very efficient laser action. For the next twelve years, I was funded by the ONR. These would be my most productive years at the Center.

Mr. H. Porter's e-mail

Promotions at the Center supposedly depend on proper position classification, using OPM-approved classification standards. Over the years, I had often observed that the Center's management promoted their favorite employees, even if they did not qualify according to the applicable classification standards. After Mr. Liddell's memo of 1969, [7] I put most of them in the trash. However, an e-mail from my division head, Mr. H.O. Porter, concerning who was and who was not promoted, proved very instructive. In this e-mail, he addressed other division heads in the department Mr. Porter wrote:

Subject: OP-IV Criteria April18, 1987

Suggested Criteria for DP-111 to DP-IV Promotion.

The following criteria have been developed over the last few years. They are not perfect but present input from a number of people. I think there are some obvious differences in promotion criteria for scientists and managers (including technical and/ or program managers) although a few people can be looked at as a combination scientist and manager. Where I can, I will indicate those differences.

Education

I think that a requirement for a DP-IV scientist should be a PhD or equivalent. However, a DP-IV manager only needs a B.S. or equivalent in their technical fields.

NOSC Experience

I think that both scientists and managers should have been working at NOSCfor a long enough time for people to really get a handle on their performance (and personality). I think this means at least 3 or 4 years at NOSC at the DPIII level. A candidate for DP-IV should already be working at the DP-IV level (especially true for a scientist). They should already have demonstrated successful accomplishments in their field. For a manager, this would mean successful development, marketing, and accomplishing of a major (in impact, not necessarily in dollars) program. For a scientist, this would mean a large number of significant papers, published in refereed journals. The recent performance rating of the employee should reflect this performance (mostly 3 or 4 points, nothing below 2).

At the DP-IV level, a person should be known in their field. For the scientist, this means internationally known. A DP-IV scientist should have given papers at international meetings, published in international journals, and be recognized by foreign scientists in the field. A DP-IV manager should be recognized by their peers in the field in the U.S. and in the appropriate community in Washington, DC. It isn't necessary, but [it] would be a plus if the manager had done some work with international organizations and participated in international meetings. The employee's peers should recognize the employee as being worthy of promotion.

To a limited degree, the DP-IV scientist should be able to work in a number of somewhat different areas. The DPIV manager should be able to handle a number of different kinds and types of programs and people.

Importance to Navy/Future Value

The expertise of any DP-IV (managers and scientists) should be in an area of importance to the Center and to the Navy. The future value of the employee to NOSC should be high.

Gut Feelings

I don't know what to say, except you should feel good about anyone you propose for Level IV promotion.[36]

There are two subjective promotion criteria contained in Mr. Porter's e-mail. The first is that the employee's work should h ave "importance to the Navy." This subjective criterion allows management to favor one employee over another by simply stating that one employee's project is of more importance to the navy than another employee's. Nowhere in any position classification standard can this criterion be found.

In fact, as I will explain later, the question of importance is moot.

The second subjective criterion, "future value," invites social speculation by management. Furthermore, the requirement that a scientist DP-IV candidate should possess a PhD or equivalent is confusing. Does this mean that a manager can bestow PhDs to employees who don't have them? Apparently, if you don't have this degree, your manager can simply declare that some past work you may have performed is equivalent to a PhD. If this is correct, why should any of us earn the degree in the first place?

Mr. Porter's e-mail also provides important insight into how employees are selected for managerial positions. Candidates should have worked at the Center "for a long enough time for people to really get a handle on their performance (and personality)." He supports the idea that only employees from the in-house pool, whose pleasant personalities (providing good gut feelings) are well known, should be preferentially selected for managerial positions.

For many years, high-quality employees were rarely hired from outside the Center, and management almost never were. When branch-head positions in the scientific or engineering fields became available at the Center, there was a specific group of employees who always applied and who were very often selected. They were scientists or engineers who were not doing well working in their assigned fields of expertise. Consequently, escaping into management was a smart professional survival strategy for these employees.

It is difficult for outsiders to imagine what wonderful goof-off positions many federal managerial jobs are. Management has available the personnel office, legal office, public relations office, contracting office, purchasing office, and others. Being part of a bureaucracy, the manager does not have to worry about the bottom line, how to pay the employees, or how to pay escalating health premiums. No advertising, no need to worry about the competition, no taxes to pay, no reports to shareholders.

The managers for military R&D laboratories today do not need an advanced degree—a bachelor's degree will do—and very little, if any, expertise or experience is required for them to perform their jobs. Moreover, they can promote and reward any employee they want. Management positions are filled from within, "after sufficient time has passed to get a handle on their personality" to assure a pleasant working environment. The managers also decide which technical or scientific projects they do or do not want an employee to perform, although they often don't have any idea what they are supposed to be supervising. What wonderful jobs the federal management positions are. They delegate all their unpleasant work to their underlings. There is no accountability; they have immunity, wonderful job security, good and regular pay, and substantial health and retirement benefits.

Pyrromethene Laser Dyes

Again, Professor Boyer and I discussed the importance of strong fluorescence. I advised him to focus on compounds related to the syn-bimanes. This time he came up with a compound belonging to the family of the pyrromethene complexes (specifically, the tetramethyl-pyrromethene complex) that exhibited strong fluorescence in the green spectral region. I was surprised when this compound exhibited laser action. Once again, we published a letter on our findings in *Applied Optics* in 1988, together with Professor Boyer and one of his coworkers.

The next dyes were the tetra-methyl-diethyl-pyrromethene complex and its disulfonated derivative. Significantly, the first complex lased about three times more efficiently in the green/yellow spectral region than the corresponding coumarin laser dye, a laser dye that was commercially available. The sulfonated compound also lased well in water as solvent but was somewhat unstable. However, using methanol as a solvent, this complex exhibited a high degree of photo stability.

We published the experimental results on these two new

laser dyes in 1989 in the journal *Optics Communications*. The development of these new laser dyes constituted a huge advance in laser dye development. The next group of three new pyrromethene complexes exhibited laser action in the yellow spectrum and lased about three times more efficiently than Rhodamine 560, a dye lasing in the same spectral region. Significantly, diethyl-pentamethyl-pyrromethene complex lased about 10 percent more efficiently than Rhodamine 6G, the king of laser dyes. Data on all three and other new complexes were published in the journal *Applied Optics*.

Finally, I had reached the most ambitious goal I had set for myself: to develop a laser dye that outperformed Rhodamine 6G. Over the following years, Professor Boyer and his coworkers synthesized many more pyrromethene laser dyes. Several of these dyes approached the efficiency of the diethyl-penta-methyl-pyrromethene complex, but none surpassed it. Altogether, about thirty of these new laser dyes were developed and published in the scientific literature. During these years, I did not attempt to be promoted, fearing that reprisal action by my managers might prevent me from completing my work on the new laser dyes. However, with the success of these new dyes, I felt compelled to try again for a promotion. Other scientists at the Center had been promoted to the DP-IV level during this time. With few exceptions, most of these employees had shown little accomplishment in the form of open-literature publications.

The International Society for Optical Engineering (SPIE) is one of the largest optical societies in the world, with chapters all over the globe. SPIE is more applications-oriented than the American Optical Society. SPIE's meetings draw huge crowds of optical engineers and physicists. Until about 1998, its yearly meetings in Los Angeles would draw in excess of six thousand participants. To accommodate the growing meetings, sessions were moved to San Jose, California. About the year 2000, the yearly meetings began to draw over ten thousand participants.

Besides presenting a paper at these meetings, participants

submit a full-fledged paper to be published in the SPIE Proceedings. The referee system requires entrants to submit a photo-ready manuscript. These days, this is easily accomplished on the word processor.

The possibility of submitting their early research results for presentation and meeting many of their colleagues at SPIE's large meetings spurs many researchers to attend. Among the hundreds of papers submitted and presented at these SPIE meetings, many are top-notch.

One of the meetings I was interested in attending took place in Paris in 1989 under the title, "High Power Lasers and Laser Machining Technology." I put together a paper titled "High-Efficiency Laser Dyes for High-Energy Dye Lasers," and listed Professor Boyer as coauthor.

In the paper, I explained that there was a great demand for high-efficiency, high-energy dye lasers for many industrial and scientific applications, which could be fulfilled with high-efficiency laser dyes. I provided a theoretical derivation that showed that laser dyes possessing reduced triplet-triplet absorption over their fluorescence spectral region could be up-scaled by using them in large dye lasers and having them pumped by large flash lamps. As an example of such improved laser dyes, I presented the pentamethylpyrromethene-BFz complex. I also mentioned its superior performance when compared to Coumarin 545.

Around this time, I also received an invitation to present a seminar on a subject of my choice at my old school, the Max Planck Institute for Physical Chemistry, in Göttingen. Unfortunately, I neither attended this SPIE meeting nor went to Germany because of a mix-up at the Center's travel office. For several years, we had been instructed not to travel with an official government passport but to use a civilian passport because of the danger of being taken hostage.

When I visited our travel office, however, I was instructed that I would need an official passport in order to be issued governmental travel documents. To speed up the issuance of a government passport on short notice, I was told I should also submit my civilian passport. Predictably, the slow-working bureaucracy returned the two passports to me the day after the SPIE meeting in Paris, and I had to cancel the entire trip.

About two years later, I received a letter from SPIE that our Paris paper had been selected for publication in their "Milestone Series," in a volume called *Laser Design*. The "Milestone Series" is a collection of classical papers from the international scientific literature on optical and optoelectronic science, engineering, and technology. Not really knowing what to expect, I did not pay much attention to this book.

Several years later, I found a copy of that volume of the "SPIE Milestone Series" in the Center's library. The purpose of the book was to collect the one hundred most significant original papers in the art of laser design. If a researcher wanted to work in a specific field of lasers, he would find the most important original papers in the field in that collection. The chapter on dye lasers contained only six papers, including the one I had written with Professor Boyer as coauthor. This aroused my interest. Out of the one hundred papers published in the collection, one author was from the army, one from the air force, and two from NASA. I was the only author from the navy. When I mentioned this fact to my supervisor, he did not seem to care, much less want to talk about how the public recognition of my expertise might affect my merit evaluation.

In 1990, Professor Boyer mailed samples of the pyrromethene complexes to several researchers for testing. He also obtained patents on these complexes and then sold the patents to Exciton, a company that sold laser dyes.

Over the years, many experimental results on the pyrromethene complexes were obtained and have appeared in a large number of open literature publications. In 1993, I was invited to participate in a colloquium on electro-optics countermeasures in Edinburgh, Scotland. Among the highlights of the meeting was a presentation by Mr. Utano from the U.S. Army Night Vision Laboratory. Working with Dr. Hermes from the Los Alamos National Laboratory and others, he reported an unheard-of 86 percent conversion efficiency from plastic samples doped with one of our pyrromethene laser dyes when pumped with a frequency doubled and Q-switched Nd: YAG laser. YAG stands for yttrium aluminium garnet, doped with about one percent neodymium.

This was an almost complete conversion of one wavelength of laser light into another wavelength. Generally, a 50 percent conversion rate is considered good. The work of Dr. Hermes and his coworkers had been published in *Applied Physics Letters* in 1993 and started a new subsection in solid-state dye lasers. Before this, solid-state dye lasers were only mentioned in a short footnote in textbooks. During the years after Hermes and Utano's team's findings were published and up to the present day, many publications appeared in the literature in this field, constituting a new class of solid-state dye lasers. In May of 1993, I visited the Army Night Vision Laboratory to give a presentation on the pyrromethene complexes. During my stay, I also talked to Mr. Grant, who was Mr. Utano's supervisor. He suggested a joint effort on laser-dye improvement between his laboratory, Professor Boyer, and me. During the summer of 1993, I made several telephone calls to Mr. Grant. He expressed great disappointment on the Pentagon's sudden and unexpected large cuts in funding for military laser programs, including his. He stated that he would not be able to support the synthesis of new laser dyes.

In December of 1993, Mr. Grant informed me that the U.S. Army Missile Command (MICOM) would receive three years of funding from Congress for the medical application of dye lasers. Several hospitals in the Boston area had approached Congress with the suggestion to make dye lasers more user-friendly. Water-soluble laser dyes would present such an improvement. In the beginning of 1994, I called Dr. J. Ehrlich several times. He said that MICOM had received some of the funding, but he did not have any to assign to our project. He asked me to provide him with a proposal. He was also interested in funding Professor Boyer to produce the improved laser dyes. The U.S. Army MICOM had also done a small part to fund our work during my last years at the Center.

I did not know that 1994 would mark the beginning of constantly declining research funding, not only for me, but also for the entire defense laboratory community. During the middle of March of that year, Dr. Ehrlich informed me that he had only $25,000 for my laser-dye improvement effort. About the same time, Dr. Peter Schmidt from ONR informed me that he could give me $40,000. In September of 1994, however, Dr. Ehrlich told me that he had received only part of the expected funding. He stated that the missing part was lost to "vultures." What this meant was that Congress had approved funding for military research projects, and as soon as this funding showed up in the Pentagon, it was swiftly reallocated in bits and chunks to other military needs that might have come up unexpectedly, like Bosnia or Kosovo. This type of raiding by "vultures" continues even to this day.

How the Demo Works in Practice

Every year, all government agencies and departments have funds available to pay their employees' wages. They also have funds to pay for their employees' yearly step increases. At the Center, these yearly pay increases are now pooled and used for the demo's incentive performance pay increases, a system that allocates socalled performance points. Zero to four points can be earned, depending on the performance rating given by the supervisor. Three points equal a one-step increase.

Because there is no performance appraisal system in place, each supervisor and manager uses his or her own subjective performance criteria to arbitrarily rank an employee's performance as outstanding, superior, satisfactory, marginal, or unacceptable. Often, the supervisor has no or only a marginal technical, scientific, or research background to properly evaluate employees' performance.

Stating it differently, the allocation of a certain number of points to each supervisor and manager presents a slush fund. Management is never held accountable as to how these funds are distributed. No one seems to care that this is actually tax payers' money.

First, the technical director of the Center receives all the points available. He takes the first cut and rewards all of the employees who report directly to him-namely, his staff and the department heads. The department heads and division heads follow similar procedures. What is left goes to the branch heads. The number of reward points they receive depends on the number of employees in their units.

However, talent and performance are very differently distributed a mong branches, divisions, and departments. It is conceivable that one branch may have many more excellent performers than another branch. Some branches have higher-performing teams than others. But under the demo, if two branches have the same number of employees, they receive the same number of performance points.

Consequently, in each branch, an employee competes against other employees for these performance points. A person's share of these points depends on the performance of the other employees in his or her branch. Such a reward system collides with basic merit principles because there is no equity. There is no objectivity. In private industry as well as in the civil service, teams mostly perform work assignments. Rewarding just some of the employees in highperforming teams destroys team cohesion.

Employees have only an in-house appeal route available when dissatisfied with their performance rankings. But how can they appeal a performance rating, even in a system where their appeal would be heard by a fair judge, without having performance appraisal and performance standards in place? When filing an appeal, it is the employee's word against the supervisor's.

Although many employees appealed their performance ratings, I never learned of an appeal that was successful. However, with the passage of time, the number of such appeals has drastically declined. Apparently, employees realized that even if they are successful, appealing their supervisors' judgment is not a good idea. The supervisor always remembers.

Under the terms of the demo, it was never explained to the Center's employees how management rewards the performance of the supervisors and managers under them. The OPM has oversight and evaluation functions over the Center's demo, so they should know how the performance-reward system for management actually works. It is conceivable that management might be dipping into the employees' pool of points to hand out rich rewards for their favorite supervisors and managers.

To illustrate the pay-for-performance and pay-banding situation at the Center under the demo, I have provided two examples. These are generalizations from real situations that actually occurred—or could have occurred. The first example tries to answer why it is wrong for management to pressure employees to solicit funding and highly reward them if they are successful.

We have a DP-III supervisor who holds a BS degree in electrical engineering. In his branch are twenty-five workers. He retired after about thirty-two years of service. During this time, on the average, he had two DP-III employees in his branch who successfully obtained outside funding. Consequently, the branch head and the two successful employees are quickly promoted to DP-IV. They receive "outstanding" performance pay every year and, because of pay-banding, move up quickly into to DP-IV GS14/15 pay range.

However, funding categories constantly change. The amount of funding available and the duration of projects depend on Congress. Also, funding may end because the sponsor at the Pentagon retires or is transferred to another position.

We can assume, somewhat optimistically, that the average funding duration of each project is about eight years. After the funding ends, the "successful" employees are only able to perform DP-III (GS-12/13) level work, but continue to receive their DP-IV GS-14/15 pay.

During the thirty-two years, the branch, including the supervisor, would have accumulated about nine promotions to DPIV. Most likely, nobody else in the branch was promoted to DP-IV because most pay-for-performance rewards went to the branch head and the eight "successful" employees. This raises an important question. Is it not the main function of supervision to give work assignments to workers who have the means to perform these assignments? If someone else performs this managerial function, what is the function of supervisors at work?

Many employees in the branch are victimized without having any workable routes available to voice their grievances. The other victims of this system are the taxpayers. Let's say a branch head holds a bachelor's degree in civil engineering, and he supervises twenty-five employees, including a group of physicists, several of whom have PhDs. They work in frontier areas of semiconductor physics. This group receives in-house independent research funding. They publish extensively in the open literature.

Most likely, their branch head has never performed any research himself. However, as the supervisor of a research group, he is now dabbling in research, deciding which research projects should be performed in his branch. This branch head would not have the slightest idea what the employees in his semiconductor group were doing, scientifically. Often, such a supervisor may have a chip on his shoulder from supervising employees who hold more advanced degrees than his own. However, yearly performance rewards, promotions, and the professional future of the group depend entirely on his whims. Let's assume the semiconductor group's leader complains to the group's branch head because of the lack of promotions and pay-performance rewards. The branch head can ignore the complaint by claiming that there were insufficient promotions and performance points allocated to the branch to properly reward all the deserving employees.

Interestingly, the real reason the semiconductor group received very few reward points and promotions could be that another group in the branch received much more performance rewards and promotions. This other group was trying to develop a more "useful Navy product"-namely, a paint that prevents the accumulation of barnacles on ship hulls.

Until such paint is developed, ships must be put on dry docks and the fouling scraped off mechanically. This is time-consuming and expensive. Such money-saving projects as the development of a barnacle-blocking paint find huge support in the navy. The manager supervising this type of project—and his branch head— "looks very good."

Besides funneling performance-pay rewards to the paint group, the branch head might also withdraw independent research funding from the semiconductor group and redirect this funding for the work in antifouling paint. Because of pay-banding, the employees working on the paint project can climb quickly up the pay-band ladder. Now, promotions come easily. Promotions to members of the paint-project group might be explained to the captain as being merited because they are doing work that is very important to the navy. The supervisor and the project leader move quickly up the pay ladder to top GS-15 pay.

However, there are two problems. First, the employees in the paint group are shallow in professional competence. Similarly important is the multibillion-dollar paint industry, which has the best-trained chemists available to work on antifouling paint. Not only the navy but also the huge commercial fleet would profit from an antifouling paint. In short, the navy should have left this type of project to private commercial research. By this time, some researchers in semiconductors will have left the group, or worse, the group may have been disbanded.

After a few years, the paint project collapses. However, all employees associated with this project, including the ones receiving DP-IV pay, continue to receive their high rate of pay, not only until retirement, but also afterward, in their pensions. Once retired, DPIV (GS-15) employees collect retirement pay in the range of $90,000 to $110,000 per year, depending on the length of their service. In addition, they will receive a yearly cost-of-living adjustment, together with copayments to their health insurance.

This is a typical example of how the American bureaucracy under the demo rewards those it deems "performing employees." There are many supervisors and managers working for the government who, during their professional careers, supported a large number of questionable projects like the example of antifouling paint, including boondoggles that fail but are never removed from their "research positions."

In 2006, a branch head, with the help of pay-banding, can quickly reach a yearly income of around $142,000, the top step of GS-15. This amount includes San Diego locality pay, namely additional pay depending on how expensive it is to live in a particular area.

All branch heads' performance rewards depend solely on the relationship they have with their division heads. Generally, their relationships are very good, because the division heads handpick the branch heads. How their branches perform, though, is often unimportant. Only in the case of funding problems would the division head get worried.

1989 and 1990 Equal Employment Opportunity Commission Complaints

By 1989, I had been working at the Center for twenty-four years. During this time, other employees had been promoted from DP-III to DP-IV. Because of the success of my pyrromethene laser dyes, I reasoned, I should file another classification appeal, seeking an accurate classification of my work and, correspondingly, appropriate pay for what I did.

On July 10, 1989, I filed a complaint with the Equal Employment Opportunity Commission (EEOC), claiming discrimination based on national origin and age. I stated that I fulfilled the criteria contained in the Level DP-IV Scientist Standard of September 25, 1980.[30] I attached Mr. Hillyer's memo in which he has emphasized the importance of formal reporting, namely that "Formal reporting is considered part of the evaluation process when considering scientists and engineers for promotion."[35] The EEOC counselor interviewed my supervisor and my division and department heads. He collected the following "facts":

The resignations, retirement, etc., of personnel in each department at the DP-IV level allows the Center to allocate the number of DP-IVs that can be promoted in that department. This year (FY) Department 50 was allocated five (5).

When selecting and nominating potential candidates, no written guidelines are used. However, each division and department has individual factors, which they consider important to the operation of their area.

Visibility, time in grade, leadership abilities, productivity, as well as abilities to work with others in related fields, serve as a mentor to others in related fields, especially younger people. Contribution to the Division, Department, NOSC, and the Department of the Navy in the technical/management fields. Recognition among peers in related fields, valuable publications (scope and depth considered versatility and notoriety).

There are more potential candidates recommended for DPIV by the division heads than there are allocations. No mention was made of any candidate's national origin, nor was it a factor in making selections for DP-IV.[37]

It is important to remember that if you perform at the DP-IV level, you must be paid at that level. The reason for limiting promotions, especially to the DP-IV level, is the over-grading and the grade-creep at the Center. In practice, "However, each division and department has individual factors, which they consider important to the operation of their areas." This refers to the need to reward cronies and employees who perform their managers' jobs—namely, obtaining funding.

Later, the June 8, 1990, edition of the Center's internal journal, *Outlook*, featured pictures of employees promoted to DP-IV. Because I had once again been unfairly passed over during this latest round of promotions, I filed a second EEOC complaint, claiming discrimination because of my Greek origin, age discrimination, and reprisal for failing past classification appeals. For the 1990 case, the counselor collected the same responses from my managers that were similar as listed above.

I continued with my 1989 complaint. The investigator who was assigned to my case collected sworn affidavits from my managers and me. When he furnished me with the copies of the affidavits, I was very surprised to find that he had attached the promotion nomination forms of the three employees who had been successfully promoted to scientist DP-IV in 1989.

The investigator had gone to the Center's personnel office and requested the personnel files of the three candidates. In these promotion nominations listed below, I have omitted the names of the scientists to avoid privacy law issues. I also changed some acronyms; others I left standing. The meaning of 6.2 and 6.3 will be explained later.

PROMOTION NOMINATION (1)

Scientist, DP-1310-III, $53,458, Time in Demo Level: 42 months

1. *This proposal is for: Scientist, DP-1310- IV*
2. *State briefly below justification for this proposed promotion and incumbent's accomplishments (past, present, &future).*

PAST: *Mr. AAA is an expert in acoustic and electromagnetic wave propagation. Prior to joining NOSC in 1985, he spent six years at Science Applications International Corporation (SAIC) as a principal scientist where he was P. I. (principal investigator) on Navy-sponsored 6.2 and 6.3 acoustic modeling projects. He has extensive experience in computer modeling analysis on a wide variety of computers. Mr. AAA's formal training has been as a physicist with a BS from Caltech and an MS in theoretical nuclear physics from the University of Washington. He is presently completing his thesis for a PhD in theoretical physics from UCS D.*

PRESENT: *Mr. AAA joined NOSC in 1985 and has been working in Code 541 on 6.2-3 environmental acoustic modeling projects in the area of undersea surveillance with major emphasis on LFA problems. He currently is working with SPAWA R-180 on LFA* *source design issues, with the active classification and bi-static sub-programs of ONT, on a tactical towed array bearing resolution projects and on parabolic equation E.M. propagation algorithm for radar program. He is a P. I. on an NOSC IR project dealing with underwater sound propagation. Since joining NOSC, Mr. AAA has been heavily involved in interdepartmental ASW projects with Codes 71, 72, 73, and 65. He is widely respected within and outside the Center.*

FUTURE POTENTIAL*: Mr. AAA is expected to continue as a leading expert in underwater acoustics and develop major new projects in simulation and modeling at NOSC. He is proposing an ambitious multi-year effort to develop a high-fidelity sonar simulation capability analogous to the computational fluid dynamics method used in aeros pace design. This project will provide a major increase in our capability to understand and design new and complex surveillance systems such as High Gain and LFA.[38]*

PROMOTION NOMINATION (2)

Scientist, DP-1310-III, $53,476, Time in Demo Level: 106 months.

1. *This proposal is for: Scientist, DP-1310-IV*
2. *State briefly below justification for this proposed promotion and incumbent's accomplishments (past, present, & future).*

PAST*: Mr. BBB received his BS in physics and a BS in geophysics from the University of Hawaii in 1971. He was promoted to a DP-III in November 1977.*

He has managed and provided technical direction for the Bionic Sonar and the Multiple-Aspect Classifier programs. He successfully demonstrated single target classification using a Bionic Sonar expert system. Mr. BBB identified critical marine mammal and human listening experiments to support the expert system base. He has proven to be a very competent and effective manager. Mr. BBB's research has been published in scientific journals and he has presented papers at technical conferences/symposium.

PRESENT: *Mr. BBB is an internationally recognized expert in the field of high-resolution sonar, acoustic, and sonar signal processing. (1) He is the program manager for the Biological Enhanced Acoustic Signal Technology (BEAST) program, which is an IED effort involving the development of a bionic sonar; (2) He manages the Movable Broadband Sonar program, which is currently funded by the Navy's Physical Security Research and Development Program; and*

(3) He is the manager of the sonar portion of a major effort resident in Code 53. Additionally, Mr. 888 is a sonar consultant for the Waterside Security System program and as such is often called upon to review technical performance, evaluate trade-offs, and recommend approaches. Mr. BBB also recently received funding from DARPA to provide technical guidance on a sonar program for the minehunting community that utilizes neutral networks.

FUTURE POTENTIAL: *After interviewing scientists from NCSC, NSWC, ARL: UT, APL, UT and NOSC, the Defense Nuclear Agency selected Mr. BBB to take over the technical direction and management of the*

Navy's 6.2 Swimmer Identification program in FY 90. In this role, he will guide the technical efforts of several research centers/universities. While Mr. BBB is capable of running a branch and often serves as acting division head, the best use of his talents is to have him continue to conduct and direct research in his specific field of expertise.[39]

PROMOTION NOMINATION (3)

Scientist, DP-1310-III, $53,458, Time in Demo Level: 255 months

1. *This proposal is for: Scientist, DP-1310-IV*
2. *State briefly below justification for this proposed promotion and incumbent's accomplishments (past, present &future potential).*

***PAST**: Dr. CCC has been a pioneer and innovator in the technology of spectroscopic instrumentation, optoelectronic devices development, and characterization. Since coming to NOSC in 1971, he has established facilities for ultrahighresolution spectroscopy, radiometric characterization of photo emitters and photo-detectors for fiber-optic and other optical communication systems, high-sensitivity Raman scattering and infrared photoluminescence. Innovations applied to these facilities have included state-of-the art digital control and signal processing schemes, which have been adopted widely in the technical community. These facilities are currently in heavy use, supporting SLC programs and several materials and device development programs at NOSC. During the past 2 years, Dr. CCC was involved in the SLC program that has identified critical areas of technology improvement for large-area deep* *red photo multipliers for the SLC receiver. These developments have resulted in greater than five times improvements in quantum efficiency in the detectors currently in the Project Y receiver and are expected to result in more than thirty times improvement in the next generation of detectors.*

PRESENT: Dr. CCC's role in the SLC program has recently been expanded to define the technical goals of the Raman Converter Technology Development program and coordinate the efforts of contractors and laboratories for the technology and industrial production capability for long-life, high-performance lead-vapor Raman wavelength converters for the SLC transmitter. These efforts have already resulted in the delivery on a very short schedule of improved vapor Raman cells for the project Y transmitter currently under final testing.

FUTURE POTENTIAL: Dr. CCC possesses an unusual grasp, both of the theoretical aspects of electro-optical devices and their practical application in Naval systems. He has demonstrated skill and effectiveness in managing the effort of contractors and in-house teams on a variety of applied research and development projects. During the current transitional period in Code 56, broad experience will be invaluable in definition of goals and management of new program, which will apply the capabilities of the Division to the development of Naval systems.[40]

Studying the above three promotion nominations, it is completely unclear which of the promotion criteria contained in the scientist DP-IV classifications standard[30] were actually met by these three scientists. In the promotion nominations, no mention is made that their "research results had a Navy-wide impact."[33] Further, insufficient specifics on their funding are provided. Besides justification for the promotion and some background, these briefs also explain why the candidates are of "future potential." If the management clique feels comfortable with the proposed candidate, he will always be of "value to the Navy" and will possess ample "future potential." Mr. Hillyer had given Code 96 the task of monitoring the Center's performance at formal reporting. Therefore, I paid Code 96 a visit. For each nominee, but also for me, I obtained copies of publication records for conference proceedings and openliterature publications for the period from 1986 to 1991.

Nominee Mr. AAA had a master's degree and was working on his doctor's degree. He had four open-literature publications and seven conference proceedings. This is a mediocre number of scientific contributions, and he is weak on qualifications.

Nominee Mr. BBB had two bachelor's degrees. He had one open-literature publication and one conference proceeding. He is insufficient in open-literature publications and conference proceedings, although in his promotion qualifications it is claimed that "Mr. BBB's research has been published in scientific journals and has presented papers at technical confe rences/symposium." Further, he has very weak qualifications. Apparently, his management was grooming him for a supervisory position but did not want him to undergo the required competitive merit-based promotion process.

Dr. CCC had a doctoral degree. He showed only one entry in conference proceedings. As a scientist working in the laboratory for many years, he is a nonperformer; his performance in formal reporting shows a failure. Over the same time span, I had ten open literature publications and six entries in conference proceedings. Altogether, I had twice as many entries in open-literature publications as all three successful candidates combined, who now were outranking me.

I knew Dr. CCC, so I inquired about his accomplishments and performance from is coworkers. His last publications in the open literature had been in the 1970s, about twenty years befor his promotion to DP-IV. In these old publications, his division head was the principle investigator. Dr. CCC had not been able to obtain his own funding for many years, so he had worked on and off in his division's test facility for radiometric characterization of photo emitters and photo detectors for many years. Finally, he had obtained an assignment as a contract monitor for the SLC. He only monitored one contract given to the Los Alamos Scientific Laboratory but was not involved in any actual scientific research. The year after Dr. CCC's promotion to DP-IV, funding for the SLC project was discontinued. Without doing much work, he retired several years later.

***

Mr. Hillyer, in a memo of July 10, 1990, again complained about the decline in formal reporting at the Center. He states:

1. *The Center is experiencing a significant decline in formal reporting, i.e., FY [fiscal year] technical reports and technical documents have declined by 13% when compared with FY89. I can see no reason for this decline in publications, as our in-house technical base work has continued to increase. This increase should be reflected by an increase in reporting and not by a decline.*

2. *I want to again emphasize that formal reporting of technical work is a fundamental precept in the scientific and engineering profession. As I have previously mentioned, it is one of the most important products of the Center. Publications, not only attest to the professionalism of your performance as a scientist or engineer, but they also provide an account of how public moneys have been spent. In addition, formal reporting if and advices a DOD and Navy requirement that is designed to avoid duplication of work and to advance national RDT&E efforts. In an era of*

declining DOD resources, publication of work is more vital than ever.

3. *As our performance in this area must be improved, I have requested the following:*
   a. *Increased emphasis be placed on formal reporting as part of the performance rating of scientists and engineers.*
   b. *Increased emphasis be placed on formal reporting as a part of the evaluation process when considering scientists and engineers for promotion.*
   c. *NOSC requirements of formal reporting be placed in the performance objectives for managers (technical department, division, branch heads).[41]*

When Mr. Hillyer sent this memo, I had worked for twenty-five years at the Center and published a total of forty-seven papers in the open literature—and had never been promoted. As reported, I had also filed unsuccessful position classification appeals.

1991 Classification-Reconsideration Appeal

On April 1, 1991, I asked the NOSC commander to form an adhoc committee of my peers to consider my promotion to DP-IV. Significantly, the demo provides for such a promotion route. However, the captain declined my request. He stated that Mrs. Smith's classification of my grade, as a scientist, level DP-III, was appropriate.

On April 23, 1991, I continued with my classification appeal, requesting classification reconsideration from the commander of the Naval Weapons Center (NWC) at China Lake, California.

On May 9, 1991, the NWC principle classifier, Mr. R. Bennion, visited me in my office to perform a so-called desk audit, to collect data on my qualifications, performance, and background that would affect my appeal. Two weeks later, he again visited me in my office to hand me his evaluation statement.[42] In his findings, he stated:

"The incumbent is considered an expert in the field of laser dye research. However, a requisite element which clearly separates level 4 [DP-IV] classification from level 3 [DP-III] is the requirement that the field of study be a major importance to the Navy." In this memo, he also stated that his decision constituted the final administrative review and agency decision. There are no further appeal routes available for employees to have their positions properly classified in order to receive fair compensation. Also he stated that I was the only demo employee who had ever filed a classification reconsideration appeal to the NWC at China Lake. He used the Scientist Level DP-IV Scientist Standard NOSCINST 14000.2B of January 27, 1987, which is an updated standard.[30] This updated version contains three additional supervisory/managerial criteria, namely:

1. *Scientists who manage and direct major projects and programs are included in this description.*
2. *At this level, the incumbent is responsible for major system development or the direction of technology base research, which has the highest significance to the Navy needs.*
3. *Management responsibilities include the area of finance, facilities, technical direction of personnel, and logistics.*[43]

The "upgraded" Scientist DP-IV classification standard now contains twenty-eight classification criteria. The classifier from the NWC used twenty-seven of them to classify my position. N avy laboratories perform both R&D. Most development projects are large and some of them are of major importance to the navy. However, I performed research, and therefore my position must be classified as a research position and not as a managerial position. According to CPI 335 OPNAVINSTR 12000.14 CH-7:

A-1 Accretion of Duties

Activities, which provide for an exception for this type of promotion must also provide for controls. Noncompetitive promotions will only be appropriate when the position is classified at a higher grade due to the accretion of duties which are directly related to the employee's major or (and grade controlling duties).

1. *In order for an employee to be eligible for a noncompetitive promotion all the following conditions must be met:*
2. *The new position must be determined to be a clear successor to the former position (that is, major duties of the replaced PD are absorbed into the new PD and the replaced PD is abolished.*
3. *The new position does not involve the addition of project leader, team leader. Or any other supervisory position to a non-supervisory position (this is when the new supervisory duties are a part of the basis for the upgrading),[44]*

Apparently, the Center's personnel office had added these managerial criteria to the scientist classification standard intended to promote scientists noncompetitively, also referred to as accretion of duties. Now, the Center's management can promote employees to supervisory and managerial positions automatically, without going through the required competitive, merit-based selection process.

However, the Center did not have the required approval from the OPM to use this newly fabricated classification standard for classifying non-supervisory scientist positions under the demo. Significantly, only one of the above managerial promotion criterion is contained in the level DP-IV Manager/Supervisor demo classification standard listed below.

NOSCINST 14000.2 25 September 1980
Level IV Manager/Supervisor (Professional)

Managers at Level IV are normally responsible for the administrative and technical supervision of a medium to large workforce (usually from 15 to 200 professional employees). Typically, the workforce consists of Level II and III employees and subordinate Level III supervisors. In some instances, Level IV employees, and supervisors are also supervised. Work is primarily in engineering, scientific, and technical fields. Organizational elements supervised are typical divisions, departments, or a major staff office. Also included are managers of major staff organizations.

In addition to the second and third level supervisor/ manager described above, supervisors at Level IV may be first line supervisors when supervisor meets the definition of Level IV engineer, scientist, or specialist, or when level of projects, expertise, and recognition by Center top management (Commander/Technical Director) warrant Level IV.

As a second level, or higher supervisor, the work is primarily coordinative and guiding through other supervisors. The supervisor maintains control through periodic reviews, briefings, reports, or observations to identify where corrective action is needed to meet task requirements. The supervisor oversees projects and programs providing assistance, advice, and guidance where problems exist or are developing. Makes decisions on work problems and administrative proposals or requirements. Works closely with other supervisors and managers outside the unit to further Center or Navy programs. Supervisor is usually the prime contact with sponsors of various programs under his/her management responsibility. Provides information and advice to higherlevel managers when the work of the unit impacts on other groups. At this level, supervisors evaluate subordinate supervisors and staff personnel. Resolves employee complaints and hears serious problems including those where disciplinary action is proposed. In addition, Level IV supervisor may also be program managers, responsible for major system development or the direction of technology base research, which has the highest significance to the Navy's needs. Managers direct the planning of resources to accomplish major blocks of engineering endeavor which commitments of Navy dollar allocations. Managers typically remain in their assignments for extended periods of their careers, and become widely recognized as the leaders, directors, and executives of a particular area of technology or family of systems.

Each incumbent serves an essential role in providing equal employment opportunities and is responsible for effecting and implementing the Center EEO policy within the area of recognizance and responsibility.[45]

The above classification standard for Level IV Manager/Supervisor is a remarkable document. There are no specific qualifications and/or experiences required for management who supervise employees performing high-tech or cutting-edge research.

Most of the above standard describes administrative functions to be performed by management. The only exception appears at the end of the above standard: "In addition, Level IV supervisors may also be program managers, responsible for major system developments or the direction of technology base research which has the highest significance to the Navy needs." This appears to me to say that it is not really necessary to perform this managerial function.

Further, the "upgraded" nonsupervisory scientist DP-IV classification standard[43]contains more managerial performance criteria than are contained in the above Level IV Manager/Supervisor classification standard.[45]However, in Mr. Bennion's memo,[42] declining my promotion request, he stated that I did not fulfill the key criteria that separate a level DP-IV from a level DP-III nonsupervisory scientist: "At this level, the incumbent is responsible for major system development or the direction of technology base research, which has the highest significance to the Navy needs." Also, this DP-IV Manager/Supervisor standard explains why the Center's administrators rushed into a demo. It states: "Managers typically remain in their assignments for extended periods of time of their career...."[45]This means that the Center's managers wanted to hang on to their administrative positions for many years. However, high-quality employees working on high-tech or cutting-edge research might revolt, protesting their incompetent management. To suppress an uprising by these employees, the Center's management needed to have total control over personnel functions to determine who is and who is not promoted and who is or who is not a performing employee, in order to protect their administrative managerial positions.

**

Dissatisfied with the result of my complaints, I requested a hearing before the Equal Employment Opportunity Commission.

Administrative judge Martin Burke was assigned to the case. I submitted a brief to the administrative judge, stating that my management improperly claimed that it had the right to suspend merit principles by ranking employees for noncompetitive promotions and also by using newly fabricated classification criteria like "importance to the Navy" or to the employee's department.

The hearings lasted seven days, stretching from November 20 to December 2, 1992. I chose not to use any attorney but represented myself. Again, my managers and their witnesses claimed that their choices were based on the importance of the work performed by the successful candidates to the navy and the candidates' departments; they doubted my project's "worth" to the navy. However, according to the demo:

> *Properly developed individual standards and unit objectives that focus on mission requirements, individual and organizational productivity, and management goals will ensure that employee rewards are tied directly to greater efficiency and improved agency operations rather than to longevity or other artificial measures of worth.*[28]

During the hearings, among other witnesses, I called Mr. W. Riley, the head of the Center's personnel office. I had some questions I wanted to ask him.

Questioning of Mr. W. Riley by T. G. Pavlopoulos

Q: Just a guess. How many people [file] classification appeals here every year?

A: Very limited number. I would say less than one percent

Q: One percent?

A: Probably less than that Sure.

Q: So you mean from [all] the professions, you have about ten classification appeals every year?

A: Not even that

Q: Not even that?

A: No. We've had only one or two in the last ten years.

Q: Okay. What about downgrading? How many people get downgraded every year?

A: None that I can think of at this moment.

Q: Nobody's been downgraded at the lab. Do you have any idea how many people are getting unsatisfactory ratings?

A: Very limited number. Again, and this won't give you an exact, it's less than probably a half percent. One person, probably.

Q: One thing I don't understand, and you probably can explain it to me, what is a maintenance review?

A: A maintenance review is a process that is no longer required at the Navy Department, and I say that for us at the Naval Ocean System Center because we are under a demonstration project, but I believe that's also true out in the GS system also. It was a process where you went through and looked at a series of documents like position descriptions. We concluded some other things here at one time and asked, "Is this up to date? Is it accurate?"

Q: When did you stop, about—

A: Well, it stopped here in 1980, in the demonstration project. I think it stopped in the Navy, and please don't hold me to the exact date, within a few years after that, because I don't think they're doing maintenance reviews generally in the Navy right now. Could be wrong. We have no requirement under the demonstration project to do that.

A: This is an industrially funded place that doesn't just operate from appropriated funds. We have to go out in the market and get business, and that's what some of the DP-IV and III guys do that make them so valuable to us. They go out and demonstrate that they have the right technologies and the right abilities to bring dollars and work, and people are attracted by that to this place.

Q: Is it not the function of management to bring in the funding?

A: That's a—I'd have you ask them that. I don't think it is. I think it's the function of everybody here. We're supposed to—recently we've heard a lot of talk about dividing our customers, and that goes right down to the project manager. I don't think their precise job is to go out and bring in funding. In my idea of this place, and you might want to ask some project engineers that, it's the engineers themselves or the project managers that go out and bring in the business.

Q: But you just said that management manages resources. There are no resources to manage if somebody else brings in the money.

A: Well, there's a lot of resources to manage in a place like this, because you have things like overhead and allocate buildings and facilities and workforce—

Q: So management does not perform its main function, which is to give assignments to employees?

A: I do not want to simplify it that much. I think that management does what they're supposed to do here. They manage the organization.

Q: Mr. Riley, what I'm saying is that Mr. Hightower, he could, with your statement that we have to rationalize here, promote many deserving people into the DP-IV if the system wasn't overloaded by over-graded employees.

A: I'm troubled by a couple of things there. I don't think—I hope I didn't use the word "quota," because we really don't have a quota.[46]

Mr. Riley's testimony above "because we really don't have a quota" seems to contradict Mr. Hillyer's statements during the U.S.Senate Hearing 32 and the EEO's Counselors report.[37]

I was very interested to learn how employees were promoted to DP-IV. I was puzzled as to why the investigator assigned to my 1989 EEOC complaint had been able to obtain the three promotion nominations, but the investigator assigned to my 1990 complaint had not. Someone in the personnel office had suggested that a Mr. Richard Cashore, personnel management advisor, should be able to answer my question. Accordingly, I put Mr. Cashore on the witness list.

Questioning of Mr. R. Cashore by the Center's Attorney

Q: Okay. And are you involved, are you not, in the DP-IV promotion process?

A: Yes, I am.

Q: I want to show you some documents. It's in the '89 EEOC file, and they are called promotion nominations. Do you recognize those documents; do you know what they are?

A: Yes. This—this looks like the format that we ask them to submit nominations in.

Q: Okay. Now, it's my understanding that for the FY [fiscal year] 90 promotion process in de partment— or Code 50. We were unable to find the unsigned completed briefs for the nominees; is this correct?

A: That's correct

Q: Can you explain why you have the '89 brief or promotion nominations but not the 1990 promotion nominations?

A: I'm not sure why you have the '89. I do not retain the nomination forms beyond the current year. [I consider those to be] informal management notes,[38,39,40]. They're not any formal system of records; there's—I'm not aware of any requirements that they be retained for any period of time whatsoever. And they're used for that period, and then they're not generally referred to again, so I don't retain them. I do—in '89, as I recall, there was an investigator, whose name I can't—Art—I don't recall now, from the Southwest region, who was looking into, I believe, a matter relating to Dr. Pavlopoulos, and he asked to see some of the records, and I showed them to him, and I think he made—he may have made some copies of them, but I really didn't pay that much attention.

Q: But you don't have the 1990 briefs?

A: I don't have the 1990 briefs; that's correct

Q: Then you wouldn't keep them for 1991?

A: I don't have the 1991 because that's the current year, but as we complete this year and move to the next year, I usually dispose of them.

Questioning of Mr. Cashore by T. G. Pavlopoulos

Q: If I understand you correctly, about after one year the reason for promotion cannot be reconstructed?

A: No, I didn't say that I just said that I don't retain those documents.

Q: How can someone like me, looking into it later on, maybe one and a half years later, or two years later, reconstruct why these people got promoted?

A: I don't know how you can do that

Q: You cannot do that?

A: I can't do that, no.

Q: Is there anybody else who could do that?

A: You can ask the people who made the decision whether to recommend people or not recommend people and ask them on what basis they decided to recommend or not recommend people. But those documents are not the basis for promotion or not promotion; that is just a part of the process and not even the most important part. The presumption is that people who are being nominated for promotion to DP-IV are doing work that is of such significance *to the Center that they are generally known by the top management people in the Center, and so their knowledge of the individual's contribution and their discussion—verbal discussion with the people who are proposing the individuals for promotion, [in] my opinion, are of far more worth than any written documentation that gets submitted on that sheet.*[46]

Finally, I had a complete picture and documentation on how employees at the Center were promoted to DP-IV. From the data provided by the above witnesses, the following procedure emerges. The Western Field Division of the Office of Civilian Personnel in 1978 had criticized the Center's"... lack of any significant documentation to support the basis for the classification action."[19]

According to Mr. Cashore's testimony, management only needs to convince the captain orally that their crony's work is very important to the navy. Or, the candidates are of high future value. Now, the Promotion Nominations are not inserted into the candidate's personnel files, but are discarded. Under the demo, the Center is promoting employees to DP-IV without any supporting documentation whatsoever. All this is a snow job, prompting the happy captain to rubber-stamp the DP-IV promotion. After the promotion, the promotion nomination, according to Mr. Cashore "... I usually dispose of them." After the incumbent has been promoted, the scientist DP-IV standard[43]is inserted into incumbent's personnel folder. This personnel folder contains no documentation whatsoever as to why they were promoted. There is no documentation that the three successful 1989 candidates for DP-IV promotions secured significant funding for any major navy projects or that they influenced the direction of any major work There is no evidence that their research results had a significant navy-wide impact, nor that these candidates provided an "expert" consultation to higher-level navy, DOD, or interagency committees. There is no evidence that they provided scientific leadership or made substantial contributions in the form of presentations or substantial numbers of open-literature publications. Significantly, according to Mr. Riley, during these years, nobody has ever been downgraded. Less than one percent received an unsatisfactory rating. The Center seems to have almost no poorly performing employees. Did the Center really need to start a demo to take care of this tiny number of poorly performing employees? And how wonderful that there are no maintenance reviews anymore. The OPM does not care that there is a high percentage of federal employees occupying over-graded positions and therefore are collecting wages they don't deserve, but at the same time totally ignoring the bloodletting of the poor taxpayer.

Because there are no performance-evaluation systems either, the performance of these over-graded employees is always well rated. Consequently, a person can be remiss year after year without ever getting an unsatisfactory performance rating, and can also collect unjustified overpayments from occupying an over-graded position.

Many hundreds of deserving employees at the Center, including blue-collar workers and secretaries, have no chance of ever being promoted due to the inflated overall high-average grades of other employees. This applies, not only at the Center, but also at many other federal departments and agencies.

All underpaid employees are simply forced to make do with less-or quit. This assures that overpaid employees occupying over-graded positions can stay on their jobs until they retire with full benefits and pensions. In his decision, Judge Burke sided with management and supported them in their decision not to promote me. He claimed the other three candidates' work was more important to the navy than mine. He cited Mr. Bennion's conclusion that their fields of study were of "major importance to the Navy."[42]

At the end of every fiscal year, continued funding for most federal DOD projects is uncertain. Congress appropriates new funding for the coming fiscal year. Whenever I appealed my position classification, the "uncertainty" of my on-and-off funding situation became a major issue. However, this did not have any importance in the promotion of the three nominees.

It appeared that neither judge Burke nor my management understood the meaning of merit principles. Instead, the judge put great emphasis on the fact that I was having funding problems, and that the Center was a NIF-funded laboratory. As I have mentioned, I was not the only scientist who had funding problems. Other scientists also battled the dilemma. Starting about 1993, almost all scientists performing research for the DOD have faced funding problems.

Funding problems are, not only the federal government's constant burden; they are also a burden for the private sector. In the private sector, a shortage of funding leads to the dismissal of employees. In the public sector, funding problems are supposed to lead to reductions in force (RIFs). RIFs happen often, resulting in newer employees losing their jobs. The Center is strictly opposed to RIFs, because it could result in the removal of some of the management's favorite employees. In my view, the Center's management was and still is trying to avoid a RIF by targeting certain "problem employees" (those who did not inspire "good gut feelings") whom the management felt should not work at the Center.

Obviously, judge Burke did not understand—or did not want to understand—the meaning of fair treatment of employees, although this is the central issue of his profession as an administrative judge handling EEOC cases. Fair treatment simply requires that management provide equal pay for substantial equal work.[9] This is the heart of the EEOC merit system. The Center's management is allowed to assign an arbitrary "Navy value" to employees' work, allowing them to create competition among employees for incumbent-developed promotions, though these should be noncompetitive. By introducing ranking, this allows management to promote anyone they want and prevents the promotion of anyone they don't want. Again, the decision about which work is or is not important to the navy is strictly a managerial decision and has nothing to do with promotions.

According to:

> (2) *The principle of equal pay for substantially equal work, and*
>
> (3) *The principle that variation in ranges of basic pay for different employees should be in proportion to substantial differences in the difficulty, responsibility, and qualifications requirements of the work performed.*[11]

Promotions are solely based on merit. Management every year makes the question about the "importance to the Navy" of an employee's assignment. Every year, work and performance objectives are assigned to each employee during the performance planning/appraisal session for the coming fiscal year. When a supervisor and the division head approve an employee's work objectives by signing off on the performance/appraisal form, they have made a legally binding statement that these assigned objectives are important to the navy. If management judges an employee's work objectives as not or only marginally important to the navy, the employee must not be allowed to continue with the work.

After management has signed off on an employee's work objectives, the question of whether or not these work objectives were more important to the navy than those of another employee is moot. Now, merit principles must be strictly enforced, requiring management to provide equal pay for substantially equal work. If management were to declare an employee's work of little or no significance to the navy, they would, in fact, be criticizing their own decision.

In an e-mail to all the Center's employees, a secretary complained:

Date: Wednesday August 8, 1994

Subject: Hotline-Secretaries

I would like to know why it is the Center's policy not to promote secretaries. As I understand it, if you are a Branch secretary, you are a DC-I; if you are a Division secretary, you are a DG-II; if you are a Department secretary, you are a DG-III, with no possibility of promotion, ever. Also, training, or any type of schooling, is not encouraged or supported at all. What kind of incentive, satisfaction, and job morale does that policy create? Especially when secretaries are taking on permanent additional job tasks, plant inventory, buyer, budget, to name only a few.

I am looking forward for your reply

Thank you,

Anonymous female[47]

Obtaining additional skills or qualifications, more responsibility, a higher academic degree, a more difficult work assignment, and so on, are not necessarily relevant for being promoted at the Center. Because of the long duration of the demo, younger employees mainly believe that promotions in the federal civil service come about by being very accommodating to their supervisors. They hope that at the next meeting of the promotion committee, their supervisors may put in a good word for them. After more than twenty-six years of the demo, most managers and employees have no idea that a classification standard, such as the Scientist DP-IV standard exist or that there is such a thing as position classification.[30]Contrary to the pre-demo performance appraisal form, the new form does not contain an entry for the supervisor to certify the currency of an employee's position description. When there is an "a llocation" of promotions, the branch head and the division head of the incumbent produce a promotion nomination.

The Center's management and the captain are completely unaware that they are required to enforce merit principles— namely, to provide equal pay for substantially equal work.[9]

However, at the Center, management acts if the merit principles read—namely, to "provide equal pay for work of substantially equal worth," meaning worth to management.

There is no accountability for management for not enforcing merit principles, despite the OPM's oversight mission to review agencies and departments' adherence to merit principles. This observation does, not only apply to the Center, but also afflicts the entire American bureaucracy. Judge Burke's ruling did not satisfy me. I decided to continue with my EEOC complaint, suing in federal court. The main issue of my appeal was that my performance and qualifications warranted my promotion to Scientist DP-IV.

Chapter 7
Appealing to the Federal District Court

The Center's Mission Statement

To better explain the issues involved in my federal district court classification appeal, I have provided some details on the mission, personnel, and funding of the Center in 1993, when I filed the appeal.

Mission Statement

The Naval Command, Control and Ocean Surveillance Center (NCCOSC), RDT&E [Research, Development, Test and Evaluation] Division (or NRaD) is a full-spectrum RDT&E laboratory serving the Navy, Marine Corps, and other Department of Defense and national sponsors within its mission, leadership assignments, and prescribed functions. NCCOSC is one of the Navy's four major warfare centers and reports directly to the Commander, Space and Naval Warfare Systems Command (SPAWAR) in Washington, DC. At NRaD we provide solutions to Navy, joint service, and national problems by generating and applying science and technology. We provide innovative alternatives to tomorrow's decision makers, enabling them to pursue new or expanded missions and capabilities.

Personnel Data

Total on board 3388; Total military 283; Total civilians 3105, (Full time civilian personnel) FTP 3086. Administrative 328; Technicians 299; Scientists and Engineers 1716; Technical specialists 328; Clerical 415. FTP-Graded Scientists and Engineers Electrical engineers 868; Physicists 171; Mechanical engineers 134; Mathematicians 101; General engineers 71; Oceanographers 16; Operations research analysts 65; Computer Scientists 168; Psychologists 33; Chemists 12; Other 77; Total 1716. Scientists and Engineers by Demo Level-I 14; DP-II 139; DP-III 1215; DP-IV 336; DP-V 3; Senior executive service 7.

Degrees—All FTP personnel: PhD 207; MS/MA 725; BS/BA 1366.

Funding by Category and Type (Percent of Total Funding)

6.1	*Research 2 percent;*
6.2	*Exploratory development 13 percent;*
6.3a	*Advanced technology development 10 percent;*
6.3b	*Advanced development 19 percent;*
6.4	*Engineering development 10 percent[48].*

Financial Handbook
R&D Categories

For planning, funding, and review processes, the Defense RDT&E Program is structured in the following categories:

6.1. *Research (Develop knowledge base)—All scientific study and experimentation efforts directed toward increasing knowledge and understanding in the physical, engineering, environmental, and life-sciences fields related to long-term national security needs.*

6.2. *Exploratory Development (Develop technology/ examine concept feasibility)—All effort directed towards the solution of specific military problems, short of major development projects. These efforts may vary from fairly fundamental applied research to quite sophisticated breadboard hardware, study programs, and planning efforts.*

6.3. *Advanced Development (Examine concept feasibility/ demonstrate system and subsystem feasibility)—All efforts directed towards projects that have moved into the development of hardware for testing. The prime result of these efforts is proof of design concepts rather than development for service use.*

6.4. *Engineering Development (Develop advanced systems) Programs in full-scale development for service use that have not received approval for production or had funds included in the DOD budget of subsequent fiscal years.*[49]

6.4 *Engineering development 10 percent*[48].

In 1993, research at the Center consisted only of 2 percent of the work performed, compared with 52 percent for development. When I started to work for the Center in 1965, about 5 percent of the work was devoted to research. Presently, this number is less than 1 percent.

I emphasize that research is in the mission statement of the Center. To rephrase the above mission statement: research provides innovative alternatives to future decision makers, enabling them to pursue new or expanded missions and capabilities. Generally, basic research projects are small in size.

Appealing to the Federal District Court in San Diego

The year 1994 was a bad one for me. In 1965, my mother had followed Helen and me to San Diego. She found a nice apartment one block from the beach, only a short walk to the Ocean Beach pier. Her apartment was also a short drive from our house, allowing me to visit her often. She died in 1994 from complications of Alzheimer's disease.

In 1994, Professor Boyer lost his funding for his laser-dye synthesis program. Also at that time, the Office of Naval Research had suffered large cuts in its basic research funding. Dr. Schmidt of the ONR, who was my sponsor at that time, stated that my laser-dye improvement program had reached a critical stage. Now that we knew how to make better laser dyes, the program had left the basic research phase and had entered the applied research stage. However, applied research was not the ONR's responsibility anymore. He decided that it was time for me to look for support from some other funding sources. During the first months of 1994, I received $44,000 from Dr. Schmidt to complete my ongoing research program.

At the same time, I had no idea that the developing shortage of research funding would affect, not only me, but also many other scientists working for the federal government.

On the following pages, I describe my appeal to the Federal District Court in San Diego. I stated at the beginning of this book that the OPM was management-biased and anti-employee. When ever management is accused of violating merit principles, the OPM seems to feel compelled to cover up for management. This is contrary to the OPM's mission, namely to administer, enforce, and execute civil service regulations, laws, rules, and merit principles. I am sure some readers will find this statement unbelievable. Therefore, I present my appeal to the OPM in some detail as an example of the OPM's pro-management bias. I hired an attorney, Mr. Robert Rothman, to represent me. As is customary, Mr. Rothman introduced a brief to the U.S. district court, stating that in my case, a violation of Title 5, U.S. Code 2301 had occurred—namely, a merit-principle violation.[50]

The district court ruled that a violation of Title 5, U.S. Code had occurred, and Mr. Rothman proposed a compromise settlement. The terms of the settlement required that "The Defendant will arrange for an appropriately experienced position classification specialist ('classifier') from the U.S. OPM to conduct a prompt review of the actual duties performed by the Plaintiff. The review will be for the sole purpose of making the determination whether the Plaintiff is currently performing at the DP-IV level at NRaD."[51]

In addition, I was able to insert the provision that the classifier should, not only classify my position according to the demo's Level DP-IV Scientist standard, but also determine my GS grade against the pre-demo classification standard, namely, the Research GradeEvaluation Guide (RGEG).[13]Mr. T. K. Dowd, the Center's attorney, stated the Center's position below to Mr. Richard Johnson, the newly appointed classifier from OPM, in his letter of January 6, 1994. Excerpts from his statements are listed below.

Mr. Richard Johnson
Office of Personnel Management
Jackson Federal Building
915 Second Ave., Seattle, WA 98174

Re: Classification Review of DP (Demonstration Project) Level of Dr. Theodore Pavlopoulos

Dear Mr. Johnson,

This is the Naval Command, Control and Ocean Surveillance Center RDT&E Division's (NCCOSC RDT&E Division) submission of written material to aid you in your review of the job classification of Dr.Theodore Pavlopoulos. This submission is made pursuant to a settlement agreement which was entered into by the United States and Dr. Pavlopoulos in order to terminate litigation he had instituted. The settlement agreement is Enclosure (1) to this letter.

NCCOSC RDT&E Division has taken a consistent position for many years that Dr. Pavlopoulos is properly classified at the Scientist, DP-III level. Conversely, Dr. Pavlopoulos has claimed that he should be classified as a Scientist at the DP-IV level. NCCOSC RDT&E Division, like its counterpart laboratory, Naval Weapons Center, China Lake, is under the Demonstration Project (DP). The DP is a congressionally authorized alternative personnel system, established under the aus pices of Title VI of the Civil Service Reform Act of 1978, which differs in a number of ways from mainstream civil service. For purposes of your review, several of these differences are important. First, the Demonstration Project has wider pay bands than does the civil service grade level system. A DP-III in the Project is a pay band, which includes GS-12 and GS-13; a DP-IV is a pay band, which includes GS-14 and GS-15.

Another general consideration for your review is the fact that NCCOSC RDT&E Division is an "industrially funded" activity with a focus on applied as opposed to basic research. NCCOSC RDT&E Division does not receive an appropriation or allotment to conduct its business, pay salaries of direct and overhead personnel, etc. Rather, NCCOSC, RDT&E Division and its employees, particularly technical employees, must seek out and secure funding from sponsors within the Federal government. It is sponsor funding which "pays" for NCCOSC RDT&E Division and allows NCCOSC RDT&E Division to pay its employees. NCCOSC RDT&E Division has direct labor rates, indirect rates and such, as would a corporation. A loss incurred by NCCOSC RDT&E Division in one fiscal year carries over and causes an increase in the labor rates for the next year. An increased labor rate then makes it more difficult to secure funding the following year. As a consequence of this funding structure and process, an ability to secure major programs and/or major funding is a consideration in DPLevel classification, particularly at the DP-IV level.

Historically, Dr. Pavlopoulos' position has not influenced major projects, proposals, or direction of major work. Dr. Pavlopoulos has not been involved with high-level Navy or DoD Committees. He is a subject matter expert in a narrow area of scientific research. While his work is advanced, it is very narrow in scope. His work has not been well-funded due to its narrow scope and lack of impact and importance to the Navy and DoD. While the research in which Dr. Pavlopoulos is engaged was of interest to the Navy, it has never been a major program nor highly significant. Indeed, as your on-site review will validate, Dr. Pavlopoulos' work is completely un-funded by sponsors this fiscal year. As a result, his position is funded solely from NRaD overhead funds. At this time, it is questionable whether his work is of any interest to the Navy or DoD.

Enclosures (4) and (5) further support our position in this matter. Enclosure (4) is a Classification Review conducted by a Principal Classifier from China Lake which was performed in 1991. The Classifier, for reasons stated therein, concluded that Dr. Pavlopoulos was properly classified at the DP-III level. Enclosure (5) is another classification review of Dr. Pavlopoulos' position, which was performed by an NCCOSC RDT&E Division personnel list in 1987. She also concluded that he was properly classified at the DP-III level. Enclosures (6) and (7) are provided as background concerning the DP and the classification/promotion process used at NRaD. I hope that this letter with enclosures will aid in your review.

If you require information during your on-site review concerning personnel-related issues, contact Ms. Margaret Malowney. As to factual and fiscal matters, Dr. Pavlopoulos' supervisors, including Mr. Peter Seligman, should be contacted.

We look forward to your on-site review. We will be happy to provide access to such individuals and documents as you may require. The continuing point of contact is Ms. Malowney of the NRaD Personnel

Department. I will be happy to discuss any and all issues with you at any time. Thank you so much for your efforts in this matter.

Timothy K. Dowd[52]

My attorney Mr. Rothman replied to Mr. T. Dowd's above letter of January 25, 1994 to Mr. R. Johnson of the OPM. It is presented below.

To: Mr. Richard Johnson

Lack of funding at NRaD, the importance of incumbent's project to the Navy, the size of incumbent's research grants are all irrelevant to position classification. The purpose of position classification is to provide equal pay for substantially equal work: The issue is fair and consistent classification of positions. It is incumbent's contention that other physicists working at NRaD, the Naval Weapons Center at China Lake, other Naval laboratories and other government facilities, who perform work of similar difficulty and possessing similar qualifications as incumbent, are receiving GS-14/15 pay. It is simply unfair and not in either the spirit or letter of civil service merit principles to filter qualified employees through a system of subjective criteria in order to deny them promotions for which they are qualified. Incumbent has been employed by employer for twenty-eight years. During this time, his work has been funded, to a large extent, through Navy grants. It is inconsistent to now claim that incumbent's work "lacks importance to the Navy." Even if such a claim were true it would not form the basis for denying incumbent a promotion for which he is qualified because of his duties and accomplishments.

Funding at NRaD.

There is a considerable block of funding, amounting to about $3,700,000 per year, provided to NRaD by the socalled Independent Research Program (IRP). The IRP is designed to support innovative basic research and allocates about $90,000 to each project per year. The purpose of the IRP is to free scientists performing research from having to devote time and effort to fund-raising, traditionally a management or supervisory duty. A copy of the 1993 IRP Policy Guidelines are submitted herewith.

Classification Criteria

Over the last 15 years, the world has seen tremendous growth in new technologies. Personnel management problems in the Navy and at NRaD have made it extremely difficult for the technical work force to keep up with rapid scientific developments. Because of "over grading" NRaD has consistently hired at lower grades, generally one grade level below other Naval laboratories. Promotions have also come much slower in order to fight so-called "grade-creep." Over the years the result has been an exodus of many bright, technically talented NRaD scientists. One consequence has been the inability of NRaD managers and supervisors to generate new programs. This has resulted in considerable loss in funding at NRaD for many of the DT&E projects. This consequence was predicted in 1978 by the WFDOCP survey submitted herewith which noted that"... Failure of the Center to correct existing PM and classification problems will ultimately impact significantly on costs and mission accomplishment." In order to combat losses in funding former NOSC personnel director Riley added three managerial/ supervisory criteria to the non-supervisory DPIV level scientists descriptors. The added criteria created a descriptor currently in use that has not been approved by OPM. Use of non-approved criteria violates the requirement of section 1 and 3 of the "Accretion of Duties" promotion criteria of CPI 335 (Appendix A-Exceptions (OPNAVINST 12000.14, CH-7)), which is submitted herewith. The idea was to move physics performing research in smaller projects into managing development of programs by providing them with incentives, i.e. promotion to non-competitive level DP-IV scientist positions. Thus there now exists at NRaD a dual management structure: the manager/supervisor who provides administrative but little or no technical leadership; and the scientific program directors that are responsible for conducting technology base research. Obtaining funding may well be a legitimate job duty for the former; it is not for those such as the incumbent in the latter positions who are conducting basic research.

Incumbent's employer, does not, indeed cannot, deny that incumbent has the experience, qualifications, and is performing the duties of a DP-IV scientist. Their rationale for denying the requested promotion is that the incumbent's work is not important to the Navy. Incumbent believes that use of this criteria is invalid and violates the fundamental principles of civil service merit based evaluation.

Respectfully submitted,
Robert B. Rothman[53]

I also prepared a position description in the format required by the RGEG.[13] I listed my major duties and contributions, controls over the position, qualification requirements, and scientific contributions. This position description was also submitted to Mr. Johnson.

Position Description of Theodore Pavlopoulos

1. Introduction

Incumbent's Scientist (Physicist/1310) position is organizationally located in the Chemistry/Biochemistry Branch Code 521. Code 521 is part of the Environmental Science Division Code 52, which in turn is part of the Marine Sciences and Technology Department Code 50. Code 521 is responsible for conducting basic and applied research in chemistry, biochemistry, chemical-sensor development, and environmental technology in support of Navy environmental requirements. The primary purpose of this position is to perform basic and applied research in projects relating to electro-optics (EO), which is part of physics.

2. Major Duties and Responsibilities

Incumbent is responsible for independently organizmg, planning, coordinating, conducting, and implementing broad research programs in the field of EO, which includes integrated optics, fiber optics, the physics of lasers, laser phenomena, and laser materials (the active laser media), and to consider the application of obtained results to the Naval environment, warfare, and communications. Presently, the incumbent carries out complex experimental and theoretical studies of dye lasers and laser dyes (a laser material). Lasers are subdivided into three major groups: Gas-, liquid- (dye), and solid-state lasers. Laser dyes dissolved in a solvent (liquid) are employed as the active media in dye lasers. Dye lasers are widely used in research as sources of tunable laser radiation. Commercially available laser dyes have limitations in lasing efficiency and photo-stability. The main objective of the incumbent's program is to improve the performance of laser dyes. Having improved laser dyes available, dye lasers can be up-scaled in output energy and efficiency. Up-scaled dye lasers have wide and important applications in the military (laser weapons, target illuminators), medicine (cancer treatment), optical communications (Naval blue-green laser sources), research (in many fields of optics, spectroscopy), and the environment (monitoring pollutants). Incumbent carries out complex spectroscopic studies (including socalled triplet-state absorption) on organic compounds (including dyes) to obtain information on the very complicated relationship between laser-dye performance and organicdye molecular structure. Among other parameters, small triplet-state absorption of dyes determines efficient laser action. At the beginning of this study, there was not available a sensitive method to measure weak triplet-state absorption. Over the span of several years, the incumbent has developed such sensitive spectroscopic equipment. The development of this equipment required a high degree of originality and creativity. This equipment allows one to identify specific organic molecules, which can be transformed by substitution (chemical synthesis) into dyes, where small triplet-state absorption is present. To obtain new and improved laser dyes, incumbent cooperates with Professor Boyer, a chemistry professor at the University of New Orleans. Incumbent asks Professor Boyer to transform the specific organic compounds he has identified into laser dyes. Professor Boyer suggests chemical synthesis routes for transforming these compounds into new laser dyes to his group of chemistry postdoctoral fellows and graduate students. After the new dyes have been synthesized, they are mailed to the incumbent for evaluation. They are tested for laser action efficiency and photo-stability. Also, their spectroscopic properties (including triplet-state absorption) are recorded. From all this data, incumbent draws conclusions on how to improve the laser dyes further.

It has been exceptionally difficult to improve the performance of laser dyes. About 5 years ago, the just-described effort led to the development of a new class of efficient laser dyes, namely, the so-called pyrromethene-BF2. Some of these dyes outperform rhodamine 6G, which was the most efficient laser dye known. This dye was discovered in 1967, and it took over 20 years to advance the state of the art of laser-dye technology to surpass rhodamine 6G in performance. Recently, some of the pyrromethene dyes have become commercially available. The incumbent is frequently called to give presentations before universities and national/ international professional conferences. These meetings are attended by high-level physicists, chemists, engineers, and managers interested in the research and development of laser devices, applications, and materials. The incumbent also has been asked to participate, to organize, and to chair conferences. The incumbent writes papers for publication in the open (refereed) scientific literature. Further, he is called upon to give technical presentations as an official NRaD representative before a variety of groups, such as the Office of Naval Research (ONR), SPAWAR, and other DoD agencies. Consults with members of other NRaD divisions, DoD agencies, and university professors regarding matters and investigations relating to lasers and laser applications. Incumbent also writes formal technical proposals for the funding of his program.

3. Controls over the Position

Immediate supervisor is the Code 521 Branch Head, a supervisory DP-III (equiv. GS-12/13) Scientist (Biologist). The incumbent has freedom to select his own field of research. Work is performed independently, and the incumbent plans and conducts investigations utilizing only his own ideas, originality, and creativity in approach. Incumbent has complete freedom for determining the proper course of action, in selecting the most appropriate approach to solve problems in the fields of his research. Further, incumbent has full responsibility for organizing, evaluating, and documenting his research results. The supervisor is kept informed of unusual results, which might call for major changes or modification of the program. Through informal discussions with his supervisor, incumbent obtains information on general administrative matters. Because the state of the art in laser research and development is advancing at a very rapid pace, all guidelines must be developed by the incumbent. Since incumbent started to work for the Navy in 1965, he has published about 45 papers in the open literature. None of his past or present supervisors have ever appeared as coauthors or contributors to his research efforts leading to these publications. This supports the claim that he is working as an independent senior principal investigator.

4. Qualification Requirements and Scientific Contributions

Incumbent holds a diploma in physics (equiv. MA, 1951) and a doctor's degree (ScD, 1953) in physical chemistry from the University of Göttingen (Germany). He spent four years with industry (Convair in San Diego) and eight years as a postdoctoral fellow at Toronto University, University of British Columbia, Tulane University, and UCLA. This position requires [the incumbent] to provide directions for the overall program, and incumbent must be able to make significant contributions to his professional field of research. He must have exceptional ability to conceive original ideas, methods, and techniques for planning, conducting, and evaluating the results of his studies. Work requires knowledge and experience in combinations of rare and unusual interdisciplinary fields. An extensive background in optical physics (including spectroscopy), EO (including lasers and laser materials) is required. This has to be combined with an extensive knowledge of organic chemistry as well as extensive experience and knowledge of the complicated field of spectroscopy of organic compounds.

Incumbent has authored and coauthored over 50 papers, which were published in the open scientific literature. A substantial number of these papers had a significant impact on the various fields of his studies. Several of these papers are now considered milestone (classical) contributions, which have led to major advances in the disciplines of his studies. In 1975, in recognition of his scientific accomplishments, incumbent was elected a member of the New York Academy of Sciences. Internationally, incumbent is a recognized authority on laser dyes. Over the last 20 years, he has been a major contributor, and over the last few years, the major contributor to the advancement of the state of the art in the field of laser dyes. Further, the incumbent is an internationally recognized authority on triplet-state spectroscopy of organic compounds. Many of his research ideas contained in his publications have formed the basis for research and development ideas of other scientists. Also, his work has been favorably cited many times in the scientific literature as well as in books. Often, he is called to review papers of other scientists for publication in scientific journals. Also, he is called by agencies to review proposals of other scientists for agency funding. His professional standing is comparable to that of a highly regarded full professor at a major university.[54]

Mr. Johnson's evaluation of my position description is listed below.

Mr. Johnson's Classification Advisory

Incumbent Dr. Theodore G. Pavlopoulos, Position: Scientist, DP1310-III Environmental Chemistry/ Biochemistry Branch, San Diego, California

Decision: Scientist, DP-1310-III Date: March 25, 1994

Introduction

This advisory is provided at the request of the Department of the Navy, Naval Command, Control and Ocean Surveillance Center, San Diego, California. It stems from a "stipulation for compromise settlement" between the Navy and Dr. Theodore Pavlopoulos, which provides that an experienced position classification specialist from the U.S. Office of Personnel Management (OPM) will review the duties and responsibilities of the subject position to determine the appropriate Demonstration Project (DP) level.

The guidance to the classifier in the stipulation document is as follows: The review will be conducted in a manner deemed proper by the classifier, based upon criteria selected by the classifier. The classifier shall consider the written submissions of the parties, conduct his classification review, and issue a written final decision. Any additional specific process, whether substantive or procedural, whether requested by a party or otherwise, shall be implemented at the sole discretion of the classifier. Based on the latitude implied in the above paragraphs, and in an effort to provide the best and most comprehensive classification review, the position was evaluated against both the controlling Demonstration Project instructions and the most appropriateOPM classification guide.

Source of Information

This advisory decision is based on information from the following sources:

Materials supplied by Dr. Pavlopoulos' attorney, Robert B. Rothman, Esq., dated January 3, 1994. These materials include general background and job information, as well as listings of presentations and publications from 1954 to the present Also included is an extensive collection of letters and memos relating to interest in Dr. Pavlopoulos' work by others. Materials supplied by the Navy, dated January 6, 1994. These materials include general background and job information, as well as internal classification evaluations of the subject position conducted by the Navy in 1987 and 1991.

A rebuttal to the Navy submission from Mr. Rothman, dated January 25, 1994.

The level/specialty designator (#845273) for the subject position dated October 1984. These designators take the place of traditional position descriptions under the Demonstration Project

On-site interviews with Dr. Pavlopoulos; his first, second, third, and fourth level supervisors; and with the classification staff at NRaD. These interviews were conducted during the week of March 11-15, 1994.

Classification Guidelines Used

OPM's Research Grade-Evaluation Guide (June 1964).

The Demonstration Project (DP) classification system features pay bands, which incorporate two or more General Schedule grades. Each pay band is described by a benchmark called a "level/specialty descriptor." The subject position has been assigned since inception of the DP to level/specialty descriptor, Level III for scientists, which includes grades GS-12 and GS-13 under the traditional system. Dr. Pavlopoulos feels the position should be at level IV, which includes grades GS-14 and GS-15. An advantage of the DP classification system is that it is easy to use by line management, who have, at the higher levels, been delegated classification authority. The role of the civilian personnel office staff is strictly advisory. However, there is a significant trade-off for this ease of use. Because Level III includes the full range of duties and responsibilities corresponding to grades GS-12 and GS-13, and because the description of this full range of duties (the entire width of the band) is described in four general paragraphs on one page, it is usually impossible to tell if a given duty or responsibility statement is intended to describe work toward the bottom or the top of the band. For example, is the statement "Technical contributions are recognized by management and peers as having significant impact on new ideas as well as ongoing projects," meant to be descriptive of all positions in the band? If so, it would fall near the low end, or at the bottom threshold of the band. Or, is the statement meant to describe some positions near the top of the band, but not include all positions in the band? There is no guidance in the implementing instructions or elsewhere about how to make this kind of determination. Therefore, we must assume that each such statement is intended to describe the mid range of the band, or that the totality of the various statements (which would chart like a scatter-gram throughout the band) would, on overage, describe the mid-range of the band. These are different concepts; however, in both cases, the practical result is that the descriptor for Level III best describes the dividing line between GS-12 and GS-13 in the traditional system. The analogous situation holds for Level IV. Level IV best describes the dividing line between GS-14 and GS-15 in the traditional system. Unfortunately, the issue at hand is whether or not the subject position should be at Level III or Level IV. The boundary between these two levels is the dividing line between GS-13 and GS-14.

Thus, although the DP descriptors were used as the primary classification reference, OPM's Research Grade-Evaluation Guide (RGEG) was also used in an attempt to better distinguish between GS-13 and GS-14 work in the subject position. Theoretically, a position correctly classified using the RGEG would also be classified into the appropriate band using the DP system. The General Schedule classification system and the demonstration project system were intended to be compatible. The RGEG, because it distinguishes between GS-13 and GS-14, is simply, by definition, a more precise classification tool.

NOTE: We are using the RGEG here for the reasons explained above, and because of the wide latitude given the OPM classifier in this specific case (as described in the Introduction).

The use of the RGEG in this case should not be interpreted by the Navy as setting a precedent. Navy is precluded from using any classification guidance not contained in NRaD Instruction 14000.1 for positions covered by the DP.

Additional Issues Raised

Dr. Pavlopoulos, either during the on-site audit or through his attorney, raised the following issues:

Relevance of Past Work and Accomplishments

Work products and innovations produced by Dr. Pavlopoulos during the 1960s and 1970s are mentioned in several places in his attorney's submissions. While these are informative and indicate a continuity of contributions, this classification decision is based primarily on the current (in about the past year) work history of the incumbent. An exception is in application of Factor IV, "Qualifications and Scientific Contributions" in the RGEG. As is shown in the body of this decision, this factor is not restricted to present and immediate past job performance.

Position-to-Position Comparison

Dr. Pavlopoulos compares the duties and responsibilities of his position to several positions classified at Level IV. By law, OPM must classify positions solely by comparing their current duties and responsibilities to OPM standards and guidelines (5 U.S. Code 5106, 5107, and 5112). Although the language in the "stipulation for compromise settlement" seems to provide additional latitude in this case, we still do not feel that position-to-position comparison would be appropriate. One reason behind the law is that position-toposition comparison could lead to comparison with improperly classified positions. Therefore, consistent with established practice, and because it is beyond the scope of this review to determine the correct classification of other positions, we are limiting our comparison of the incumbent's position to the DP level descriptors, and to the criteria in the RGEG.

Non-Approved Changes to Level IV for Scientists

The incumbent noted that "managerial/supervisory" criteria were added to the Level IV descriptor for scientists. "The added criteria created a descriptor, currently in use, that has not been approved by OPM." The implication here is, that since Dr. Pavlopoulos does not have supervisory responsibilities, he has been unfairly penalized by the addition of these criteria.

We compared the July 1980 version of the Level IV descriptor for scientists with the current one. Project and program management language has been added. However, we interpret this language as indicative of the scope of the project or program; it does not imply a requirement for full supervisory responsibilities. This interpretation is consistent with the fact that there is a separate DP career path for managers and supervisors. In any event, our review of DP implementation guidelines in the Federal Register, Vol. 45, No. 77, dated April 18, 1990, did not find any requirement that OPM must approve any changes to level descriptors. The agency has informed us that they also do not know of any such requirement

Funding

Dr. Pavlopoulos contends that outside funding/ sponsorship, or the lack thereof should not be a classification issue. We disagree. Funding by other components of DoD and by outside sponsors would be one indicator of the importance of research to others. The size and importance of research projects and programs managed are classification criteria under the DP classification system, and these criteria are normally linked directly to funding levels.

Miscellaneous Contentions about the Agency

Several written statements were made about lack of fairness and poor management practices on the part of the agency. Our only concern here is to make our own independent decision on the proper classification of the subject position by comparing the duties and responsibilities of the position to relevant standards and guidelines. Therefore, we have considered these statements only insofar as they are relevant to our making that comparison.

Position Information

The primary purpose of the incumbent's work is to improve the performance of mainly water-soluble laser dyes with respect to their lasing efficiency and photo stability. To do this, he conceptualizes promising organic compounds, which are then prepared according to his specifications by a university-affiliated chemist. Upon receiving the compounds, he exposes them to various and complex spectrographic tests and studies to determine their lasing efficiency and photo stability characteristics. These characteristics vary with the molecular structure of the organic dye compounds. Part of the equipment and the techniques used to perform these tests and studies were originally designed and developed by the incumbent more than twenty years ago and have been periodically refined ever since. Dr. Pavlopoulos is considered a specialist and expert in the field of laser dyes. Dye lasers, using improved laser dyes, many of which have been developed by the incumbent, have been used in weapons systems, medical applications, optical communications, and in research conducted by the Navy and others.

Dr. Pavlopoulos works under very general administrative supervision, and his technical findings are considered authoritative by the agency and his peers. Through his publications and presentations over the years, he has developed an international reputation.

Application of the Research Grade-Evaluation Guide (RGEG)

The subject position, for reasons discussed in the Introduction, is also evaluated by application of the Research GradeEvaluation Guide (RGEG). The RGEG is used in the traditional General Schedule classification system to determine grade levels of research positions.

Part of the RGEG is used to evaluate positions at GS-II through GS-15 that are engaged in basic or applied research in the sciences, when the functions involve the personal performance, as the highest level function and for a substantial portion of the time, of professionally responsible research. Part I includes four factors that are considered and rated separately, with the total point value then being converted to a grade level by use of the grade conversion chart provided in the RGEG.

Each factor is evaluated at one of five-degree levels. Three of these levels (A, C, and E) are defined in the RGEG. An intermediate level (B or D) may be assigned when a position is evaluated between levels

A and C or levels C and E, respectively. Factor 1: Research Situation or Assignment

This factor deals with the nature, scope, and characteristics of the studies being undertaken by the employee. It is intended to reflect the situation or assignment in the current job, rather than a summation of the employee's assignments over a long period of time.

Degree A describes scientific investigations of limited scope, with readily definable objectives, which require only fairly conventional techniques. Projects at this level may involve applying existing theory or methods to new classes of subjects, or to classes of subjects previously experimented with, under various controlled changes in conditions. Projects at this level are expected to result in a publishable addition to scientific knowledge.

The subject position fully meets and somewhat exceeds Degree A. Testing dyes to determine and record their properties can be considered investigations of limited scope. However, Dr. Pavlopoulos must also conceptualize new and modified compounds, which exceeds this level. The objectives (enhanced performance of water-soluble dyes) are readily definable. Although he designed much of the equipment and procedures twenty years ago, he has constandy modified and improved the equipment and procedures. Some of the apparatus (especially that dealing with the study of weak triplet-state absorption) only exists in that configuration in his laboratory. The techniques used to perform tests using this equipment cannot be characterized as "only fairly conventional."

He experiments with new compounds and variants of old compounds, subjecting them to a variety of controlled tests. The results are periodically published in respected journals and/or presented at scientific gatherings.

Degree C is not fully met because the research situation cannot be considered to meet the criteria of "considerable scope and complexity." Laser-dye research is considered a very narrow research area. Also, his current work has not led to the kinds of innovation, validation, or modification of scientific theory or methodology, or resulted in the kinds of important changes of existing products, processes, techniques, or practices envisioned at this degree. (Some of his work twenty years ago in the development of new equipment and procedures may have met some of these criteria at that time, however.)

Degree B (4 points) is assigned for this factor. Factor II: Supervision Received

This factor deals with the supervisory guidance and control exercised over the researcher in the current job situation. Degree A describes a much closer level of review than is evident in the subject position. At this degree, the supervisor defines the research problem, provides ongoing guidance, and the employee's writtwork receives fairly close scrutiny.

Degree C is almost an exact match with the subject position. The overall area (laser-dye research) is assigned to the incumbent, but he is allowed to work with substantial freedom within his area of primary interest. He is allowed to identify, define, and select specific dye compounds for study and is responsible for determining what approaches to use. As is described at this level, Dr. Pavlopoulos is responsible with little or no supervisory assistance for formulating hypotheses (new or modified dye compounds which might yield desirable results), for developing and carrying out his research plan, for coping with any novel and difficult technical problems requiring modification of standard methods, for analyzing and interpreting results, and for preparing comprehensive reports of findings. As at Degree C, the scientist is expected to keep his supervisor informed of general plans and progress and major changes in important lines of investigation; however, his professional judgment is relied on to such an extent that his recommendations are ordinarily followed. As is typical of this degree, Dr. Pavlopoulos has full responsibility for decisions regarding the use of equipment and available resources. His completed work and reports are reviewed principally to evaluate overall results.

Degree E is not met in that this degree is characterized by management's expectation that the researcher will, within broad agency policies, locate and explore the most fruitful areas of research in relation to the agency's program and needs and the state of the science involved. There is no evidence that the incumbent has met this expectation. He has remained very focused in an extremely narrow specialty area, which, according to agency management, has very limited current interest to the Navy. In fact, according to interviews with management, the incumbent has resisted attempts to involve him in related research in optics, which the agency feels has broader applicability to its mission.

Degree C (6 points) is assigned for this factor. Factor III: Guidelines and Originality

This factor deals with the creative thinking, analyses, syntheses evaluation, judgment, resourcefulness, and insight that characterize the work performed in the current job situation.

Degree A describes a situation where existing theory and methods are generally applicable to most, though not necessarily all parts of the problem. At this level, some originality is required in development of a research design, but only a limited amount of innovation or modification of procedures and techniques is required. As mentioned earlier, the incumbent has continued to modify equipment and procedures he designed twenty years ago. The originality required to hypothesize more efficient water soluble laser dyes somewhat exceeds the originality envisioned at Degree A.

Degree C, however, is not fully met. Experimentation on new and enhanced laser dyes has been conducted for many years. Although the water solubility problem has not been satisfactorily resolved, and the search for higherperformance dyes is ongoing, basic research in laser dyes is not "novel." At Degree C, because of the novel nature of the research, a high degree of originality is required in defining problems, which are very elusive and/or highly complex. Applied research at this degree typically involves development and application of new techniques and original methods of attack to the solution of important problems presenting unprecedented or novel aspects. Because of the established nature of research in dye lasers and laser dyes, we do not find the level of originality or lack of guidelines and precedents present in the subject situation to an extent required to fully meet the intent of Degree C.

Degree B (4 points) is assigned for this factor. Factor IV: Qualifications and Scientific Contributions

This factor measures the total qualifications, professional standing and recognition, and scientific contributions of the researcher, insofar as these bear on the dimensions of the current research situation and work performance. It is given twice the weight of the other factors. Degree A describes a fully qualified and functioning, but beginning, researcher. At this degree, some publication has occurred, but major contributions to the field have not been made.

At Degree C, the researcher has demonstrated his ability as a mature, competent, and productive worker. He will have authored one or more publications of considerable interest and value to his field, as evidenced by favorable reviews, by citation in the work of others, and/or he will have contributed inventions, new designs, or techniques which are of material significance in the solution of important applied problems. At this degree, he is beginning to be sought out for consultation by colleagues who are, themselves, professionally mature researchers. This degree describes emerging recognition as an expert in a specialization.

Dr. Pavlopoulos has published more than 80 [proceedings and] articles over the past 40 years and continues to do so with at least six publications or co-publications during the past two years in recognized scientific journals. His work has been liberally referenced by others over the years, and he is regularly asked to present papers at national and international gatherings of scientists. His reputation in dye-laser and laser-dye research is well established. His qualifications and scientific contributions in his specialization exceed the criteria at Degree C.

In several respects, Degree E is also met for this factor. As is described at this degree, Dr. Pavlopoulos has demonstrated considerable attainment in a narrow but intensely specialized field of research. As is typical of this degree, he has authored a number of publications, and contributed inventions, new designs, and techniques. He is also sought as a consultant by colleagues who are, themselves, specialists in his field, and he speaks authoritatively regarding his field in contacts within and outside the Federal government. As mentioned above, and as is typical of this degree, he is invited to address national and international professional organizations, and is often recognized in the literature of his field through favorable reviews and numerous citations.

However, to fully meet this level, at least some of the publications would have had a major impact on advancing the field, or would have opened the way for extensive further developments, or have solved problems of great importance to the scientific field, to the agency, or to the public. Contributions at this degree are of such importance and magnitude that they serve to move the art forward to the extent that other researchers must take note of the advance in order to keep abreast of development in the field.

Our on-site audit, our review of the material submitted, and our interviews with the four levels of supervision and management over the subject position have led us to the conclusion that while Dr. Pavlopoulos' contributions have been extensive and consistent, the contributions have not had "major impact on advancing the field," are not regarded as "major advances," and he has not resolved problems of "great importance" within the intent of the standard. Also, there is no hard evidence that his contributions have been of such importance and magnitude that they have moved this branch of science forward to the extent described for this degree. This is not to say that his contributions have not been considerable and substantial, but that they are not of the scope and impact required to fully meet Degree E, the highest degree described in the Guide.

Because Degree C is significantly exceeded and Degree E is not fully met, Degree D (16 points) is assigned for this factor.

Conversion of Points to Grade Level

Factor I: Degree B, 4 points
Factor II: Degree C, 6 points
Factor II: Degree B, 4 points
Factor IV: Degree D, 16 points

According to the conversion scale in the RGEG, the total of 30 points falls in the GS-13 range (26-32 points).

Decision

Based on the above application of both the DP classification criteria, and the RGEG, we find that the subject position is appropriately classified as: Scientist, DP-1310, Level III.[55]

Did Mr. Johnson Properly Classify My Position?

1. Funding

Although I performed at the DP-IV Level, the Center's management succeeded in convincing the classifier Mr. Johnson that I should not be promoted to DP-IV because I had funding problems. From this conclusion it was speculated that my narrowly focused research project must not be of high value to the navy. However, all basic research projects are narrow in scope, unlike development projects.

The simple fact is that all scientists performing research and working in federal laboratories started to have funding problems—and now are having even bigger ones. These funding problems escalated after 1993. As a result, at the Center, many scientists, including many scientists with DP- IV ratings, have landed behind desks, pushing papers. However, no cuts in pay resulted for these scientists.

After January 1994, I received some funding and in the following years, funding was off and on. However, I was able to continue with my research, and I continued publishing in the open literature.

In a letter to Mr. Johnson, the classification advisor, my attorney, Mr. Rothman, had stated that the Center had available $3.7 million in independent research (IR) funding. This allowed the Center to support about forty employees in their research. However, at that time, there were less than forty employees working at the Center who were capable of performing independent research. If some boondoggles in the IR program could have been eliminated, there was definitely sufficient funding available for my research project. However, since about 1990, I had not received any of the in-house IR funding due to the negative ranking of my IR proposals by my biased management. I had similar problems in 1982.

2. Was Mr. Johnson Qualified to Classify My Position?

Although my attorney and I had requested an "appropriately experienced position classification specialist," Mr. Johnson seemed not to be qualified to classify positions of scientists performing basic research. According to Mr. Johnson, he interviewed my supervisor and managers in all of the four managerial levels above me. However, none of these managers held doctoral degrees, nor had they any training or experience whatsoever in physics or in laser research. I am sure that none of them had ever studied any research publications on lasers, not to mention dye lasers and laser dyes. According to Mr. Johnson's findings, my GS-13 (DP-III) position was correctly classified—namely, as a journeyman-level performance. This is the level that I had shared under the demo with about 1,200 other journeymen, most of them holding BA or BS degrees. I had mentioned in my position description submitted to Mr. Johnson that since 1975 I had been a member of the New York Academy of Sciences. Specifically, the RGEG states:

4. The qualifications, stature, and contributions of the incumbent have a direct and major impact on the level of difficulty and responsibility of the work performed.

5. Research capability as demonstrated by graduate education and/or research experience is a significant requirement in selection of candidates.[13]

I wonder whether there are any institutions besides the Center that pay the same wages to members of the New York Academy as they pay their scientists and engineers who hold bachelor's degrees. During my thirty-seven year stay at the

Center, I am not aware of any other scientists and engineers at the Center having been selected as members of the New York Academy of Sciences. Below, I list my comments on Mr. Johnson's classification criteria.

Factor 1: Research Situation

I received only four points from Mr. Johnson, which is simply insulting. If my research situation was of such a low level of complexity, how was it possible for me to have had my research results extensively published in the most prestigious journals of my field? Even back in 1973, I had received six points for this evaluation category. Further, Mr. Johnson conceded that:"... he has constantly modified and improved the equipment and procedure. Some of the apparatus (especially that dealing with the study of weak triplet absorption) only exists in that configuration in his laboratory."

Factor II: Supervision Received

I received only six points, even though Mr. Johnson agreed that my first-line supervisor, a biologist without a doctorate, was unqualified to provide me with any technical or scientific guidance. Why, then, did I not receive the ten points possible for this category? For the twenty-nine years I had worked at the Center at that time, I had worked and published without any supervisory assistance.

Factor III. Guidelines and Originality

I received only four points in this category, which, again, is nothing short of insulting. How was it possible for me to have had my research results extensively published in the most prestigious journals of my field? Even back in 1973, I had received six points for this evaluation category.

Factor IV: Qualifications and Scientific Contributions

I received only sixteen instead of twenty points. However, Mr. Johnson, in his evaluati on statement, agreed that I had a large amount of documentation to support my exceptional qualifications and contributions.

Intra-Agency Classification Consistency

Mr. Johnson acknowledged and then quickly dismissed these significant documents and also refused to perform a position-to position comparison. He also expressed his belief that miscellaneous contentions about the Center's poor management were of no concern in my position classification appeal. My attorney, Mr. Rothman, had also submitted to Mr. Johnson the WFDOCP's report on the disastrous state of position classification at the Center, which reported massive over-grading of employees' positions.[19] This over grading violates Title 5, U.S. Code, which requires consistency in intra-agency classifications. This issue was specifically stressed in my attorney's letter to Mr. Johnson.[53] This issue is addressed in the OPM bulletin listed below:

OPM, FPM Bulletin No 511-33

Subject: Intra-Agency Classification Consistency

September 15, 1992

Heads of Departments and Independent Establishments

Ensuring equal pay for substantially equal work is an important responsibility of Federal agencies in the administration of position classification. The principle of equal pay is stated in three different places in Title 5, U.S. Code: in chapter 23 as a merit-system principle, in chapter 51 as a principle of GS classification, and chapter 53 as a principle of the Federal Wage System.

As part of its oversight responsibility, the OPM requires agencies, upon receipt of OPM classification appeal decision, to review the agency classification of identical, similar, and related positions to ensure that these positions are classified consistently with the OPM appeal decision (section 511.612 of Title 5, U.S. Code of Federal Regulations). Agencies are reminded that this requirement exists, whether or not OPM has also required a report of intra-agency classification consistency as described below.

When OPM has reasons to believe, either as the result of its own investigation or as a result of a substantiated allegation of an appellant, that an agency has positions classified inconsistently with an appealed position, it will require the agency to conduct a classification consistency review and report the results to OPM, as described in Appendix C of FPM Chapter 511 [emphasis added]. Consistency reviews are levied on agency headquarters to ensure that a nationwide approach is taken to achieving consistent classification.[56]

As an officer of the OPM, Mr. Johnson was required to report to his management the widespread classification inconsistencies at the Center. As stated in the above FPM bulletin, this in turn would have required an investigation and potential reclassifications of all positions, not only at the Center, but also throughout the navy. We can thus speculate that such inconstancies were most likely also present at other agencies and departments—and still may be. Nationwide reclassification of federal employees' positions would have saved billions of dollars for American taxpayers.

President Clinton is swindled by the OPM

The Center's internal journal *Outlook* featured an article with the title: "Demonstration Project is made permanent." A shortened version of this article is presented below.

> On October 5, 1994, President Clinton signed the National Defense Authorization Act for Fiscal Year 1995, S.2182. This legislation carries a provision, which makes the Navy Personnel Demonstration Project, carried out by NCCOSC [the Center] and the Naval Air Warfare Center Weapons Division, permanent. It also authorizes the Department of Defense to conduct similar demonstration projects elsewhere in Department of Defense (DOD).

> The Personnel Demonstration Project or "Demo Project" originated in 1980 at the Naval Ocean System Center and the Naval Weapons Center, China Lake. It was the first demonstration project authorized by the U.S. Office of Personnel Management under the provisions of the Civil Service Reform Act of 1978.

> Evaluations conducted by OPM have shown positive results in the Demo Project's ability to recruit and retain high performers, significant paperwork reduction, and higher employee satisfaction with all features of the system.

> "It is a great pleasure to see the system made permanent," said Randy Riley, NCCOSC Human Resources Officer, who initiated the project in 1979. "It is a credit to our management who designed, implemented, and managed the system responsibly and effectively. It is a model for all other substantial

changes, which have been and are being proposed elsewhere in the government."

The basic concepts of the system were developed by the personnel office staff, in concert with the staff of the School of Public Administration at the University of Southern California, and approved by the Office of Personnel Management Demo Project classification and performance appraisal systems have changed very little since inception. The pay system has seen the most change, increasing the options and flexibility available to managers to recognize performance.[57]

At the start of the demo, the Center's personnel office had pledged, "When methodologically justified, control-group data will be obtained from other Navy laboratories not involved in the project."[28] Also, documentation was supposed to be collected, showing that extra pay to performing employees had resulted in an improvement of the overall performance at the Center. No such data were collected over the fifteen-year duration of the Center's demo, even though defense laboratories routinely produce several measurable performance criteria. These include rates of openliterature publication, conference proceedings, technical notes, and patents applied for and granted. These criteria were available and could have been used to measure the Center's performance and therefore allow a comparison.

When the demo started in 1980, its proponents claimed that upon its conclusion, the University of Southern California (USC) would undertake a detailed scientific evaluation of the impact of the demo on the Center's overall performance. Specifically, USC would be working "on the design and execution of the evaluation package."[28]

However, no such "evaluation package" was ever produced. The primary purpose of the demo was to provide pay-for-performance. However, proper appraisal of employees' performance was impossible when the Center failed to develop a performance appraisal system and performance standards for all its employees at the beginning of the demo. The evaluation function of USC became superfluous, and the OPM took over USC's evaluation of the demo. However, the OPM failed to inform Congress of the demo's failure. In its white paper, the OPM specifica lly states:

> *Of course, it is also important to remember that any compensation system changes that increase an emphasis on a performance linkage will only succeed to the extent that credible, reliable measures of that performance are readily available.*
>
> *A rigorous performance management system that employees trust to make appropriate performance distinctions is the sine qua non for stronger linkage, both for setting clear expectations and accountability and for establishing measures that can bear the burden of driving pay decision.[1]*

When planning to use pay-for-performance concepts, every agency and department is required to develop its own performanceevaluation systems that meet its needs. However, no "credible, reliable measures of that performance" were ever developed at the Center. Obviously, having no performance-evaluation system in place can be used to meet incompetent management's needs for job security. By simply rating marginally performing employees as satisfactory year after year, but not providing pay-for-performance rewards for performing employees whom management feels don't belong, management can force the performers out of their jobs. Is this the way "to attract the best and brightest into public service where performance and results are rewarded"[1]?

As a result, over the last twenty-six years, since the beginning of the demo, all the Center's management has been exercising detrimental judgment in the appraisal processes of many high performing employees. However, no member of management has ever been held accountable, suffered any loss in pay, or been removed from his or her managerial position. During the first five years, and continuing during the demo's ten-year extension, the Center's personnel office mailed attitude-survey questionnaires to employees. These inquiries were anonymous. Most of the questions were concerned with employees' satisfaction under the demo. These collected surveys formed the sole "scientific" basis for the OPM's fifteen years of evaluation of the Center.

Several employees who visited the Center's personnel office during that time stated that Personnel Office staff bragged to them about removing negative surveys before their evaluation. I do not know if the OPM also discarded some of the more negative survey forms on the demo. Nevertheless, I perceive two reasons for high employee satisfaction at the Center. Both of them were predictable. First, any pay-for-performance system rewarding some employees for "performance," justified or not, will generate a group of happy employees. This will show up automatically in any attitude survey. Second, a very large percentage of the Center's employees had entered the demo occupying over-graded and, as a result, overpaid positions. Many of these employees collected better wages than private industry could offer, together with solid job security. Of course, all these overpaid employees were very happy to have the demo make their inflated pay rates permanent. However, it eludes me how this type of employee satisfaction proves that the overall performance at the Center had improved.

Besides these attitude surveys, no other documentation or any other measurable performance criteria was ever collected at the Center. There is no shred of proof that the demo resulted in an increase in employee performance that resulted in an increase of effectiveness and efficiency at the Center. This renders the OPM's evaluation of the demo worthless.

Proper oversight by the OPM during the navy's fifteen-year-old demo—namely, interviewing the Center's employees personally—would immediately have exposed gross violation of basic merit principles by the Center's management. It appears that the OPM still views federal employees as file clerks, such that it was beneath the OPM's dignity to have any contact with them. In the introduction of this book. I mentioned that in the 1940s, 70 percent of the federal workforce consisted of white-color filing clerks. Had such interviews been conducted, the OPM would also have discovered that the Center was hiding hundreds of overpaid, over-graded employees, a high burden for taxpayers. The OPM's mission includes oversight of agencies' and departments' adherence to merit principles, including oversight over demos.

However, the OPM mostly prefers to deal with and listen to "clerk-type" management. Contrary to its mission, the OPM acts as the self-appointed whitewash agency to cover up mismanagement, including management's deliberate violation of basic merit principles.

I don't know whether Mr. Johnson reported gross mismanagement, such as the lack of consistency in job classification at the Center, to his management at the OPM. If he had, from early 1994 until September 11, 2001, the OPM would have had sufficient time to replace incompetent management with high-quality management, not only at the Center, but also in other federal agencies and departments.

Better management might have been better able to put together available information and could possibly have prevented the events of September 11, 2001. Improvements in the quality of management could also have prevented widespread mishaps at the CIA, the FBI, and other agencies and departments. With most high-quality employees leaving or having left the Center, "organizational effectiveness" has declined, seriously affecting the Center's spending and its ability to accomplish its mission.

It appears to be a conflict of interest for the OPM to perform an oversight function over demos—and at the same time to perform an evaluation function. On top of this, due to the complexity of the scientific evaluation process originally proposed by USC, the OPM was unqualified to take over the function of evaluating the Center's demo.

Reporting the Demo's Shortcomings to Congress

I put great effort into presenting my classification case to Mr. Johnson, the OPM reviewer who classified my position. Now the demo was possibly headed for adoption by other federal agencies and departments. I had misgivings about the future of the American bureaucracy, but nobody seemed to care. It appeared to me that United States might be facing failures and catastrophes in the future, with its federal bureaucracy becoming more and more dysfunctional.

In January of 1995, after a long period of soul-searching. I decided to write a report on the working of the demo and submit it to both houses of Congress. This document carried the title: The Navy's Demonstration Project as a Model for the Proposed Reform of the Federal Civil Service: A Report on How the Project Works in Theory and Practice.[58]

The report I presented is a mini version of this book, and I had enclosed most of the documents contained here. I mailed my report to the U.S. House of Representatives Subcommittee on Civil Service, addressed to representatives John Mica, Dan Burton, Ben Gilman, James Moran, Connie Morella, Frank Mascara, and Bernard Sanders. The report was also mailed to the Senate Subcommittee on Civil Service, addressed to se nators William Roth, Daniel Akaka, Thad Cochran, Byron Dorgan, John

McCain, David Pryor, Ted Stevens, and Bob Smith. I did not receive any replies from the representatives. From the Senate, I received a reply from Senator D. Pryor. He thanked me for my thoughtful letter regarding the proposed reforms to the federal civil service. However, he stated, "Unfortunately, as a ranking minority member on the Subcommittee for Post Office and Civil Service, I do not have the staff necessary to work on individual cases."[59]

Chapter 8
Employees Speak Out

Merit System Protection Board
Surveys on Employees' Attitudes

Until now, I have reported mostly on my own experiences working under the navy's demo. I have no personal experience regarding employee relations and over-grading at other federal departments and agencies. Further more, other federal employees reading this may criticize me for being too negative in assuming that the working of all federal bureaucracies are as negative as that of my workplace. Evidence shows otherwise.

Over the years, several rankings of the performance of federal departments and agencies have appeared in trade magazines and other publications. Among these reports, the highest ranking goes to NASA, often followed by the National Science Foundation. DOD departments rank in the middle of the scale, with the air force often leading, then the army, followed by the navy. Whenever I meet people who have worked for other federal department or agencies, I ask them their opinion about their respective bureaucracy. Of course, judging the Department of the Navy as mediocre does not mean that all employees working for this department are mediocre; instead, this ranking presents an average of employees' performances, with performance levels spanning excellent, good, mediocre, marginal, and poor. However, all these performance levels are distributed on a Gauss curve, also called a bell curve. An average performance means that about 50 percent of employees are mediocre, about 20 percent are putting in a good performance, and about 20 percent are marginal. About 5 percent of performances are excellent, and about 5 percent are poor.

Before starting to write this book, I was often troubled by questions and doubts: was I simply a malcontent? Was I reporting sour grapes? Therefore, I collected the reactions of other federal employees, and their comments are listed below. These employees from other federal workplaces report experiences similar to mine.

The MSPB is required, under Title 5, U.S. Code, 1204 (a) (3), to conduct surveys to obtain information on the working of the American civil service. These MSPB reports are available on the internet from studying these findings, listed below, one important question arises: why is nobody, including the president, Congress, and the OPM, paying any attention to these observations by the MSPB on the sad state of affairs in the American bureaucracy? Why has the OPM not conducted more surveys on employee attitudes and reported them to the president, Congress, and the American people? Such monitoring is the OPM's duty as the president's agent and advisor for the government's human-capital practices.

From the 1994 survey on "Working for America," the MSPB obtained information on whether the federal civil service is protected from prohibited practices violating merit-system principles. These are some of the survey responses:

> *I am totally shocked by the way some employees do not work and the waste of time that is tolerated. My agency and supervisor provide very little feedback on my performance. It is difficult to obtain any performance rating except 'fully successful.' My supervisor does not agree with the policy of giving awards or recognition, so he doesn't. When*

a supervisor is selected, not only do they need to be qualified, but they need to be able to work with people and understand people.

The extreme secrecy with which cash awards are given leads me to believe that inequities exist. An award, cash or otherwise, should be a public honor.

I have to rate employees based on a quota system. I was ordered to lower two ratings to meet quotas. Quality of work was never mentioned as a reason to lower these ratings.

People who have started years after me with even less education are up for GS-9.

My organization is a good place to work. I have the freedom to do my job well. I would not discourage my kids from being civil servants. [This was submitted by a GM-14 supervisor.]

Affirmative actions and whistleblower policies are useless if a first-line supervisor can manipulate the facts in a believable manner and retaliate against an employee!

My supervisor is a master in manipulating the system to suit his needs and the needs of a few favorite employees!

The reality is that going against your supervisor-fair or unfair-kills your career.

I have been in the same job for eighteen years! I have been turned down for five promotions even after making the best-qualified list each time. My agency does not promote people with skills. You must be a good friend of management or be a white male! [This was submitted by an African-American woman.]

The government could use employees much more effectively. Presently, people are being stifled. What people are capable of doing is not considered as important as whether or not they fit into the system.

The government isn't using my knowledge and talents to the best of its ability. There are no challenges and no training to get ahead, so I just do my job. I wish it were different.

Although I am an excellent secretary, I am bored and uninspired with my job now. I am going to college parttime for a degree in accounting.

Increased budget cutbacks are causing incredible levels of tension, stress, and pressures to perform and produce without sufficient staff to do the work. Employees are burning out with increased expectations of job performance.

I received an "outstanding" performance rating last year and was told that even though I deserved and should receive one again this year, I could not be given outstanding rating two years in a row. That is utterly ridiculous.

Further excerpts from the survey are listed below. This survey includes employees' responses to specific personnel problems.

Problem: *Many federal employees do not feel they are treated fairly.*

Response: Fewer than half of federal employees in 1992 felt treated fairly when it comes to job assignments (45 percent), awards (37 percent), training and promotions (34 percent).

Problem: A significant percentage of federal employees believe they are the victims of discrimination or other prohibited practices.

Response: One of five employees believes they were denied a job promotion in the last two years because another applicant was given an unlawful advantage. About one in nine employees said they experienced discrimination based on race, gender, or age.

Problem: Employees rate their organizations as less than satisfactory on several important factors.

Response: Fewer than half of employees said their organization does a good job communicating its policies and procedures; 50 percent said they share the values of their organization; and only 41 percent said their organization inspires them to do well. While 43 percent said their unit has enough people to accomplish its mission, 48 percent said it does not.[60]

The MSPB Report: "Adherence to Merit Principles in the Workplace."

Some discussions of employees' perceptions in this report are presented below.

Problem: Are competitive promotions and selections based on merit and subject to fair and open competition?

Response: A significant minority of employees thought their agencies had a "major problem" (i.e., they fail at least 30 percent of the time) in upholding both of these goals for promotions. These responses made competitive promotions, along with the closely related area of favoritism, the second most negative area of concern for respondents to our survey.

Problem: Is poor performance handled well?

Response: Nearly half of all respondents said their agencies have a major problem correcting poor performance, and even more said this in regard to firing poor performers, making the issue of handling poor performers the single most negative area of concern or our respondents.

Problem: Is equal pay given for equal work?

Response: While one third of respondents said this was not a problem, or only a minor one, a sizable minority of respondents saw a major problem here. Roughly one-fourth of survey respondents thought their agencies do a poor job of ensuring that employees receive equal pay for equal work.[10]

And here are the responses from the 2001 MSPB Survey on: "Th e Federal Merit Promotion Program."

Problem: Employees, supervisors, and union representatives all have reservations about how well the merit promotion process is working in the federal government with regards to the end result

Response: Only 45 percent of the employees reported that their supervisors promote the best-qualified available persons when there are jobs to be filled in their organization. Likewise, a significant portion of the supervisors responding to the survey did not think that their organization's merit promotion program allowed them to select the best-qualified applicant for the job to be filled.

Problem: *Supervisors believe their promotion decisions are made on merit-based considerations, but employees believe that is often not the case.*

Response: *According to supervisors, the most important factor used to compare applicants is their technical qualifications, followed by their estimation of the applicant's potential and, when possible, the direct observation of the candidates' work. In contrast, many employees as well as many of the union representatives surveyed were not particularly confident that hiring policies are based on those factors that most would agree are indicative of applicant's potential to perform the job for which they are applying. Instead, they thought that non-merit factors such as loyalty to the supervisor and connections to other important people in the government were the most important factors in determining who is promoted.*

Problem: *The source that supervisors used most frequenly to fill their vacancies was those employees who already worked in their organization.*

Response: *Forty-six percent of the selections made by supervisors were people who already worked for their organization. The next largest source of hiring was applicants who worked outside government (29 percent). The remaining 25 percent of selections were applicants from other federal organizations.*

Problem: *Most often than not, before a merit promotion opportunity is announced, supervisors believe they know which employee in their organization would be the person for the job, and most of the time they select that person.*

Response: *Supervisors told us that during the past two years, 54 percent of the time they had already identified one of their own employees whom they thought they would promote into the vacancy. They also told us that 80 percent of the time they actually selected that person to fill their vacancy. Moreover, the vast majority of supervisors said that they were very satisfied with the people they chose to fill their vacancies.[61]*

A Letter to the Federal Times

In a letter to the *Federal Times* in 1999, Rosann Goodrich states:

Self-Serving Managers

I read your July 12 article "Jerks in the Workplace?" and wondered how Federal Times could have missed the much bigger picture that exists in all federal offices. The biggest jerks in the workplace are the so-called managers who take managerial positions only for the power, prestige, or additional money. These managers are self-serving and have no desire to oversee the workplace and their staff's needs. It's very easy for employees' behavior and work habits to deteriorate when the leadership is weak and indifferent to begin with. Ken Lloyd and Dick

Oppendisano mention that jerks get away with all kinds of nonsense because managers do not want to deal with the problems or risk getting themselves in trouble with EEO complaints or MSPB hearings.

I have been wondering for 23 years why so many employees who are given managerial positions are not removed or disciplined when it is obvious that they lack the skills and interests in becoming trustworthy, decisive, and impartial leaders for their staffs and for the public we are supposed to serve.

The obvious reason is because those managers above them also just pass the situation on because they don't want to document things. When the government makes more effort to hire good managers who have some backbone and leadership skills, and are able and willing to deal with all their subordinates fairly and humanely, the "jerks" in the workplace will have to shape up. The most profound fact I have learned as a federal career employee is this: When the wrong people are put in charge, everyone suffers—including the taxpayers.[62]

Federal Supervisors and Poor Performers

In 1999, the MSPB produced a research report with the title: "Federal Supervisors and Poor Performers." In part, this report relied on input from employees. This document was addressed to the president, the president of the Senate, and the speaker of the House of Representatives. Some excerpts are presented.

After literally decades of research, discussions, and discussion about poor performance—not to mention 20 years of experience under civil service reform legislation specifically designed to improve the situation—there remains a widely held perception that the federal government is not doing enough to deal appropriately with federal employees who do not do their jobs adequately. Often implied in this perception is the notion that there is an unacceptably large proportion of the workforce who falls into the "poor performance" category. However, evidence to support this contention is lacking, and it is fair to ask whether the prevailing perceptions are an accurate reflection of reality.

Regardless of the actual number of poor performers, however, a consensus has formed over time on two issues. One, even a relatively small percentage of poor performers can have a disproportionately large and negative effect on an organization. Secondly, federal departments and agencies do not do a good enough job of confronting and resolving individual instances of poor performance. In fact, based on its recent study of the experiences of federal supervisors ("Poor Performers in Government: A Quest for the True Story"), OPM estimates that poor performers make up only 3.7 percent of the federal workforce.

Although Congress attempted to influence this situation in 1978 by revising legal and procedural requirements to make it easier to demote or fire workers whose performance is unacceptable, removing or demoting inadequate performers still remains relatively rare in the civil service. However, according to the Sixth Merit System Principle, 5 U.S. Code: "Employees should be retained on the basis of the adequacy of their performance, inadequate performance should be corrected, and employees should be separated who cannot or will not improve their performance to meet required standards."

There is a powerful piece of conventional wisdom that holds that federal supervisors do not observe this sixth merit principle very well—that they tend not to address the problem of poor performance in their work units, and when they do deal with poor performers their action lacks force and effectiveness. An equally powerful tradition maintains that government regulations and procedures make it too difficult to fire poor performers. As is often the case with conventional wisdom, there is both truth and error in these beliefs.

The fact is, most supervisors do act in response to poor performance, but usually in an informal way that avoids adversarial postures. And they seldom fire or demote poor performers, not necessarily because government rules truly make it so difficult, but often because of agency culture that encourages such beliefs and because of the difficulty inherent in confronting a nother human being whose work has been judged inadequate.

Unfortunately, there are also federal supervisors who do little or nothing about problem performers, choosing instead to look the other way, sometimes letting the better performers pick up the slack— hoping, perhaps, that the performance problem will cure themselves or that the inadequate performers will voluntary leave the unit. This sort of supervisory inaction can create problems far beyond that of a single incompetent worker. It can turn the unit's better performer[s] into overworked, resentful employees who, noticing the absence of penalties for

> *inferior performance, may reduce their own efforts*
> *as a result.*[63]

Again, there is always this excessive worry by management about the poorly performing worker who seems to present major problems for the efficient operation of the American federal bureaucracy. No one seems to worry about the poorly performing manager.

Whenever the poor performance of the American bureaucracy is criticized, management successfully claims that their lack of power in personnel matters prevents them from getting tough with poorly performing employees. For management in bureaucracies, there are no stock options or other financial rewards for improving overall agency performance. As a result, they are mainly interested in their welfare: job security, job comfort, and stability. Therefore, nonperformers are tolerated, and performers are stifled, causing many high-performing and high-quality employees to quit their jobs. The above MSPB report failed to emphasize an important subject—namely, how incompetent management interacts with highly qualified employees. I hope this book fills that void.

Chapter 9
Decline of the Federal Bureaucracy

High-Performance Organizations

In the early 1990s, it dawned on the Center's management that the overall performance and productivity of the Center had plummeted. The output of patents and publications, the amounts of outside funding obtained, and other measurable indicators of performance had declined. There was widespread dissatisfaction in the workforce. Especially troublesome was the reduction of the Center's capability to write successful proposals for obtaining project funding. In addition, as stated, the amount of funding for research and development available from the Pentagon had further declined. Slowly but steadily, the WFDOCP's assessment, made in 1978, on the future of the Center had become reality:

> *For example, the failure to resolve a combination of position management/classification problems is blocking effective use of the high-grade quota for employees now performing at levels above their present classification in work, which NOSC considers highly mission essential. Failure of the Center to correct existing personnel management and classification problems will ultimately impact significantly on cost and mission accomplishment.*[19]

Around 1998, I first heard about HPO, or High-Performance Organizations. HPO is dedicated to individual and collective involvement in organizational improvements.[64]

These courses were first offered only to the Center's upper management. Soon, however, the entire staff of the Center was required to attend these three-day courses. The centerpiece of HPO is the development of an organizational vision. This vision is communicated throughout the organization, and then individual and cooperative efforts are aligned with the mission. For the Center, the vision is "To be the nation's preeminent provider of integrated C4ISR solutions for warrior information dominance."[65] C4ISR stands for Command, Control, Communication, Computers, Intelligence, Surveillance, and Reconnaissance.

According to HPO, there are four different organizational systems. The first is the worst, namely the exploitative and autocratic system. The fourth is the participative system.

The exploitative autocratic systems views workers as selfish, lazy, and inept. They work only when closely supervised. The exploited workers have no recourse. They are incompetent and fear the loss of pay. The structure of the organization is one of a steep hierarchy. Only management posseses all the "important" knowledge, and therefore there is no need to consult Outputs of such organizations are, at best, only mediocre.

The participating system stands at the opposite end of the scale. It uses a collective of workers with widely distributed backgrounds of ability, knowledge, and creativity. The norm is consultation within the organization. Managerial hierarchy is flat. Now, workers are capable of performing many managerial responsibilities that, in the past, were solely management's functions. Groups of employees in self-directed work teams perform managerial and leadership functions. The claim is that these organizations have the highest outputs.[64]

Despite the influence of the HPO training, the Center's autocratic managerial hierarchy is still intact, having total control of all personnel functions, including performance pay and promotions. Furthermore, despite the dynamic new vision statement that they developed with HPO, the Center's management still has no vision whatsoever. All of them are comfortable, having entered semiretirement when they were promoted into management—a perfect example of the Peter Principle, which states that everyone in an organization is eventually promoted to the level of his or her incompetence. The Center's management is without any outside overview or accountability, well paid, and mostly underworked; they occupy very secure jobs and look forward to full retirement to collect substantial pensions.

HPO is also focused on rewarding high-performing workers providing pay for performance. Accountability and the active, daily practice of consulting leadership are combined. The centerpiece of H PO's philosophy is the so-called Balanced Scorecard that is supposed to translate strategy into operational objectives—specifically, objectives that can be measured.[64] Although HPO is in its eighth year, the Center has not made any attempts to develop any measurable performance objectives.

In my opinion, HPO principles will never work at the Center. For HPO's concepts to work, the first step would be to abolish the demo, which is an "exploitative, autocratic," incompetent, managementcentered, oppressive civil service system. In a lengthy e-mail, Captain Flynn addressed, on November 2, 2002, all Center employees.

Subject: SSC SD and DOD Transformation,

Coming soon to Old Town, Seaside, Topside, Bayside, and Hawaii will be Town Hall Meetings that explain the Road to Higher Performance (the three-day HPO seminar was only the first step), and how the Balanced Scoreboard will propel us on this journey. Management does not have a monopoly on good ideas. More often than not, the best solutions on any ship come from the deck plates. This Center places a premium on participative management and consultative leadership. Bring your ideas to the Town Meetings and/or send them up to our chain of command.

I strongly encourage you to read the speech below [by Secretary of Defense Donald H. Rumsfeld]. DOD's transformation will succeed because it must I want the Center to be surfing the wave of transformation ... not careening out of control in the undertow.

Very respectfully,
Tim Flynn

Below, the rest of Captain Flynn's e-mail of November 2, 2002, is presented. It contains a speech delivered by former Secretary of Defense Donald Rumsfeld to Pentagon personnel on September 10, 2001, one day before the terrorist attack. This speech carried the title: "War on Bureaucracy." To save space, some suggestions on possible Pentagon savings have been omitted.

War on Bureaucracy

The Pentagon, Monday, September 10, 2001

The topic today is an adversary that poses a threat, a serious threat, to the security of the United States of America. This adversary is one of the world's last bastions of central planning. It governs by dictating five-year plans. From a single capital, it attempts to impose its demands across time zones, continents, oceans, and beyond. With brutal consistency, it stifles free thought and crushes new ideas. It disrupts the defense of the United States and places the lives of men and women in uniform at risk.

Perhaps this adversary sounds like the former Soviet Union, but that enemy is gone: our foes are more subtle and implacable today. You may think I'm describing one of the last decrepit dictators of the world. But their day, too, is almost past, and they cannot match the strength and size of this adversary.

The adversary is closer to home. It's the Pentagon bureaucracy. Not the people, but the processes. Not the civilians, but the systems. Not the men and women in uniform, but the uniformity of thought and action that we too often impose on them. In this building, despite this era of scarce resources taxed by mounting threats, money disappears into duplicative duties and bloated bureaucracy— not because of greed, but gridlock. Innovation is stifled—not by ill intent but by institutional inertia.

Just as we must transform America's military capability to meet changing threats, we must transform the way the department works and what it works on. We must build a department where each of the dedicated people here can apply their immense talents to defend America, where they have the resources, information, and freedom to perform. Our challenge is to transform not just the way we deter and defend, but the way we conduct our daily business. Let's make no mistake: The modernization of the Department of Defense is a matter of some urgency. In fact, it could be said that it's a matter of life and death, ultimately, every American's.

A new idea ignored may be the next threat overlooked. A person employed in a redundant task is one who could be countering terrorism or nuclear proliferation. Every dollar squandered on waste is one denied to the war fighter. That's why we're here today challenging us all to wage an all-out campaign to shift Pentagon's resources from bureaucracy to the battlefield, from tail to the tooth.

We know the adversary. We know the threat. And with the same firmness of purpose that any effort against a determined adversary demands, we must get at it and stay at it. Some might ask, how in the world could the Secretary of Defense attack the Pentagon in front of its people? To them I reply, I have no desire to attack the Pentagon; I want to liberate it. We need to save it from itself.

The men and women of this department, civilian and military, are our allies, not our enemies. They too are fed up with bureaucracy. They too live with frustrations. I hear it every day. And I'll bet a dollar to a dime that they too want to fix it. In fact, I bet they even know how to fix it, and if asked, will get about the task of fixing it. And I'm asking.

They know the taxpayers deserve better. Every dollar we spend was entrusted to us by a taxpayer who earned it by creating something of value with sweat and skill—a cashier in Chicago, a waitress in San Francisco. An average American family works an entire year to generate six thousand dollars in income taxes. Here we spill many times that amount every hour by duplication and by inattention. That's wrong. It's wrong because national defense depends on public trust, and trust, in turn, hinges on respect for the hardworking people of America and the tax dollars they earn. We need to protect them and their efforts.

Waste drains resources from training and tanks, from infrastructure and intelligence, from helicopters and housing. Outdated systems crush ideas that could save a life. Redundant processes prevent us from adapting to evolving threats with the speed and agility that today's world demands.

Above all, the shift from bureaucracy to the battlefield is a matter of national security. In this period of limited funds, we need every nickel, every good idea, every innovation, every effort to help modernize and transform the U.S. military.

We must change for a simple reason—the world has—and we have not yet changed sufficiently. The clearest and most important transformation is from a bipolar Cold War world where threats were visible and predictable, to one in which they arise from multiple sources, most of which are difficult to anticipate, and many of which are impossible even to know today.

Let there be no question: the 2.7 million people who wear our country's uniform—active, Guard, and Reserve—and the close to 700,000 more who support them in civilian attire comprise the finest military in the history of the world. They stand ready to face down any threat, anytime, anywhere. But we must do more.

We must develop and build weapons to deter those new threats. We must rebuild our infrastructure, which is in a very serious state of disrepair. And we must assure that the noble cause of military service remains the high calling that will attract the very best. All this costs money. It costs more than we have. It demands agility-more than today's bureaucracy allows. And that means we must recognize another transformation: the revolution in management, technology, and business practices. Successful modem businesses are leaner and less hierarchical than ever before. They reward innovation, and they share information. They have to be nimble in the face of rapid change, or they die. Business enterprises die if they fail to adapt, and the fact that they can fail and die is what provides the incentive to survive. But governments can't die, so we need to find other incentives for bureaucracy to adapt and improve.

The technology revolution has transformed organizations across the private sector, but not ours, not fully, not yet. We are, as they say, tangled in our anchor chain. Our financial systems are decades old. According to some estimates, we cannot track $2.3 trillion in transactions. We cannot share information from floor to floor in this building because it's stored on dozens of technological systems that are inaccessible or incompatible.

We maintain 20 to 25 percent more base infrastructure than we need to support our forces, at an annual waste to taxpayers of some $3 billion to $4 billion. Fully half of our resources go to infrastructure and overhead, and in addition to draining resources from war fighting, these costly and outdated systems, procedures, and programs stifle innovation as well. A new idea must often *survive the gauntlet of some seventeen levels of bureaucracy to make it from a line officer's to my desk. I have too much respect for a line officer to believe that we need seventeen layers between us.*

Our business processes and regulations seem to be engineered to prevent any mistake, and by so doing, they discourage any risk. But ours is a nation born of ideas and raised on improbability, and risk aversion is not America's ethic, and more important, it must not be ours. Those who fear danger do not volunteer to storm beaches and take hills, sail the seas, and conquer the skies. Now we must free you to take some of the same thoughtful, reasoned risks in the bureaucracy that the men and women in uniform do in battle. To that end, we're announcing today a series of steps the Department of Defense will take to shift our focus and our resources from bureaucracy to battlefield, from tail to tooth.

Today's announcements are only the first of many. We will launch others ourselves, and we will ask Congress for legislative help as well. Harnessing the expertise of the private sector is about something more, however. The De partment of Defense was once an engine of technological innovation. Today the private sector is leading the way in many respects, yet [the] DOD makes it harder and harder for us to keep up and for those who do keep up to do business with the department. Consider that it takes today twice as long as it did in 1975 to produce a new weapon system, at a time when new generations of technology are churned out every eighteen to twenty-four months. That virtually guarantees that weapon systems are at least a generation old technologically the day they're deployed. Meanwhile, our process and regulations have become so burdensome that many businesses have simply chosen not to do business with the Department of Defense. To transform the department, we must take advantage of the private sector's expertise.

Many of the skills we most require are also in high demand in the private sector, as all of you know. To compete, we need to bring the Department of Defense the human resources practices that have already transformed the private sector. No business I have known could survive under the policies we apply to our uniformed personnel. We encourage, and often force, servicemen and women to retire after twenty years in service, after we've spent millions of dollars to train them and when, still in their forties, they [are] at the peak of their talents and skills. Because our objective is to produce generalists, officers are most often rotated out of assignments every twelve to twenty-four months, giving them a flavor of all things but too often making them experts at none. Both policies exact a toll in institutional memory, in skill, and in combat readiness. To that end, we intend to submit revised personnel legislation to Congress at the beginning of fiscal year 2003.

If a shortcoming on the uniformed side is moving personnel too much, on the civilian end we map hardly any career path at all. There, too, we must employ the tools of modern business—more flexible compensation packages, modern recruiting techniques, and better training.

Let me conclude with this note. Some may ask, defensively so, will this war on bureaucracy succeed where others have failed? To that I offer three replies. First is the acknowledgement, indeed this caution: change is hard. It's hard for some to bear, and it's hard for all of us to achieve.

There's a myth, sort of a legend, that money enters this building and disappears, like a bright light into a black hole, never to be seen again. In truth, there is a real person at the other end of every dollar, a real person who's in charge of every domain, and that means that there will be real consequences from, and real resistance to, fundamental change. We will not complete this work in one year, or five years, or even eight years. An institution built with trillions of dollars over decades of time does not turn on a dime. Some say it's like turning a battleship. I suspect it's more difficult.

That's the disadvantage of size. But here's the upside. In an institution this large, a little bit of change goes a very long way. If we can save just 5 percent of one year's budget—and I have never seen an organization that couldn't save 5 percent of its budget—we would free up some $15 billion to $18 billion, to be transferred from bureaucracy to the battlefield, from tail to tooth. Even if Congress provides us every nickel of our fiscal year '02 budget, we will still need these extra savings to put toward s transformation in this Department. Second, this effort is structurally different from any that preceded it, I suspect it begins with the personal endorsement, in fact the mandate, of the president of the United States. President Bush recently released a management agenda that says that performance, not promises, will count. He is *personally engaged and aware of the effort that all of you are engaged in. The battle against a stifling bureaucracy is also a personal priority for me and for the Service Secretaries, one that will, through the Senior Executive Council, receive the sustained attention at the highest levels of this department. We have brought people on board who have driven similar change in the private sector. We intend to do so here. We will report publicly on our progress. The old adage that you get what you inspect, not what you expect, or put differently, that what you measure improves, is true. It is powerful, and we will be measuring.*

Our strongest allies are the people of this department, and to them I say we need your creativity, we need your energy. If you have ideas or observations for shifting the department's resources from tail to tooth, we welcome them. In fact, we've set up a dedicated e-mail address— www.tailtotooth@ osd.pentagon.mil —where anyone can send in any thoughts they have.

Finally, this effort will succeed because it must. We really have no choice. It is not, in the end, about business practices, nor is the goal to improve figures on the bottom line. It's really about the security of the United States of America. And let there be no mistake, it is a matter of life and death. Our job is defending America, and if we cannot change the way we do business, then we cannot do our job well, and we must. So today we declare war on bureaucracy, not people but processes, a campaign to shift Pentagon resources from the tail to the tooth. All hands will be required, and it will take the best of all of us. Now, like you, I've read that there are those who will oppose our every effort to save taxpayers' money and to strengthen the tooth-to tail ratio. Well, fine, if there's to be a struggle, so be it. So as we all remember that if you do something, somebody's not going to like it, so be it. Our assignment is not to try to please everybody. This is not just about money. It's not about waste. It's about our responsibility to the men and women in uniform who put their lives at risk. We owe them the best training and the best equipment, and we need the resources to provide that. It's about respect for taxpayers' dollars. A cab driver in New York City ought to be able to feel confident that we care about those dollars. It's about professionalism, and it's also about our respect for ourselves, about how we feel about seeing GAO reports describing waste and mismanagement and money down a rat hole. We need your help. I ask for your help. I thank all of you who are already helping. I have the confidence that we can do it. It's going to be hard. There will be rough times. But it's also the best part of life to be engaged in doing something worthwhile.

Every person within earshot wants to be a part of a proud organization, an organization that cares about excellence in everything it does. I know it. You know it. Let's get about it. Thank you very much.[66]

***

Secretary of Defense Rumsfeld deserves to be applauded for his openness and his concern for the suffering American taxpayer. He has no idea what is wrong with the Pentagon's bureaucracy and asks for help. The same applies to Captain

Flynn. However, the answer is simple and always the same: the Pentagon, the Center, and many other federal departments and agencies are overloaded with incompetent management, mostly performing administrative functions, and poor- to mediocre-performing employees- often over-graded and overpaid.

The OPM should have been aware of these shortcomings of the Pentagon's and other federal bureaucracies and informed the president and Congress many years ago.

Declining National Reconnaissance Office

Another example of a dysfunctional federal agency is the National Reconnaissance Office (NRO). A 2003 U.S. News & World Report investigative report carried the title "How America's Troubled Satellite Agency is Failing the War on Terrorism," by D. Pasternak, on the problems of the NRO.[67]

According to this article, the DOD established the NRO in 1961. Its mission was to develop and operate spy satellites for the CIA. At its beginning, the accomplishments of this agency were highly regarded, allowing the United States to spy on Russia, many thousands of miles away from America. Today, such a spy capability is still highly valued, providing intelligence that might be helpful to foil terrorist attacks.

The NRO launched two spy satellites in 2001 that developed technical problems. However, no follow-up satellites were launched in the meantime. The future looks dim, claims U.S. News, for America to maintain this important advantage in space.

This secret spy satellite agency has cost Americans two hundred billion dollars over the last forty years. Despite an annual budget of seven billion dollars, NRO satellites are behind schedule, and there is a lack of intelligence. NRO spy satellites do not always function as promised. Intelligence and national security experts have warned that NRO problems may jeopardize American's superiority in space.

Robert Kohler, a retired senior CIA officer, was honored as a Pioneer of the NRO in 2000. In 2002, he wrote an article entitled "The Decline of the National Reconnaissance Office," published in the CIA's internal journal, *Studies in Intelligence*. Some excerpts from Mr. Kohler's article are presented below:

> *The National Reconnaissance Office was once the benchmark organization for excellence in acquisition and program management. It had a reputation for designing and procuring the most sophisticated unmanned satellite and aircraft reconnaissance systems in history. These acquisitions were mostly accomplished on time and within budget, and they performed as promised. Despite an occasional problem, the NRO's record of accomplishment was unsurpassed by any organization, considering the high technical risk that goes with developing state-of the-art systems. A team of dedicated military and civilian personnel stood behind these accomplishments. Unfortunately, the NRO today is a shadow of its former self. Its once outstanding expertise in system engineering has dra stically eroded.*

> *NRO management adopted the principle that anybody could run anything, regardless of skill, background, or experience. People were shuffled around so that any semblance of loyalty to their parent organization was lost; carrier planning fell by the wayside; and experience as a criterion in the position assignment process was discarded.*

Now, they no longer need that kind of experience to be senior officers in the NRO. The CIA no longer sees development of future civilian leaders in this business as its responsibility. The current crop of experienced SIS officers at NRO is retiring, and no replacements with comparable talent and dedication are being actively developed. The current structure is more attuned to the "joint ness" model preferred by DOD, but it is certainly less effective than the old model. It is pushing the organization on a downward slide to mediocrity that the country cannot afford.

Mediocrity in the NRO will result in less innovation and risk taking, more reliance on contractors who are less accountable than government staff, and more cost overruns and schedule delays. Acquisition cycles will be longer. It will become harder and harder to attract the high-caliber people needed to keep this "first-class" organization. Evidence of these problems is already surfacing.[68]

Spy satellites are technically complex. NRO's management lacks qualifications and/or experience, and is unable to provide technical leadership to its employees. The poorly qualified, overpaid, and leaderless workforce is also unable to handle the complex work assignment. However, as at the Center, the managers and employees at the NRO have no incentive whatsoever to leave their agency. Again, all these factors result in high-quality employees leaving the organization, high costs for the taxpayer, and difficulty—if not impossibility—in accomplishing its military missions. Again, where is the OPM?

After September 11th, 2001, many people wondered whether the terrorist attacks could somehow have been prevented. Since protecting America was the business of several different department and agencies, combining them into one department to improve cooperation made sense. The Homeland Security Department (HSD), with 170,000 employees, came into being. Congressional hearings and discussions on homeland security revealed what the president, Congress, and most Americans did not know. The country's federal civil service faces a serious human resource problem that threatens the security and future of America. The country is burdened with a serious shortage of highly skilled and qualified applicants for employment, because most of these workers prefer to work for the better-paying private sector.

Many young people are not interested in working for the government, where wages for top job categories are frozen. The Executive Summary of the 2002 MSPB report on "Making the Public Service Work" states:

> *The federal government's widely acknowledged human capital crisis threaten the government's ability to meet the expectations of the American people. This crisis is the product of a variety of factors, including changes in missions and public expectations, a decade of downsizing, evolving technology, and workforce demographics. To adequately address this crisis, improvements in the public service and in management of human capital must be made. Incremental improvements have been attempted in recent years, but they are not enough. Bold and sweeping changes to the system and structures of the public service and to the practice of human capital management are needed.[69]*

In the name of improved efficiency, the Bush administration suggested putting all employees of the new Homeland Security Department under a new civil service personnel system. The OPM suggested that the failures of the present civil service system could be corrected by replacing the old system with parts of the China Lake project. Among others, they included new job-classification syste ms, pay-banding, and no employee appeals to the MSPB.

About three years ago, the HSD won approval to create its own in-house appeal process. Somewhat later, the DOD also won the authority to establish its own in-house appeal system. The OPM is still hiding the fact that the Center's demo is a total failure. The OPM has known this since 1982. Without a working performanceevaluation system in place, pay-for-performance is a swindle. This primitive and phony civil service system all but guarantees the failure of the HSD and DOD to fulfill their missions, threatening the security and future of America.

During congressional hearings in the fall of 2003, Mr. Rumsfeld and Undersecretary Mr. Chu requested to have their seven hundred thousand DOD employees under a civil service system similar to the demo. The rationale for this request was to be able to fight terrorism more effectively. Also here, Mr. Chu complained that DOD managers were unable to properly reward top performers, which had forced many employees to depart the DOD for the private sector. The most seriously considered new personnel system was the China Lake Project. During these congressional hearings, Mr. Chu claimed, "Only China Lake has undergone substantial review."[70]

For the OPM to recommend the incompetent-management centered civil service system of the demo to the DOD and HSD borders on treachery. This will put only more cronies into powerful managerial positions that they are unable to handle as soon as difficult decisions have to be made. Without a performance appraisal system and without outside appeal rights, DOD management can shuffie huge performance awards to favorite employees and deny rewards to those employees management feels do not belong. This will very quickly force good employees to vote with their feet, abandoning the DOD for the private sector.

Some final thoughts: According to Dr. P. Light, citing a 2001 statistic by the Brookings Institution, a sampling of seven hundred thousand federal civil servants found that only a fraction of 1 percent received unsatisfactory performance ratings.[71]

Also, according to Mr. W. Riley's sworn testimony of 1992: "One person, probably,"[46] received an unsatisfactory rating. These results show, at least on paper, that considerable parts of the federal civil service are virtually without any poor performers. This is a very strange result. As we have seen throughout this book, whenever management is asked to explain the overall poor performance of the federal bureaucracy, the reason given is always the same: management's legal inability to get tough with a large number of poor performers. How can you get tough with poor performers when, literally, there aren't any? Where are all the underachievers, whose removal, with help from the China Lake demo, would transform a dysfunctional federal government workplace into efficient organizations? At many federal workplaces, as a fact of life, incompetent management and knowledge workers don't get along well. Under these conditions, hiring and keeping the urgently needed, highly qualified workforce is an impossible task.

No Terror Expertise Necessary for FBI Management?

For decades, the FBI has enjoyed a fine reputation among federal agencies and departments as the top crime-fighting agency in the country. But during the last decade or so, mainly due to management problems, its image has been tarnished. Before we discuss the case of the FBI agent Bassem Youssef, let's examine some shortcomings of FBI operations that have been recently criticized.

In 1986, agents from the Bureau of Alcohol, Tobacco, and Firearms tried to infiltrate a white-supremacy group in Idaho. These agents tried to sell two illegal shotguns to Mr. Randy

Weaver. From there on, details on events get murky. It is claimed that four hundred armed federal agents, including some from the FBI, conducted a siege of Weaver's cabin at Ruby Ridge in 1992. During this siege, Weaver's wife, Vicki, and his son were killed.

Weaver, after being found innocent of all major charges, was awarded $3.1 million in civil damages. In 1995, the Senate conducted hearings on the Ruby Ridge siege, and the FBI was criticized in the Senate report.

Another interesting case involved FBI agent Robert Hanssen, a senior counter intelligence officer who spied first for the Soviet Union and continued to spy for Russia. In 1979, he sold the name of a Russian officer who was selling Soviet secrets to the United States to the Russians. Hanssen continued to trade American secrets for many years to the Russians until he was arrested on February 20, 2002. For his spying activities, he had been rewarded with cash and diamonds. The FBI had to pay seven million dollars to a Russian intelligence officer to smuggle Hanssen's file out of Russia. Bad publicity for the FBI resulted from the discovery that there had been a spy among its agents for so many years. This poses an interesting question: over all the years Hanssen had been spying, where was his management?

The FBI and other federal agencies have been criticized for the intelligence failures that allowed the September 11th attacks to happen. Much of the criticism focused on the FBI's unwillingness to cooperate and communicate with other federal, state, and local lawenforcement agencies.

During his confirmation hearing in July 2001, FBI Chief Mueller assured the Senate judiciary Committee: "All institutions— even great ones like the FBI—make mistakes. The measure of an institution is in how it responds to its mistakes; I believe the FBI can and must do a better job of dealing with mistakes. I will make it my highest priority to restore the public confidence in the FBI to re-earn the faith and trust of the American people."

In 2005, John Solomon of the Associated Press wrote an article entitled, "FBI Didn't Seek to Hire Terror Experts," describing the case of an Egyptian-born FBI agent named Bassem Youssef. Some excerpts and summation of this article are presented below.* (The following material is used with the permission of the Associated Press Copyright © 2007. All rights reserved.)

On July 10, 2002, FBI agent Youssef filed a complaint against his agency, claiming discrimination and reprisal based on his national origin. At that time, Youssef had been an FBI agent for fifteen years. He was an expert on the Middle East and counterterrorism, with a highly successful career. During a meeting with an Egyptian official in 1993, he was praised for improving relations between the FBI and the Egyptian police. Because he was familiar with customs of the Muslim world, he was able to smooth gaps between the FBI and its Middle East colleagues.

He returned in 2000, after serving as the FBI's attache in Saudi Arabia. However, he was unable to continue in his field of expertise, namely, counterterrorism. After the September 11 attack, the FBI promoted many agents to managerial positions in counterterrorism, but none of them had any wide experience, including in Middle Eastern affairs, similar to Youssef. After he complained in 2002 about not being promoted, he was transferred to an off-site budget office to tag and process evidence. After he filed his complaint, he was informed at a meeting that another agent had taken over his assignment. He was removed from his position and was not allowed to attend meetings. Youssers chances for being promoted had vanished. During the court hearings, top FBI management stated that expertise on Middle East terrorism was not an important criterion in selecting agents to top managerial positions in counterterrorism.

Executive Assistant Director Gary Bald, chief of the FBI's terrorfighting division, stated that he received his first training on terrorism "on the job" after he transferred to headquarters two years prior to supervise antiterrorist strategy. Recently, questioned on his background and on the history and culture of the Middle East, he replied. "I wish that I had it. I would be nice."

Sometime later he stated: "You need leadership. You don't need subject matter experience ... It is certainly not what I am looking for in selecting an official for a position in a counterterrorism managerial position." Bald again emphasized that: "Probably the strongest leaders I know on counterterrorism have no counterterrorism in their background."

After the terrorist attack on September 11, Congress allocated billions of dollars to fight terrorism. During subsequent Congressional hearings, Mueller emphasized that he was planning to build a new agency, staffed with new experts with proper qualifications to possibly stop terrorist attacks before they occurred.

Bald's testimony agrees with other sworn statements made after September 11 by FBI management that many agents promoted to top terrorist-fighting positions did not have any terrorist experience or Middle East background. These testimonies contradict statements made to Associate Press by Assistant Director Cassandra Chandler, claiming that changes had occurred in criteria used to hire special agents and intelligence analysts, ensuring they receive the necessary skills, knowledge, and experience needed to face today's threats. She also stated: "New agents receive personalized training from Muslim leaders. Street agents and managers in every field office have gotten to know the Middle Eastern and Muslim communities in their territories and regularly attend training sessions sponsored by community leaders."

Daniel Byman, a national security expert, was hired by the court to analyze the Youssef case. He had participated in presidential and congressional investigations on terrorism and intelligence failures of federal agencies. Byman concluded that Youssef was one of the Bureau's most qualified FBI agents to fight terrorism. Further, he affirmed that overall the FBI lacks depth in expertise on Middle East affairs and also is weak in expertise to cooperate with friendly foreign governments to fight terrorism.[72]

In the Youssef case, unqualified FBI management hired other unqualified ma nagers from the in-house pool. Just as at the Center, they looked for birds of the same feather. The main prerequisite is that the managerial clique in power is comfortable with the new candidates. Agents' qualifications and/or experience are rather unimportant. Apparently, the FBI also promotes unqualified managerial candidates in violation of the first merit principle. There is no "selection from all sections of society based on merits after fair and open competition, which assures that all receive equal opportunity."[9]

In summary, Mr. Youssef is simply a high-quality employee whose management has no use for him because his exceptional qualifications present a threat for the clique in power. He might have become aware of their incompetence and complained. I wish I had good advice for him. In my opinion, his professional career with the FBI is over. The managerial clique never forgets-nor forgives.

And a final question: was it not the OPM's mission to build a high-quality and diverse federal workforce?

Chapter 10
How to Improve the
Federal Civil Service

The OPM Must be Abolished

The OPM claims its solution for improving America's bureaucracy has been to let management manage and provide payfor-performance. In reality, however, the navy's demo allows in competent management to mismanage and provide performance rewards and promotions for cronies. The OPM provides no oversight, nor does it hold management accountable.

My failed attempts to be promoted or receive any recognition for my performance from my management left a bitter taste in my mouth. During all those years working at the Center, there were many other employees who had either not been promoted or who were not properly rewarded for their efforts. It took me considerable time to understand the social dynamics of this "research project," the demo. Finally, one day I realized what the problem was. I remembered that historically, besides the system being centered on mostly incompetent management at the Center, there had once been an even bigger autocratic and incompetent-managementcentered bureaucracy that had failed miserably.

The navy's demo, with eager support from the OPM, had simply rediscovered a variant of the phony and primitive communist-style civil service system. There are several similarities between the failed communist system and the navy's demo civil service system.

Myth that Non-Performers are Concentrated in the Workforce

For many years, and for good reasons, the American bureaucracy has been criticized for its poor performance. Federal managers, many of them incompetent, have successfully defended themselves by claiming that too many poor performers were concentrated in the workforce. Advocates of the China Lake demo claim that the demo's system can improve the performance of the American civil service by simply providing management with more power and flexibility in personnel matters to deal with poorly performing employees. Similar to the communists, they claim that this quick fix would allow their federal bureaucracy to operate as efficiently as the private sector. The reasoning behind the demo system is that more managerial flexibility will automatically be used to reward performing employees and punish nonperformers. However, under the demo, nonperforming employees are not removed, and deserving employees are often not promoted or otherwise rewarded for their performance. Unqualified managers deliberately abuse their increased power to improve their job security and job enjoyment

For over seventy years, communist management very successfully used the same excuses to explain the poor performance of their bureaucracy. During this time, the Soviet Politburo swallowed this nonsense, heaping more and more power in personnel matters on its incompetent civil service management. No improvement was ever observed. In the end, much of the responsibility for the collapse of the USSR in 1991 rested on the poor performance of its huge bureaucracy.

Propaganda about Fair Treatment of Employees

According to communist propaganda, freeing workers from capitalistic exploitation and providing them with civil service protection would create a workers' paradise. Similarly, when working for the American civil service system, we are supposed to work for a bureaucracy that operates under the umbrella of merit principles. The OPM's fiscal year 2002 mission statement states:

> *It is OPM's job to build a high-quality and diverse federal workforce, based on merit-system principles that America needs to guarantee freedom, promote prosperity, and ensure the security of this great Nation.*[73]

Unfortunately, after twenty-eight years of OPM guidance, there is no twenty-first century, high-quality workforce in place. The MSPB states: "the merit principles send a clear message that all individuals have the opportunity to participate in the operation of our government if they desire and are qualified."[10] However, under OPM oversight and support, management has trampled on merit principles, resulting in loss of security with no guarantee of freedom—and all to a huge cost to taxpayers.

OPM's bureaucrats eagerly follow management's suggestions on how to improve the American bureaucracy. However, under the demo, position classification has been abandoned, and no performance-evaluation systems are in place. There is no guarantee of fair rewards when such decisions depend on the whims of management that is largely incompetent, self-serving, and interested in protecting only their cronies. However, we are told that the demo presents "an expanded application of the merit pay concept."[28]

Moreover, employees are no longer protected from abuses of merit principles by their management, having mostly highly biased in-house appeal routes for performance ratings and position classification available. At some length, I have reported my attempts to get promoted by having my position properly classified. However, the demo claims:

> *It is anticipated that the project will demonstrate that public managers can be trusted to take these new and changed responsibilities seriously, and that they will act in the best interest of the public service, their organization, and their personnel.*[28]

Autocratic and Incompetent Management

The demo, similar to the communist civil service system, is highly autocratic and in competent-management-centered. As the demo's project objective states:

> *The purpose of the project is to demonstrate that the effectiveness of federal laboratories can be enhanced be allowing greater managerial control over personnel functions.*[28]

Openings for managerial positions in the communist civil service system were mostly reserved for Communist Party members only, where subject knowledge, experience, and/or qualifications were unimportant. Similarly, the Center's management clique reads the first merit system principle routinely as: "Recruit individuals only from your in-house pool and advance only those you feel are loyal, compatible, with no fair or open competition, which assures that nobody else receives any opportunity." I wish to remind the reader of the first merit-system principle, which begins, "Recruit qualified individuals from all sections of society."[9]

This statement seems to me to say that any American can apply and should have a fair chance to occupy a federal management position, "if he or she chooses to apply and qualifies." Further, the demo claims:

> *Finally, the project will actualize the principle that public managers, once given the tools and resources, should be held accountable for their decisions and practices with regard to personnel administration and that such accountability is an essential ingredient of effective and efficient administrative action.*[28]

On first reading, this statement makes good sense. However, in practice, the demo's "accountability" statement is hollow communiststyle propaganda. None of the Center's managers have ever been held accountable for their failure to provide fair treatment for their workers by enforcing merit principles. Similarly, the Communist Politburo very rarely held communist management accountable for their mismanagement. In summary, just like the Soviet bureaucracy, the China Lake demo is a false and autocratic civil service bureaucracy centered on the whims of a management caste that is mostly incompetent. It should not be allowed to become the model to be followed by all federal agencies and departments.

Is the OPM Responsible for 9/11?

Many of the shortcomings and disasters in recent memory involving the American bureaucracy, especially those that became visible after the September 11 attacks, go back to the shortcomings of our federal management. This management is simply too incompetent and too detached to make the proper choices and decisions under pressure. The OPM is responsible for our incompetent management's failure to put the available pieces of information together that led to the September 11 catastrophe. Better management might have prevented the attack

With oversight over federal departments and agencies, the

OPM should have been aware that competitive managerial positions are too often filled without any fair competition from the in-house pool of employees. When selecting employees for promotion, basic merit principles are violated. Work is arbitrarily judged to be of high navy value, and employees with high future value—which really means that management had good "gut feelings" about them—are preferentially promoted. These subjective selection processes have been in use for many years, in many departments of the federal civil service. During the last twenty-six years of the demo, the OPM has looked the other way, never providing any oversight and never reporting to the president and Congress on management's widespread merit-principle violations under the navy's demo.

The OPM—together with the China Lake demo and similar civil service schemes—should be immediately abolished. The OPM, a fraudulent agency, should provide documentation on the number of managers that have been held accountable over the last twenty eight years for their mismanagement, including flagrant and deliberate violations of merit principles. Significantly, the MSPB also has proposed the closing of the OPM:

> *However, OPM's oversight and program evaluation efforts have, at times, reflected OPM's institutional concerns and the interests of the Administration more than the concern for the long-term health of the merit systems and the public service. OPM should be divested of oversight responsibilities for discrimination and for compliance with violation of merit principles. Both the oversight and program evaluation functions should instead be performed by an independent organization.[69]*

Who should perform the important independent oversight functions of enforcing merit principles? Possibly a university should take over these functions.

Improving Federal Civil Service Management

The major shortcoming of the American bureaucracy results from the way open managerial positions are filled. Using the in-house pool of employees, without the required fair and open competitions, and discarding subject knowledge, qualifications, and/or experience must come to an end.

There is a rather easy method to improve the performance of our federal management. This is how it works. Openings for supervisory/managerial positions (mostly in the scientific and technical fields) are advertised the usual way. This allows selecting qualified individuals from all segments (but not from one) of our society to apply for this opening. The ones excluded are the employees of the advertising agency (i.e. often cronies). However, they can always apply to all other position openings so long as it is not their place of work. This selection method creates a professional climate rather than a buddy-buddy situation, where the manager who handpicked the candidate is always inclined to protect his crony every time criticism is voiced.

Further, employees holding PhDs, especially senior professionals should not be supervised by management that holds only a BS or BA degree. These days, qualifications and/or experience are of critical importance and a must to manage a highly qualified twenty-firstcentury wor kforce.

In a recent report, the MSPB came to a similar conclusion:

> *Despite adequate tools and systems, agencies need supervisors and managers who have the capacity, and the will to manage their human capital resources. Unfortunately, too many employees believe their supervisors and managers lack the necessary competence to carry out their managerial responsibilities. This is a critical problem because*

many studies have found that the most common reason employees leave an organization is because of poor supervisors and managers. Therefore, ensuring high-quality federal supervisors and managers is very important.[69]

How are new technical directors selected? Well qualified and well-paid directors should run agencies and departments. They should also be selected according to the above suggestions. However, they should be rotated after four to six years of service, before continuing to another assignment. These directors perform mostly administrative functions and don't have much impact on the mission performed by their organization. This would prevent a director from becoming a loyal supporter of the local managerial clique, settling down and protecting the local clique until it's time for him to retire. Any complaints on mismanagement and merit principle violations could be directed to this director for resolution. He should not have any civil service protection, making it possible to remove him at any time.

It's not just government bureaucracies that need qualified management, but also colleges and universities. There is a saying that poor faculty drives out good faculty. Following the departure of good faculty is the departure of good students.

How to remove unqualified supervisors and managers?

There is a rather simple method already available. This only requires comparing the position descriptions of supervisors and managers with the mission objectives of their agencies or departments. All federal branches, divisions, departments, and agencies have mission statements. If there is any discrepancy between the mission objectives of these units and the qualifications and/or experience noted in the position descriptions of the supervisors and managers, they should be downgraded.

Even if it turns out that the newly hired candidate for a supervisory or management position does not perform as expected, he or she could be more easily removed from the new position. This creates a professional climate rather than a buddy-buddy situation, where the manager who handpicked the candidate is always inclined to protect his crony every time criticism is voiced.

Building a High-Quality Federal Workforce

We urgently need to put a twenty-first century federal workforce in place. It is my conviction that high-quality employees will only work for the government if two conditions are fulfilled. Number one: they must be fairly treated. This can only be accomplished by strictly enforcing merit principles. This in turn implies there must be proper position classifications in place. Position classifications determine the pay employees receive.

Number two: their management must be highly qualified. However, this will never happen as long as the federal workforce is treated unfairly and its management is never held accountable for mismanagement and merit-principle violations.

I reported in some detail how the Center's management protected a large number of employees occupying over-graded positions by entering a demo. Before the demo, the Center's management had falsely certified on the yearly performance evaluation forms that many positions were properly classified, when many were not. Now, on the demo's yearly performance evaluations forms, there are no such certifications necessary.

Consequently, many employees occupy misclassified positions. Because of the long duration of the demo, one can expect that a large part of DP-III level employees is collecting GS-13 pay, but performing only GS-12 level work. Similarly, a large part of the DPIV level employees is collecting GS-15 pay, but performing only GS-14, or GS-13, or GS-12 level work.

Again, it must be emphasized that incompetent management

has the potential to convert pay-for-performance schemes into powerful weapons to drive out high-quality employees. This can be accomplished simply by denying step-increases to high-quality employees who would otherwise be entitled to receive them under the old GS system. These employees quickly get the message that they are not welcome at their place of work. Why would a socially astute manager do this? Many fear the dangerous combination of expertise and honesty.

Another shortcoming of the American bureaucracy is the present trend advocated by management to abandon or weaken proper position classification. I have outlined the reason for the neverending hostility of incompetent management toward appropriate position classification. In classification standards, pay scales for employees as well as management are strongly tilted in favor of qualifications, knowledge, and/or experience— the very criteria that incompetent management and their cronies lack.

Further more, appeals challenging performance ratings and the accuracy of position descriptions should be handled by the agency replacing the OPM. This agency must conduct an independent investigation. This will prompt many over-graded, overpaid employees to retire, automatically opening up many positions. This would make it possible to hire high-quality employees and also promote qualified in-house employees. In addition, this would immediately result in considerable savings for taxpayers. To assure equitable position classifications for all employees, the same classification sta ndards should be used nationwide throughout the federal civil service. Also, one must realize that it might be impossible to obtain 100 percent accuracy in classifying all positions. Specific classification standards like the ones established for the demo should be abandoned. Also, management should be prevented from developing their own private classification criteria that allow them to promote their cronies at will but prevent the promotion of qualifying employees. The last thing we need is a chief classifier—a person whose function is similar to a communist commissar—in the form of a captain, rubber-stamping DP-IV (GS-14/15) promotions.

Management can easily snow the captain by claiming that their candidates are of "of high future value" or "of high value to the navy." The OPM has eagerly supported incompetent management's intent to weaken position classification and to put position classification solely into management's hands, making classification specialists superfluous. Management's successful fight to abolish position classification for the federal bureaucracy is documented in a recent OPM report (Issue 21-4 *Brief Review*), available on the internet. This report contains data on how human resources professions had changed from 1991 to 1998, including classification specialists. This report stated that the numbers of classifiers have dwindled, and they may be getting close to becoming an endangered species. Their numbers declined 58 percent, from 2,079 in 1991, to 868 in 1998.[74]

The agency replacing OPM should hear employee classification appeals. This agency should also perform periodic but also unannounced position management and position classification reviews, similar to the one performed in 1978 by the WFDOCP at the Center, ensuring that all positions are properly classified. This reviewing agency must also have the power to order the reviewed agency or department to conduct such a position management and classification review and promptly, where necessary, take corrective actions. Personnel offices in all federal departments and agencies should not report to the department or agencies they work for but should report directly to the agency that has the new oversight function. Personnel offices that report to the agency or department they are presently working for are highly dependent and easily prone to pressure from their employer's management in personnel matters.

Pay-for-Performance and Pay-Banding

The China Lake demo seeks to remove poor performers from the federal payroll by rewarding high performers financially. Supposedly this is accomplished by providing pay-for-performance and denying nonperformers the guaranteed step-increases provided by the old General Sched ule (GS) system.

Where pay-for-performance must be provided, there must be performance evaluation systems in place. Departments and agencies without performance evaluation in place should not be allowed to hand out pay-for-performance rewards.

The OPM's administrators are apparently unable develop or guide the development of such performance appraisal systems for all federal job categories. Consequently, this difficult task is simply dumped on each federal agency and department to develop their own performance-evaluation systems according to their needs. Presently, there is no information available on how many federal agencies and departments hand out performance rewards arbitrarily to their cronies, without having proper performance-appraisal systems and performance standards in place. I doubt that this flagrant violation of basic merit principles and waste of taxpayers' money was what Congress had in mind when it authorized pay-forperformance legislation during the 1978 Civil Service Reform Act.

If one wants to provide pay-for-performance for employees, one should develop performance-evaluation systems for employees nationwide. There are groups of job categories for which performance is difficult to evaluate and rank. Possibly, these groups should continue to be paid according to the GS system. Further, payfor-performance should only be provided during each year where there was performance and only as a one-time, lump sum cash payout—a bonus. It should not automatically lead to a promotion, namely from pay-banding, that can be enjoyed for many years to come. This generates "grade-creep," preventing many qualified employees from being promoted.

We have already discussed some other downsides of pay banding. Employees performing at a satisfactory level should continue to receive step-increases, possibly stretching out to twenty or twenty-four years, instead of the eighteen years that is now common. Also, these step-increases could be smaller in size, leaving funds available for pay-for-performance rewards. Having less than ten steps within a grade is an idea worth considering. In order to simplify position classifications, having less than fifteen GS grades might also be an option.

Chapter 11
The Last Years

Struggling to Obtain Funding

Starting almost unnoticed around 1993 to 1994, it became more and more difficult for defense laboratories to obtain funding for basic and applied research. Even some development funds from the DOD had become scarce. To make it even harder, universities and private industry became very serious competitors for these funds. This left the defense laboratories with an even smaller piece of the pie.

During the Gulf War in 1991, the American military exhibited huge battlefield superiority—the same that they showed in Afghanistan and in 2003 in Iraq. In part, this superiority is a result of the research and development performed at military laboratories.

The shortage of funding for the defense laboratories, including the Center, caused them to lose highly qualified technical and scientific employees. I cannot stress enough what a major national tragedy this is. To lose these employees gravely affects the future defense and security of the United States. It is important to understand that in-house scientists from these laboratories give expert advice to the military on new and emerging technologies. Many of these scientists also evaluate proposals and monitor military government contracts given to universities and private industry. Government scientists can critically evaluate reports prepared by these contractors and determine how these programs are progressing. By visiting these contractors, the government scientists can make sure programs are on track and that taxpayers' money is not wasted. Without technically and scientifically knowledgeable employees to act as contract monitors, the government runs the risk of wasting billions of tax dollars.

During February of 1994, my branch head asked me to provide assistance in listing and classifying hazardous materials, mostly chemicals that had accumulated in the division's chemical inventory storage. Over many years, employees had accumulated many chemicals in their laboratories. All these chemicals were moved to the chemical storeroom when the employees either were transferred to other positions or retired. Over time, the division had accumulated over six thousand different chemicals, some of which were very old, and some that presented serious health and safety hazards. With many new environmental safety regulations in place, the cataloging and disposal of some of these chemicals as hazardous waste had become a complex procedure, involving considerable effort and paperwork. I could not escape the conclusion that my management had assigned me this dirty, unpleasant, low-level technician work to drive me to retire or quit. Many other employees and contractors could have performed this work just as easily.

By this time, I was starting to experience a backlash of reprisal actions from my management for having gone to the federal court in my attempt to press for fair work evaluation. On my performance evaluation form in 1994, there were time restrictions in percentages attached to each of my objectives, like writing papers for publication, working in the laboratory, and working on the inventory.

Using the $40,000 I had received from Dr. Schmidt, I performed some work in the laboratory. The ongoing experiments were exceptionally successful. I discovered a new absorption mechanism present in specific organic compounds called heterocyclics, which are compounds that have nitrogen substituted for some of their carbon atoms. Although their conventional absorption spectra compared to the unsubstituted compounds are very similar, the triplet absorption spectra of the heterocyclics are considerably weaker than unsubstituted compounds. This effect seems to result from vibronic spin-orbit interactions. This reduction of tripletabsorption intensity is of key importance to laser-dye improvement.

It suggests that by concentrating on heterocyclic compounds as laser dyes, one can ignore large groups of other organic compounds, with rings made entirely of carbon atoms, as having little potential as efficient laser dyes.

As I might have expected, I had a collision with management during my next performance evaluation six months later. I received a "marginal" performance rating. My management heavily criticized me for not keeping strictly to the time limits attached to each of my assigned objectives. I had never seen time limits on performance objectives. I had no doubt that my management was planning to rate my work "unsatisfactory" on successive evaluations to provide them with sufficient reason to remove me from my position. So I filed an age-discrimination and reprisal complaint with the Center's EEO Office. I believed my management was retaliating against me for my having filed various appeals.

After I had completed the experiments on heterocyclics, I submitted the resulting paper to *Applied Optics* in 1996, and it was published in 1997.

In 1996, I was forced to assume responsibility as my division's Hazardous Waste/Hazardous Material (HzW/HzM) coordinator. I was required to ensure that proper safety practices and procedures were properly implemented for the division's laboratories. In addition, I had to provide HzW/HzM training to division personnel; check all division laboratories weekly for safety violations, including the proper working of eyewashes and fire extinguishers; and make sure that all chemicals were properly labeled.

The EEOC investigator had gone to the personnel office and obtained the 1995 yearly performance-evaluation forms of all my coworkers in my branch. None of them had any time limits assigned to the objectives listed in their yearly performance-evaluation forms. I later dropped my EEOC complaint, because at that time I found myself under new management. Because my funding was intermittent, the time I was able to spend in the laboratory was also intermittent. Therefore, I did not complain about the chemical inventory assignment. It left me with some time to perform research, write research papers for publication in the open literature, and write proposals for obtaining future funding.

A huge loss for the laser-dye program—and for me—occurred when Professor Boyer died on December 10, 1996. One of the last complexes that Professor Boyer had mailed me in 1995 was an 8-ethyl-2, 6-dicyanotetrametyl-pyrromethene-complex. Trying to test this new laser dye in my small flash-lamp pumped dye laser, I obtained in conclusive and confusing results. It seemed that the power supply for the flash lamp in the small dye laser was not working. I was advised that I should replace the main components of the power supply, starting with the capacitor. However, this did not help. Then I ran out of funding. After I was able to obtain some funding from the U.S. Army MICOM, considerable time passed before the power supply could be repaired and was finally working properly. However, I was rewarded for my efforts. The new compound was an excellent laser dye. It showed exceptional photo stability when hexane, a liquid constituent in gasoline, was used as a solvent. I published these results in *Applied Optics* in 1998, also naming Professor Boyer and Dr. Sathyamoorthi as coauthors.

In the previous fifteen years, solid-state laser media, especially those pumped with laser diodes and laser-diode arrays, had experienced unprecedented advances in efficiency. These lasers are compact, user-friendly in the laboratory, and widely available commercially. However, solid-state lasers have serious scale-up limitations. Large solidx`-state laser media are difficult to fabricate with a high degree of optical homogeneity, and they are also expensive to produce. Because most of the pump light is converted into heat, the biggest problem for solid-state lasers results from the difficulty of removing excess heat from the solid medium, because transparent solid media are poor thermal dissipaters. Overheating often results in permanent damage to the solid. Therefore, large laser systems generating high-energy and high average power outputs are either gas (including chemical) or liquid dye lasers. Flowing gases or liquids through a heat exchanger can efficiently cool these laser media. Regarding their scaling potential as laser media, it seems that practically all gas and chemical lasers have been extensively studied. Although dye lasers have been with us for more than thirty-five years, they constitute one of the few unfinished fields of laser physics. Dye lasers employing high-efficiency laser dyes and pumped with large flash lamps or laser diode arrays possess up-scaling potential, because by simply circulating the dye solution, they can be efficiently cooled.

Using the repaired dye lasers, I began testing the photo stability of several new pyrromethene dyes. I presented the resulting data presented at an SPIE conference in 1998 and published the results in *Proceeding SPIE* in 1999. By this time, I was considered the leading expert on the relationship between laser-dye structure and their spectroscopic properties.

In February of 1998, I received $75,000 from the U.S. Army MICOM for my project, allowing me to spend considerable time in the laboratory.

On January 28, 1999, I received the Center's 1997 Publication of the Year Award for the best publication in the open literature in recognition of the paper on heterocyclics that I had published in 1997 in *Applied Optics*. The Center's technical director stated in his citation:

I am pleased to present you with the Publication of the Year Award for 1997. The article titled "Spectroscopy and Molecular Structure of Efficient Laser Dyes: Vibronic Spin-Orbit Interactions in Heterocyclics" was determined to be the top publication for 1997 in Category 5, Articles in the Open Literature. Formal reporting of technical work is a fundamental precept in the scientific and engineering profession, and publications are one of the most important products of SSC Diego. Your publication attests to your professionalism in your field. You are commended for your fine work and for the contribution you have made to SSC San Diego and to the Navy.

-R.C. Kolb[75]

A committee of employees had evaluated and ranked the different Center publications categories on a yearly basis. These categories include technical notes, conference proceedings, and open-literature publications. This committee consists solely of Center employees—no management. The 1997 award was for the publication detailing my experiments in 1995, the same year I had received the "marginal" rating. In our library, I found the 1996 demo attitude survey, which contained the performance ratings of Center's employees. During 1995, only two among all the Center's three thousand workers received "marginal" ratings. It appeared that I was one of the two failures, thus proving that managerial ratings under the demo are truly based on social preferences, not merit.

During my workdays at the Center, I visited the technical library at least once a week to keep up with advances in scientific fields that were of interest to me. In the early days, many employees, including management, often went to the library. Over the years, management's presence there shrunk.

During my last years there, hardly any of the Center's employees could ever be found in the library. During one of my visits to the Center's library in November 1999, an article in *Nature* caught my attention. It was a report on East Germany, where I had spent the years after World War II. The author reported on the progress that the East German science community had made after ten years of reunification. When the Wende (change) in East Germany came, only limited research was performed at the universities.

The East Germans had followed the example of the Russian universities. Most of the research effort was being conducted at their overstuffed Academies of Sciences. Consequently, the universities had to be aligned with Western standards, causing considerable reorganization. In addition, the universities, as well as the Academies of Sciences, had to be cleaned of ardent communist followers as well as from Stasi (East German KGB) informers. The article included an interview with an East German professor from the University of Leipzig. This professor complained about the unfair treatment he had received because he had not joined the Communist Party. He stated that Communist Party members were promoted to the grade of professor after five years. However, the ones who did not join the party had to wait twenty-one years.[76]

I was much inclined to write to this professor and tell him that he really was not that bad off and should not complain too much; at that time, I had worked thirty-four years for the U.S. Navy and had never been promoted, nor was there a chance that I ever would be.

Between 1993 and 2002, I had written a large number of proposals for my laser-dye project and submitted them to several agencies, including the Office of Naval Research (ONR), the Defense Advanced Research Project Agency (DARPA), the Ballistic Missile Defense office (BM D), and the Kirtland Air Force Base project office, all without success. I learned that most of the support in lasers was geared toward high average-power solid-state lasers.

In 1998, Mr. W. Friday, from the U.S. Army MICOM, and I visited Professor H. Freeman, from the University of North Carolina at Raleigh, to discuss a laser-dye development program. The U.S. Army MICOM would fund this program. During our visit at the university, Professor Freeman suggested that I write a review paper on laser dyes. Using some of my old proposals, I wrote a lengthy review paper with the title "Laser Dyes: Their Structure and Spectroscopic Properties," which was published in 2000 in *Colorants for NonTextile Applications*. Unfortunately, MICOM was unable to come up with any funding for the proposed joint program.

Dr. R. Scheps, a laser physicist also working at the Center, informed me in April 2001 that he had $45,000 available for my dye-laser project. He informed me that he could provide me with full funding for the entire fiscal year of 2001. He further suggested that I invest some time in writing a review paper on the pyrromethene laser dyes. I agreed, and it was entitled "Scaling of Dye Lasers with Improved Laser Dyes." Many applications in industry, research, and medicine require large laser systems. Especially for the near-UV, visible, and near-IR portion of the spectrum, we still lack laser systems that provide inexpensive, highenergy, and high-average power outputs. For this spectral region, I had proposed to use large dye lasers and improved laser dyes as the active media to be pumped by large flash lamps.

Again, I started with one of my proposals that had failed to find support. The review paper was published in 2002 in *Progress in Quantum Electronics*. I studied some nitrogen heterocyclics of phenanthrene and obtained interesting results that supported my results on the anthracene heterocyclics. The results were published in the *Journal of Photochemistry and Photobiology: Chemistry A* in 2002.

Among the large pile of proposals I had written to obtain funding, I had suggested using blue/green high-energy dye lasers for underwater illumination for deep-sea search, salvage, and other applications. Developing a high-efficiency blue/green laser dye for these dye lasers had been the last goal I had set for myself. From these proposals, I had sufficient material to write a paper, which was published in 2002 in the *Naval Engineers Journal*. In 2002, I had published three lengthy papers in the open literature. Although the total number of employees' open-literature publications had declined drastically at the Center, I received only a "satisfactory" performance rating for that year.

Retirement

The decline in research funding at the Center had also affected the library, with the number of journals and magazines subscriptions falling over the years. Many of the standard American scientific and technical journals were missing due to their high prices. Among the physics journals, *Physical Review D, Physics Letters B*, and *Nuclear Physics B* became unavailable. This prevented me from searching these journals for publications on the limits of the special theory of relativity, which was still my private obsession. It was healthy for me to avoid the steady disappointment that my work had not generated any interest.

In November 2001, all employees received an e-mail from the Center's library. The head librarian informed employees that the library now had electronic journals available. Through the internet, hundreds of scientific journals were now accessible to the Center's employees. This included many journals that had disappeared from the library shelves during the last ten to fifteen years. I could not help but check the *Physical Review D* and *Physics Letters B*, both of which published papers on theoretical physics on the STR.

Reading some of the titles and abstracts of STR articles published in these journals, I took one of the biggest mental rollercoaster rides of my life. I was lifted high up and then came crashing down. Never in my life had I expected to see physics publications that carried titles containing "Lorentz Violations" (also referred to as "Breakdown of Lorentz Invariance," the title of my own work on the STR) or similar titles. Some of the titles and abstracts contained "dispersion relations, or superluminalvelocities" and related phrases that had been used in my paper. For a considerable time, I did not know if I was just dreaming or if this was real. Over the last ten years or so, completely unknown to me, physicists had started to reexamine the general validity of the STR. Lorentz violations had become one of the most studied subjects in theoretical physics. This new physics seemed even stranger than the STR. However, I received a jolt checking the references of these papers. Nowhere was my 1967 paper ever mentioned. Because so much time had passed since the publications of my papers, the new generations of physicists were completely unaware of the existence of my work

Nevertheless, I was content. The fact that my work was not mentioned in the references of the newer publications did not affect me much. With time, this could be corrected. I only needed one author to mention my paper in his references to become known to the physics community interested in Lorentz violations.

Because these papers carried the addresses of the authors and sometimes also noted their e-mail addresses, I contacted several of them. At work, I again tried to obtain funding for my laser-dye improvement project. However, there was no funding available for fiscal year 2003. In addition, my main instrument, the CW ion argon/krypton laser tube, burned out. The flash lamps of my small dye-test laser had also burned out. Without funding, I could replace neither the laser tube nor the flash lamps. This put an end to the work I was able to perform in my laboratory.

I had no hope that this shortage of funding would turn around in the near future. I was again assigned my old job as HzM/ HzM coordinator for the division. Because of my blue/green laser dye project's uncertain future, I retired from my position with the navy at the end of February 2003. Sometime during 2004, Professor T. Jacobson from the University of Maryland, who works on Lorentz violations, contacted me by e-mail. He informed me that he and his coworkers had included my 1967 paper in the references of their next publication to appear in the June 15, 2003 issue of the *Physical Review D*.

Some of my readers may wonder why I stayed so long with the navy and did not quit. In retrospect, and having recovered from the pain of old wounds, I hold no grudges. I immensely enjoyed all the years at the Center when I was able to perform basic research. Of course, it would have been nicer if I could have done more research, but it also could have been much worse.

During my thirty-seven years at the Center, I authored and coauthored over fifty-seven papers in the open literature. In short, I had set a very specific agenda for what I wanted to accomplish at the Center, and I did it. I also valued the camaraderie with my coworkers, and living in San Diego, with its blue skies, is paradise.

During the last ten years, I had suffered through shortages in research funding. However, this shortage was a widespread trend that had its origin in the Pentagon and in Congress. Instead of directing sufficient research funding into the Pentagon, Congress is directing more and more funding to industry and universities. This also affected many of my scientist coworkers. Despite this, a question still nags at me: how many others would want to work for the federal government under the conditions I have described in this book?

Dysfunctional Department
of Homeland Security

When I retired in the beginning of 2003, the DHS had become a reality. While writing this book, I heard many reports on TV and read even more in the newspapers on the poor performance of this department. This event compelled me to add the following section. There is an urgent need to resolve the American civil service crisis as soon as possible.

In August 2005, the Federal Emergency Management Agency (FEMA), now under the supervision of the DHS, mishandled the aftermath of the destruction caused by Hurricane Katrina in New Orleans and a long the Gulf Coast.

In 2001, Congress had finally mandated the OPM to conduct employee attitude surveys biannually. The first report was published in 2002 under the title "Federal Human Capital Survey." The OPM mailed survey forms to federal employees in all departments and agencies. About a hundred thousand employees responded.

The second survey took place between August and December 2004, with the DHS participating for the first time. Over 147,000 employees from thirty agencies and departments completed the survey forms. The evaluation and analysis of the survey were published in 2005 and are available on the internet. On the first page of the report, OPM Acting Director Dan G. Blair summarized the survey results in his message to employees. In addition to some other observations, he made the following critical statements:

> *Last fall, we asked federal employees across the nation and around the world to tell us how well agencies manage their most important resource- their human capitol. There is a strong perception that excellent performance is not properly recognized and that action is not taken against poor performers. Further, federal agencies have more work to do to increase employees' confidence in the leadership they receive. These results provide federal leaders with the information and guidance necessary to act on the results and build a strong*

framework to support the president's human capital initiative and his management agenda.[77]

For many years, the OPM had considered management its most important federal human capital resource, eagerly listening and supporting management as they deliberately demolished merit principles. Suddenly, apparently trying to be fashionable, Mr. Blair stated in his message that the federal workforce's most important human capital was its employees.

This indicates that there must be something very wrong with the OPM, since they still do not get the message. For gross mismanagement, the only advice Mr. Blair has to give management is to use the collected information for "guidance." At the DHS, we still have the same incompetent federal "clerk-type" management in place that is responsible for many past, present, and, most likely, future catastrophes.

Whenever you have a bureaucracy where employees feel that excellent performance is not recognized and action is not taken against poor performers, you have a communist-style bureaucracy. As I have demonstrated in detail, in order to enhance their job security, many federal managers protect poor performers and discourage good performers from working for the federal bureaucracy.

It did not dawn on Mr. Blair that it is past time for housecleaning; it is time to hold in competent managers fully accountable for their mismanagement

The Center for American Progress (CAP) is a nonpartisan research and educational institute dedicated to promoting a strong, just, and free America that ensures opportunity for all. Recently, the CAP used the above OPM survey results to provide an analysis of attitudes in thirty federal departments and agencies. Significantly, the OPM survey also used input from DHS employees, who provided ten thousand responses.

The CAP's article on its findings, by Scott Lilly, carried the subtitle "What a Recent Government Survey Tells Us about

Our Efforts to Protect Ourselves against Terrorist Attacks and Respond to Natural Disasters." This report is available on the internet, and I strongly recommend studying the entire report.

The OPM attitude survey asked seventy-eight questions that covered a wide range of employee concerns. The answers present a rich source of information. For example, four questions were concerned with employee job satisfaction from the thirty agencies and departments surveyed. This survey provided answers on the best and worst agencies and departments:

> Q8.   *I recommended my organization as a good place to work.*

> Q11. *How would you rate your organization as a place to work compared to other organizations?*

> Q67. *Considering everything, how satisfied are you with your organization?*

> Q69. *Considering everything, how satisfied are you with your job?*[78]

If 100 percent of employees ranked their workplace "very good" with the above four questions, the agency or department would have received a ranking of 100. Most highly ranked was NASA at 72; followed by the National Science Foundation (NSF), 71; and the General Service Administration (GSA), 68. The worst four places to work were Education Department (EDU), 43; the Department of Transportation (DOT), 38; the Small Business Administration (SBA), 35; and, significantly, the DHS, with a rating of only 20—dead last.

In ratings resulting from other questions, the DHS ranked last the most often out of all thirty agencies under review. It also had the most next-to-last place rankings of all the agencies, and it landed in 28th place on seven more questions. DHS employees ranked the performance of their leadership as abysmal. Out of the eighteen questions concerned with leadership, the DHS was ranked last in fourteen areas. They were second from last in three, and third from last in two.

> The CAP states: *But even the least negative of the two sets of results is devastating in its implication about how well government has taken on the important job of protecting the country against attack and preparing for the aftermath if an attack takes place.*[78] The CAP further states: *Managers at DHS appear to have failed completely in developing any level of constructive rapport with their agency workforce. The level of employee discontent evidenced by the survey creates the type of situation in which those federal workers with the highest skill levels, who are the most attractive to other employers, are likely to leave the department and perhaps the federal work force.*[78]

Because of the disastrous results obtained from the DHS survey, the CAP suggested revising civilian personnel rules:

> *One of the demands which the Bush administration made in establishing the new department was that administrators be given much greater power and flexibility and that a number of the rules protecting the rights of employees should be waived. Whatever one might think about the merits of these proposals in theory, it is painfully obvious that the enhanced administrative authority that was granted to departmental administrators was handled poorly, not only to the detriment of DHS employees, but the public and, in particular, the taxpayer as well.*[78]

Nobody should be too surprised about the revulsion expressed by employees working for the DHS, and one must wonder how well the DHS will be able to fulfill its mission in the future. The demoralized DHS employees feel that there is something very wrong by following the China Lake demo introduced on the OPM's advice.

Nevertheless, in October 2005, the Congressional Government Reform Committee conducted hearings on the administration's proposal, "Working for America." This proposal attempts to make the DHS and DOD's personnel system, which was modeled after the navy's demo, the personnel system of the entire federal government.

Appendices

1. The Special Theory of Relativity

Albert Einstein was born in 1879 in Ulm, Germany, and died in 1955 in Princeton, New Jersey. In 1900, he completed his studies at the EidgenÖssige Technische Hochschule (Swiss Confederate Institute of Technology) in ZÜrich. After completing his studies, he worked as a patent examiner for the Swiss Patent Office in Bern. It was during this time that he formulated his special theory of relativity (STR), performed studies on Brownian motion, and explained the photoelectric effect by claiming that light consists of particles (light quanta). All three important papers were published in 1905 in the *Annalen der Physik*.

Einstein occupied faculty positions in Bern, ZÜrich, Prague, and Berlin before he was appointed as director of the Kaiser Wilhelm Institute in Berlin. In 1921, he received the Nobel Prize. Interestingly, Einstein did not receive the Nobel for his contributions to the STR but for explaining the photoelectric effect. With the Nazis coming to power in Germany, he left for the United States and became a member of the Institute for Advanced Study at Princeton, in 1933.

Generally, Einstein is given credit for formulating the STR, although Poincaré, Lorentz, and others contributed bits and pieces of this theory. Both Poincaré and Lorentz derived the so-called Lorentz transformations. Einstein's main contribution to this theory was the formulation of two basic postulates:

(1) The speed of light, c (c = 300,000 km per second), is

independent of the motion (speed v) of the light source and the observer.

(2) The laws of physics are the same in all inertial frames.

From the above two rather simple postulates, all the accomplishments of Einstein's discovery could be derived, including the Lorentz transformations. Inertial frames are a fundamental concept of physics. This concept states that inertial frames are all equivalent. A physicist inside a closed box that is moving with constant velocity is not able to determine experimentally his velocity.

In classical physics, for two observers moving at the constant speed v relative to each other we have: $x^1 = x-v\,t$, with t = time. However, in the STR, this simple relationship is replaced by the Lorentz transformations. A crucial experiment conducted in 1887 by Michelson and Morley showed that the velocity of light, c, is independent of the speed of the observer. Many other experiments also show that the STR holds up well in experiments. When an electron is accelerated in particle accelerators to speeds very close to the speed of light, c, one obtains the correct increase of its mass as a function of the electrons' speed. According to the STR, the mass of an electron should go to infinity when the speed of the electron reaches the speed of light, c. The STR forced a rethinking of classical mechanics. There are two remarkable results of the STR:

(a) The famous equation $E = mc^2$ (E = energy, m = mass), which Einstein derived from relativistic mechanics.

(b) Nothing can move faster than the speed of light.

The general theory of relativity deals with accelerated inertial frames.

An observer inside a closed box, far out in space, can determine if he is accelerated or not. However, his acceleration might also be the effect of gravity. Experimentally, he cannot distinguish which force is responsible for his acceleration. This brings gravitation into the picture, with the results that space is curved.

Einstein's theory of general relativity was published in 1915 and 1916. This theory is viewed as one of the greatest accomplishments in physics. The STR and quantum mechanics are the pillars of modern physics. Together, they describe a large portion of our physical world.

After quantum mechanics, relativistic quantum mechanics was developed. This theory is used to describe high-energy physics. Predictions of relativistic quantum mechanics had many experimental triumphs. However, despite the efforts of the most talented theoretical physicists, relativistic quantum mechanics has not been able to calculate the masses of elementary particles, like the electron, proton, neutron, and so on. Although the masses of many elementary particles are listed in dictionaries, these values have been obtained from experiments. A theory that would allow us to calculate the masses of elementary particles would be one of humankind's greatest achievements.

2. Quantum Mechanics

By studying the riddle of the so-called black body radiation, physicists discovered quantum mechanics. A black body is a cavity with a small hole. Inside the cavity, the surface is colored black. Black surfaces efficiently absorb all colors of light. Any radiation entering through the small hole is absorbed practically 100 percent due to multiple scattering inside the cavity. When in equilibrium with its surroundings, a black body also emits radiation of all wavelengths.

Physicists performing early experiments with black bodies measured the wavelength distribution of the emitted radiation. They observed a definite intensity maximum. With increasing temperature, the intensity maximum of the emitted radiation moves to shorter wavelengths. Theoretically, Wien had derived a relation that connected the spectral location of the radiation maximum with the temperature of the black body. However, this did not describe the entire black-body radiation curve.

In 1900, Max Planck (1858-1947), a German physicist, tried to derive a theoretical expression for the experimentally measured radiation curve. However, he succeeded only when he introduced a new constant, h (called Max Planck's constant, in his honor), into physics. He stated that an oscillator, like an oscillating electron with frequency v, could only absorb or emit discrete levels of energy quanta E_n, $E_n = n h v$, with n = 1, 2, 3,... m, and h = 6.626 x 10^{-34} Joules seconds.

Max Planck is considered the founder of quantum mechanics. Things really became strange in 1923, when the French physicist Louis de Broglie wondered whether, because light had the properties of both waves and particles, it was possible that particles such as electrons could also have wave properties like light.

Davisson and Germer performed an experiment in 1927 at Bell Laboratories to investigate this idea. They reflected slow electrons from a surface of nickel. The reflected electrons formed a pattern that would only be observed if the stream of electrons had wave properties. Physicists and chemists had known for a long time that atoms and molecules exhibit unique spectra. When vaporized, atoms and molecules absorb and emit light often in sharp, spectral lines. Explaining the existence of these lines posed a difficult problem for physics. Observing sharp lines suggest that they result from discrete energy levels (E_n) present in atoms and molecules.

Niels Bohr, in 1913, was able to provide a simplified quantummechanical theory that made it possible to calculate the spectral lines of the simplest atom, hydrogen. However, quantum mechanics did not advance significantly until the 1920s when Werner Heisenberg and Erwin Schrodinger discovered how to calculate the energy levels of other atoms and molecules.

Heisenberg was born in Germany in 1901. He studied physics at the University of Munich, and was awarded a PhD in 1923. He spent several years at the University of Göttingen, working as an assistant to Professor Born. There, he developed quantum (matrix) mechanics in 1925. The uncertainty principle that carries his name is one of the most significant contributions to physics. In 1932, he received the Nobel Prize in physics.

During this time, Göttingen became the international center for quantum mechanics. Many American physicists who were later associated with the Manhattan Project, which developed the atomic bomb, spent some time studying in Göttingen. This included J. Robert Oppenheimer and Edward Teller.

Another key figure in the development of quantum (wave) mechanics was Erwin Schrodinger. Born in 1887 in Vienna, Schrodinger was intrigued by de Broglie's suggestion that particles may also possess wavelike properties. He reasoned that there must exist a wave equation that describes the wavelike behavior of particles. His four papers published during 1926 constitute one of the most important contributions to physics. In the first paper, he published his famous wave equation, which was later named after him. In the last paper, he showed that quantum (wave) mechanics and quantum (matrix) mechanics are equivalent. In 1933, he received the Nobel Prize with Paul Dirac, a British physics professor.

3. Fluorescence

Human eyes can recognize light, a very small portion between 400 to 700 nm (nano meter) of the electromagnetic spectrum. This range is also called the visible spectrum. At shorter wavelengths, the electromagnetic spectrum is called ultraviolet (UV) radiation and is followed by X-rays and gamma rays. On the other side, at longer wavelengths, the infrared (IR) spectrum starts and is followed by microwaves and then radio waves. Fluorescence has been known for considerable time. When one illuminates minerals and gemstones with UV light, sometimes visible radiation is emitted. This radiation is called fluorescence. When the UV illumination is cut off, fluorescence almost immediately disappears, indicating the short lifetime of this type of radiation.

With advances in chemistry, scientists observed that all atoms and molecules absorb infrared, visible, and ultraviolet light. Each atom or molecule possesses its own characteristic absorption spectrum. Every element or compound absorbs light differently than every other element or compound. Studies have shown that the nuorescence of organic molecules depends on their chemical structure and the environment in which the fluorescence spectra are measured.

When organic compounds are illuminated in solution with, for example, UV light, compounds may exhibit fluorescence. This discovery prompted the question: Why do some compounds show fluorescence but not others? Obviously, the excitation energy absorbed by some molecules is converted into heat (radiation less transitions). Not all aspects of radiation less deactivation of organic molecules are understood.

At the Max Planck Institute, I also tried to measure the so-called quantum-fluorescence yields of organic compounds. These yields are a measure of how much light energy has been converted into heat. These yields are the quotient formed by the number of light quanta emitted as fluorescence relative to the number of light quanta absorbed by the organic compound. Unfortunately, this proved to be an exceptionally difficult experiment. Even today, there is a lack of data.

Most illuminated organic compounds exhibit photo decomposition to various degrees. Their molecular structure changes, with the molecules either breaking up or undergoing a chemical reaction with the solvent. All these observations raise many questions. What is the precise mechanism that causes for organic compounds to decompose? The science of photochemistry studies all these questions.

4. Pressure-Broadening of Mercury Lines

In physics and chemistry, cells, especially optical cells, are widely used. A battery is an electric cell. Optical cells are used to measure the absorption spectra of liquids, like an organic compound. These cells have two windows arranged parallel to each other. The liquid fills the space between the two windows, allowing a light to pass through the liquid.

When small amounts of liquid mercury are placed into an optical quartz cell under a vacuum, some of the mercury evaporates. Passing light through this cell, one observes the narrow mercury absorption lines. When gasses like nitrogen or helium are introduced, one observes a slight broadening of the mercury-absorption lines due to the interaction of the mercury atoms with the fill gas. When the pressure of the fill gas is increased, the mercury-absorption lines are further broadened, due to increased interactions. New mercury absorption lines appear next to the broadened mercury lines under very high pressures.

During the 1950s, there was considerable interest in making the connection between experimental observations and theoretical predictions. Mercury atoms in a vacuum present an undisturbed quantum mechanical system. Introducing a gas will perturb the originally undisturbed system. Increasing the gas pressure means more perturbation. Going to high gas pressures simulates a situation in which mercury atoms are imbedded in a solid. Does the used quantum mechanical perturbation theory describe all these observation, or are refinements on these perturbation theories necessary?

5. Early Copying Methods

Around 1956, there was a demand for a simple method of making copies from photographic negatives without going through the photographic copying process, which would have required using chemical developing solutions. The new copying material we studied consisted of a thin sheet of transparent Mylar covered on one side with another thin transparent film. This film contained a diazonium compound consisting of molecules that contained a pair of nitrogen atoms connected by triple bonds. A positive copy of the negative film is produced in two steps. First, one puts the photographic negative on top of such a film and exposes these films to UV light. In the exposed parts of the Mylar film, the diazonium molecules decompose, producing gaseous nitrogen, which is dissolved in the film. When the film is heated, the nitrogen gases form a huge number of small bubbles that reproduce the positive image. The aggregation of these small bubbles causes multiple scattering of light. However, the formed images have a low optical contrast because light is only scattered among the bubbles, rather than absorbed.

I found a method to increase the optical densities of the Mylar films. Higher optical densities could be obtained by adding a tiny amount of a light-absorbing dye to the film. Light would now experience considerable absorption with multiple scattering from the many tiny bubbles.

6. Phosphorescence and Triplet-Triplet Absorption

Phosphorescence emission is produced at a somewhat longer wavelength than fluorescence for a given compound. The emission lifetime of phosphorescence is considerably longer than that of fluorescence. Phosphorescence is related to the so-called triplet state of organic compounds. Generally, phosphorescence is not observed from organic compounds in liquid solution, because energetic solvent molecules efficiently deactivate molecules in their triplet state. However, in solid solutions—that is, a glasslike solution like frozen ethanol, phosphorescence is often observed.

Most organic compounds have their outer orbital occupied by two electrons, with their spins aligned antiparallel to each other. This means that electrons spin clockwise and counterclockwise. Absorption of light will excite one electron into a higher energy level, and the excited electron maintains its spin orientation. This process is called the "singlet-singlet" absorption. After being excited into higher energy levels, the electron returns to the first excited state without radiation, and its excessive energy is converted into heat. From the first excited singlet state, the electron can return to the ground state by either emitting fluorescence or radiation less. Significantly, from the excited first singlet state, the electron may switch its spin orientation and become aligned parallel to the spin of the other electron. This switching of spin orientation is due to socalled spin-orbit interactions. With this type of spin alignment, the molecule is now in what is called the triplet state. In this state, the molecule can be excited into higher triplet energy levels, referred to as "triplet-triplet" absorption.

In the triplet state, molecules have different chemical and physical properties. For example, the triplet-triplet absorption spectra will be different from the conventional, singlet-singlet absorption. Further, most photochemical decomposition involves molecules in their triplet state.

From the lowest triplet state, the molecule may return to the ground state radiation less, or, when in the solid state, phosphorescence may be emitted. However, from the triplet state, the return to the ground singlet state must switch its electron's spin orientation. According to Pauli's principle, two electrons having the same spin orientation cannot occupy the same orbital. Because the spin switching is time-dependent, triplet-state molecules have a rather long lifetime compared to the lifetime of singlet-state molecules. Triplet-state molecules are referred to as "meta-stable"—or "transient"—because they return to the original ground singlet state by flipping their spins.

The most important photochemical reaction on earth

involves the triplet-state of chlorophyll. It makes life possible on Earth. Chlorophyll is the green substance present in leaves. The chlorophyll molecules absorb sunlight and this energy is used to photosynthesize carbohydrates and oxygen from carbon dioxide and water.

7. Lasers

"Laser" stands for "Light Amplification by Stimulated Emission of Radiation." Lasers consist of three parts: the gain, or the active medium; the pump source, delivering the energy to excite the active medium; and the optical resonator. The resonator, also referred to as the cavity, consists of two mirrors. One is called the high reflector, possessing almost 100 percent reflectivity. The other is the output coupler, possessing some transmission for the laser light. The pump source could be another laser, an electric discharge, or a flash lamp. The gain medium could be a gas (gas laser), a liquid (mostly dye lasers), or a solid (solid-state lasers). The gain medium is positioned between the two mirrors.

For example, a dye solution positioned within a laser cavity and pumped with a flash lamp will first excite electrons from its ground energy state into higher energy levels. These electrons will decay radiation less to the first excited state. From the first excited state they will decay into the ground emitting fluorescence in all directions.

However, some fluorescence will also be emitted in the direction of the two laser mirrors. This fluorescence light is reflected back into the gain medium, interacting with electrons occupying the first excited singlet state of dye molecules. This interaction will stimulate these excited electrons to combine their energy with the fluorescence light quant, lengthening the pulse duration. These increases of pulse length are the beginning of coherent radiation. Every time the electromagnetic pulse passes through gain medium, it is reflected back by the mirrors into the medium. The electromagnetic pulse gains in energy and becomes more monochromatic.

8. Integrated Optics

All around us light is reflected from surfaces, including glass plates and from mirrors.

A light beam hitting the interface of an air/glass-plate will be partially reflected from the glass surface, the rest will enter the glass. When hitting the other glass-plate/air interface, some light will be reflected back into the glass-plate, the rest will enter the air.

Similarly, a light beam originating within the glass-plate will split when hitting glass-plate/air interface. One part will pass into air; the rest will be back reflected into the glass-plate. Significantly, a light beam hitting this interface at a certain small angle will be reflected back into the glass, without any light exiting its surface. This is called total reflection. This happens because the index of refraction of glass is larger than the index of refraction of air. Again, the light will be reflected back into the glass, when the light hits the other glass-plate/air interface. The light is now zigzagging within the glass plate.

Similarly, optical fibers consist of two parts: namely the core and the cladding. The cladding is wrapped around the core. The core has a higher index of refraction than does the cladding. An optical signal coupled into the optical core at a sufficiently small angle zigzags within the core. This causes the light signal to propagate through the fiber.

The materials used for fibers must be of very high optical quality, meaning they must have exceptionally small absorption rates at the wave length of the optical signal in order for the signal to be transmitted over long distances without being absorbed within the fiber.

Notes

1. K.C. James, "A Fresh Start for Federal Pay: The Case for Modernization," OPM Report 2002.
2. S.E. Ambrose, "American Heritage: New History of WWII," Viking 1997.
3. Dr. S. Goudsmit's letter of October 4, 1965.
4. Dr. W.E. Parry's letter of October 16, 1965.
5. Dr. S. Goudsmit's letter of November 30, 1966.
6. T.G. Pavlopoulos, Physical Review 159, 1106-1110, 1967.
7. D.W. Udell's memo of September 12, 1969, Subject: Promotion justification—Information on.
8. President J. Carter's Federal Civil Service Reform Message to the Congress, March 2, 1978.
9. Merit System Principles, Title 5, U.S. Code 2301.
10. MSPB Report, "Adherence to Merit Principles in the Workplace: Federal Employees' Views,"1996.
11. FPM (Federal Personnel Manual) Chapter 511, 1-1. The General Schedule Classification System.
12. FPM Chapter 511, 3-2. Mandatory use of Standards.
13. U.S. CSC Research Grade Evaluation Guide, 1964.
14. W. N. Rudman, "The Legal Ties that Bind," Government Executive, March 1998.
15. FPM Chapter 511, 4-5. Periodic Review of Descriptions and Classification.
16. NELC Calendar, November 21, 1975.
17. R.R. Kraatz's memo of May 26, 1976, Subject: High-Grade Situation at NELC.
18. W.R. Riley's memo of June 27, 1977, Subject: Factor Evaluation System (FES) Requires new Position Description Format
19. WFDOCP Report of January 1978.
20. R.R. Gavazzi's memo of May 5, 1978, Subject: Position Management Review and Classification.
21. R.R. Gavazzi's memo of May 19, 1978, Subject: Position Management Review and Classification Survey of High Grade Positions.

22. R.R. Gavazzi's memo of May 19, 1978, Subject: Request for Demotion Delay.
23. Department of Defense Directive #14900.26 of July 28, 1978.
24. L.T. Rickwa, memo of March 12, 1979, Subject: Review of NOSC Classification Results.
25. NRL Instruction 12340.4 of March 20, 1978, Subject: Performance Appraisal and Promotion of Professionals in the Research Directory.
26. Title 5, U.S. Code 4701.
27. H.E. Drayton's memo of March 20, 1979, Subject: Classification Survey of High Grade Positions.
28. "An Integrated Approach to Pay, Performance, and Position Classification for More Effective Operation of Government Organizations," Federal Register, Vol. 45, No.77, April 18, 1980.
29. D.J. Wilcox's memo of May 7, 1981, Subject: Classification Reconsideration.
30. NOSCINST 14000.2, Level IV Scientist, September 25, 1980.
31. Call for FY 2000 Independent Research Proposals.
32. Hearings Before the Subcommittee of Civil Service, Post Office, and General Services, Committee on Governmental Affairs, U.S. Senate, 99th Congress, Second Session (San Diego), 1986, U.S. Printing Office.
33. H.R. Talkington's memo of July 16, 1987, Subject: Classification Reconsideration.
34. R.M. Hillyer's memo of December 8, 1985, Subject: Invention Identification and Reporting.
35. R.M. Hillyer's memo of August 13, 1987, Subject: NOSC Formal Reporting.
36. H.O. Porter's memo of April 18, 1989, Subject: DP-IV Criteria.
37. EEO Counselor's Report of August 24, 1989.
38. Promotion Nomination (1) in 1989.
39. Promotion Nomination (2) in 1989.
40. Promotion Nomination (3) in 1989.
41. R.M. Hillyer's memo of July 10, 1990, Subject: FY90 Publications by NOSC Scientists and Engineers.
42. R. Bennion's memo of May 21, 1991, Subject: Demonstration Project Classification Appeal of Dr. T.G. Pavlopoulos.
43. NOSCINST 14000.2B, Level IV Scientist, January 7, 1987.
44. CPI (Civilian Personnel Instruction) 335 OPNAVINSTR 12000.14 CH-7.
45. NOSCINST 14000.2 Level IV Manager/Supervisor (Professional), 25 September, 1980.
46. Excerpts from the EEOC Hearing, November 20 to December 2, 1992.
47. E-mail of August 8, 1994 to all the Center's employees, Subject: Hotline-Secretaries.

48. Naval Command, Control and Ocean Surveillance Center's Mission Statement, NRaD Brief of July 1993.

49. Financial Handbook (A Definition of Terms), Technical Document #1695, Naval Ocean System Center.

50. R.B. Rothman, Brief of February 1, 1993, submitted to the U.S. District Court, Southern District of California.

51. R.B. Rothman, Stipulation of November 29, 1993, Submitted to the U.S. District Court, Southern District of California.

52. T.K. Dowd, letter of January 6, 1994, addressed to Mr. R. Johnson, OPM.

53. R. B. Rothman, letter of January 25, 1994, addressed to Mr. R. Johnson, OPM.

54. Position Description of Theodore Pavlopoulos.

55. R.L. Johnson's Classification Advisory of March 25, 1994.

56. OPM FPM Bulletin No. 511-33, Subject: Intra-Agency Classification Consistency, September 15, 1992.

57. NRaD Outlook, "Demonstration Project Made Permanent," November 4, 1994.

58. The Navy's Demonstration Project as a Model for the Proposed Reform of the Federal Civil Service: A Report on How the Project Works in Theory and Practice, January 30, 1995.

59. Senator D. Pryor's letter of February 15, 1995.

60. MSPB Survey "Working for America: An Update," July 1994.

61. MSPB Survey, "The Federal Merit Promotion Program," 2001.

62. R. Goodrich, "Self Serving Managers," letter to Federal Times, August 9, 1999.

63. MSPB Report, "Federal Supervisors and Poor Performers," 1999.

64. T. Pickering and G. Brokaw, "Building High-Performance Organizations for the Twenty-First Century," Commonwealth Center for High Performance Organizations, Inc., Charlottesville, VA (Unpublished Participant Text).

65. Outlook, of September 27, 2002.

66. An e-mail from Captain Tim Flynn, SPAWAR, November 2, 2002, Subject: SSC SD and DOD Transformation.

67. D. Pasternak, "Lack of Intelligence," U.S. News and World Report, August 11, 2003.

68. R. Kohler, "The Declining of the National Reconnaissance Office," Studies in Intelligence, Vol. 46, 13-20, 2002.

69. MSPB Report, "Recommendation for Change," Executive Summary, September 3, 2002.

70. S. Zeller, "Smashing the System," Government Executive, November 2003.

71. P.C. Light, "Great Expectations," Government Executive, April 2003.
72. J. Solomon, "FBI Didn't Seek to Hire Terror Experts," Associated Press, June 19, 2005.
73. OPM Fiscal Year 2002 Performance & Accountability Report.
74. A.C. Hyde, "Federal Human Resource Employment Trends," OPM Reports, Issue-21-4.
75. R.C. Kolb, Citation of January 28, 1999, Subject: 1997 Publication of the Year Award.
76. A. Abbott, "Tough Measures Bring a Scarred Science Back to the World Stage." Nature 401, 14 October 1999.
77. OPM Survey, "What Do Federal Employees Say?" Results from the 2004 Federal Human Capital Survey.
78. S. Lilly, "An Analysis of Employees' Attitudes at Federal Departments & Agencies," Center for American Progress, www.americanprogress.org.